Study Guide for Plotnik's

Introduction to
Psychology

4th Edition

Matthew Enos
Harold Washington College

with a
Language Enhancement Guide
by Jack Kirschenbaum

Brooks/Cole Publishing Company
I(T)P® An International Thomson Publishing Company

Pacific Grove • Albany • Bonn • Boston • Cincinnati • Detroit • London • Madrid • Melbourne
Mexico City • New York • Paris • San Francisco • Singapore • Tokyo • Toronto • Washington

Sponsoring Editor: *Faith B. Stoddard*
Production Coordinator: *Dorothy Bell*
Cover Design: *Vernon T. Boes*
Cover Illustration: *Jerry E. Fruchtman*
Printing and Binding: *Patterson Printing*

COPYRIGHT © 1996 by Brooks/Cole Publishing Company
A division of International Thomson Publishing Inc.
I(T)P® The ITP logo is a registered trademark under license.

For more information, contact:

BROOKS/COLE PUBLISHING COMPANY
511 Forest Lodge Rd.
Pacific Grove, CA 93950
USA

International Thomson Editores
Campos Eliseos 385, Piso 7
Col. Polanco
11560 México D. F. México

International Thomson Publishing Europe
Berkshire House 168-173
High Holborn
London, WC1V 7AA
England

International Thomson Publishing GmbH
Königswinterer Strasse 418
53227 Bonn
Germany

Thomas Nelson Australia
102 Dodds Street
South Melbourne, 3205
Victoria, Australia

International Thomson Publishing Asia
221 Henderson Road
#05-10 Henderson Building
Singapore 0315

Nelson Canada
1120 Birchmount Road
Scarborough, Ontario
Canada M1K 5G4

International Thomson Publishing Japan
Hirakawacho Kyowa Building, 3F
2-2-1 Hirakawacho
Chiyoda-ku, Tokyo 102
Japan

Printed in the United States of America

10 9 8 7 6 5 4 3

ISBN 0-534-33846-1

Contents

Introduction

Welcome to Psychology

You are taking a challenging course, but I think you will enjoy it, because psychology is one of the most exciting and relevant fields of college study today. An explosion of new ideas and research in psychology is creating a vast accumulation of knowledge that is radically changing the way we understand ourselves and other people. To participate fully and effectively in today's world, we need a kind of psychological literacy, just as we need computer literacy and other new technological abilities. This course can help you acquire the skills and information you need to be psychologically literate.

Let's Work Together

Forgive me for using the personal pronoun "I" in this Study Guide. As a teacher, I can't help imagining you working your way through psychology and Rod Plotnik's exciting new textbook, and I'd like to help. I want to speak to you as directly as I can. Even though I don't know you personally, I am sure I have had a student very much like you in my own classes.

Rod Plotnik's New Introduction to Psychology (4th Edition)

You're going to love your new psychology textbook. More than one of my own students has asked, "Why can't *all* textbooks be like this?" Dr. Rod Plotnik, a psychologist and professor on the faculty of San Diego State University, is an experienced teacher and writer who sees examples of psychology's importance everywhere he looks and loves sharing his observations with us. You'll find Dr. Plotnik's book as fresh as your morning newspaper or your favorite talk show. At the same time, you'll see that his book meets the requirements of solid scholarship. He covers the relevant research and carefully explains the major theories. It's how Rod tells it that I think you will find especially rewarding.

Rod's book is different. An expert in learning psychology, Rod knows we *understand* what we can visualize in a picture and *remember* what we can organize into a story. Consequently, he filled his book with pictures and stories (and not many words like "consequently").

Excellent as his book is, I wouldn't want you to passively agree with everything Rod says. Instead, try to become actively involved in a dialogue with the book. You'll notice how often Rod *asks you a question*. Argue with him. Write notes in the margins. Highlight the important stuff. Make reading and studying this new textbook an adventure.

Kick The Tires and Slam the Doors

By now you've probably paged through your new psychology textbook to see what it's like. If you haven't, I suggest that you do so as soon as you finish reading this introduction. It's a good idea to get the feel of a new book before you begin working in it. That way, you have some sense of where you are going and how to pace yourself for effective study.

What Is a Module?

You may have noticed that Dr. Plotnik calls his units "Modules" instead of "Chapters." He wants his textbook to be as flexible as possible so instructors and their students can adapt it to their own needs. There are 25 modules in all. For most college courses, that might work out to about two modules per week in the typical semester, but instructors can set it up however they wish, and you can read any modules that interest you, even if they are not assigned.

Each module tackles an important aspect of psychology. If you mastered everything in every module, you would have a near-perfect understanding of modern psychology. (You might also flunk your other courses.) When you read a single module, you learn the main facts and ideas about one area of interest in psychology.

Pay attention to the modules your instructor has assigned (our first job is to pass the course, after all), but remember that there's no law against reading an unassigned module that interests you. [Hint: if you do, tell your instructor about it and you'll make a good impression.]

How This Study Guide Works

The bottom line for this Study Guide is that it must help you earn the grade you want in your psychology course. I tried to include materials that have worked for my own students. Some information is highly specific, aimed straight at getting more questions right on the next test. There are observations about the field of psychology, because, as I explain in my Study Guide introduction for Module 1, if you can't tell the forest for the trees, you're lost. Still other parts have the general goal of helping you become a more effective student (and where better than in a psychology course?). The Study Guide is organized as follows:

Module Introduction

Each module in the Study Guide begins with an observation I think may help you tackle the module in the textbook more successfully. These Introductions are not summaries, but thoughts about how to orient yourself toward understanding what you are reading in the textbook.

Effective Student Tip

Next, you will find a specific tip on how to become a more effective student. Some Effective Student Tips tell you how to study better, but most are general ideas about the psychology of effectiveness. Please read the first tip, which explains more about this feature of the Study Guide.

Key Terms

Rod Plotnik has carefully selected the words or phrases (I call them Key Terms) he believes are the most important for beginning psychology students to learn. He puts each Key Term in boldface type in the text and immediately provides a brief, clear definition of the term. These terms are also collected in a Glossary at the end of the textbook.

If you did nothing but memorize the Key Terms, you would pass most psychology exams and have a pretty decent command of the vocabulary of the discipline. Of course it wouldn't be much fun that way, and you need the story to understand psychology in any depth. Still, I can't stress enough the importance of learning the basic vocabulary.

To help you focus on these Key Terms, I have placed them (in alphabetical order) in the Study Guide right before the outline of the module. I have also included each Key Term in the outline and placed it in **boldface** type so you won't miss it.

Outline

Each module in the Study Guide includes a topic outline of the module in the text. My outlines stick very close to Dr. Plotnik's organization. I think working with the Outline will help you read and master the textbook.

There is one thing wrong with my outlines: I wrote them instead of you. Much of the benefit of an outline comes from the process of building it. Therefore, your job is to turn each Outline into your own by writing all over it and revising it as you study. Make each outline a personal set of notes that will help you prepare for your tests. If you will add your own notes and details to my outlines, you will have an excellent summary of each module.

Notice that throughout the outlines I have scattered questions for you to think about and answer. Why not write your answers right on the outline?

For Psych Majors Only...

In some modules you will find a paragraph of text or a brief quiz titled "For Psych Majors Only...." The purpose of these exercises is to suggest ideas of interest to students who intend to take more psychology courses. I guess I wouldn't really mind if an English major or chemistry major tries these materials.

Language Enhancement Guide

Following each Outline, there is a special Language Enhancement Guide prepared by Dr. Jack Kirschenbaum of Fullerton College in California. This guide is intended specifically for native and non-native speakers who are still building their language skills, but since English is such a powerful and complicated language, *anyone* who reads these pages will gain greater insight into the intricacies of our wonderful language.

Even if you don't think you have time to do the special language exercises that Jack Kirschenbaum has prepared, you will surely benefit from at least reading through his explanations of how the English language works. See the special introduction by Jack Kirschenbaum (pages 5-8) for a fuller description of the Language Enhancement Guide.

Self-tests

Following the Language Enhancement Guide, there are three sets of questions that will help you review and give you an idea of how thorough your study has been. Answers are provided at the end of each module in the Study Guide.

True-False Questions

First, you will find 10 True-False questions intended to indicate how well you understand the main ideas in the module. In some modules, on the same page you will find a special quiz. You might enjoy these quizzes.

Flashcards (Matching Questions)

Next, there are 20 matching questions based on the more important Key Terms in the module. I call these questions "Flashcards" in the hope that you will study and test yourself on the Key Terms more than once.

Multiple-Choice Questions

Finally, 15 multiple-choice questions explore important facts, concepts, and theories presented in the module.

Answers Page

All answers are on the last page of each Study Guide module. No peeking!

Feedback Form

On the last page you will find a special mail-in form by which you can let us know how well this Study Guide worked for you and what suggestions you have for helping us make it better. Please send it in at the end of the semester. We would love to hear from you.

Enjoy Your Study Guide

I hope you enjoy working with the Study Guide. Think about the Effective Student Tips as you write your responses to them. Make real flashcards for the Key Terms, if you have time. Add your own notes and comments to the Outlines.

By the way, if an occasional question of mine makes you laugh..., I'll be delighted. I don't believe learning has to be deadly serious all the time. So when I was writing questions and couldn't take it any longer, I sometimes indulged myself in what I hoped would be a bit of humor. The results may be too corny, but you be the judge.

Introduction to the Language Enhancement Guide

(By Jack Kirschenbaum, author of the Language Enhancement Guide sections)

Teachers have adopted Rod Plotnik's introductory psychology textbook for many reasons. The main reason is that they as well as their students like the book. First, Plotnik makes sure that each sentence and paragraph is clear and understandable. Secondly, the topics he selects are interesting so you will want to read them. Third, he provides many study aids in the chapter to help you understand and memorize the material. One study aid consists of printing all new technical terms in bold face type. These words are then immediately defined and followed by clear examples.

There is a problem for some students who have read Rod Plotnik's text. Plotnik has written his textbook for college students with English as their native language and he also uses a college level vocabulary that can be easily understood by students who can read at the 12th grade level. However, if you are not a native English speaker or do not have a 12th grade level or college level vocabulary, Plotnik's vocabulary may give you problems. You may find that you need to look up many words in a dictionary. Looking up words requires many extra hours of study and can be a frustrating experience for some students. Students with this problem tell me that they need help in learning new words. I have written this Language Enhancement Guide to meet this need.

HOW TO USE THIS LANGUAGE ENHANCEMENT GUIDE

To use this Language Enhancement Guide effectively you should know how it was designed and how you can use each section to help you better read and understand the text and increase your vocabulary.

The first section of each module of this Language Enhancement Guide is entitled, **IDIOMATIC EXPRESSIONS AND CULTURAL TERMS.** An idiom consist of words or phrases that are not directly translatable into other languages. Native English speakers immediately know the meaning of these phrases but students who are not native speakers, and even some who are native speakers, are confused by them. This study aid consists of a list of idiomatic expressions and cultural terms used on each text page and their definitions. Each definition contains the meaning of the term as used by Plotnik on the page indicated.

The second section of each module in the Language Enhancement Guide is called **VOCABULARY BUILDING**. This section contains many aids to help you increase your vocabulary and improve your understanding of the textbook. One of these aids, called **Word Analysis**, is based on the fact that many words in the English language are made up of separate parts that have been borrowed from many other languages such as Latin, Greek, Spanish, German, French, etc. When you can break up a word into its parts and you know the meaning of each part you can then determine the possible meanings of the word. The exercises in this section will help you master the common parts of words so you will be able to figure out their meaning without the need to look them up in a dictionary.

Vocabulary Building and Three Levels Of Verbal Precision

The major goal of this guide is to help you build (increase) your vocabulary. Why is building your vocabulary so important? A large working vocabulary and skill in using words at the correct level of precision is essential for effective communication, thinking and mastery of a scientific field of knowledge like psychology. College textbooks, newspapers, news magazines and professional journals require a college level vocabulary. When you apply for a job that requires a college education you will be judged by your pronunciation, your vocabulary and how you use words to express your thinking. Therefore, a major goal of a college education and of this class is to help increase your vocabulary and improve your communication skills.

Words can be classified into three levels of usage and precision: (1) Everyday words, Slang and Idioms, (2) Standard Dictionary and Cultural References, and (3) Professional Technical terms. As we move from the Slang to the Professional level, the degree of precision increases and vagueness and uncertainty decreases. Now let's take a close look at the details of each level of precision and how this study guide will help you better understand the text and help you develop a larger vocabulary.

Level 1. Slang, Idioms, and Everyday Vocabulary

Slang. Slang is the everyday level at which many people talk. "Hi. How ya' doin? Pretty darn good. How's about you? Not so good. I bombed on my last exam." If you are a native English speaker you have learned English at this level. This level is "good enough" for everyday use when we don't need to be very precise and accurate. After all, we use slang everyday and you "kinda know what I'm sayin, don't ya?" The problem with slang is that it varies from one region of the country to another. Plotnik's book avoids slang.

Idioms. An idiom consists of words or phrases that are not directly translatable into other languages. Native English speakers immediately know the meaning of these phrases. People who are not native speakers and even some who are native speakers are confused by them. Plotnik uses many common idioms in the book. Here are a few. How many of them do you know?

- to get along with
- to make up
- to focus on
- to keep track of
- to rule out
- to follow up on
- street smart
- to cram
- relatively good
- a quirk of nature
- plan of attack
- and then some
- a train of thought
- to boot out

It's not always easy to guess the meanings of idioms in context (that is, as a part of the whole sentence or paragraph in which they occur). There are many of these expressions throughout the text. The most difficult in each module are listed in the first study aid, **Vocabulary, Idioms and Cultural Concepts**. Many idioms have more than one meaning. The definition accompanying each idiom corresponds to the way the author uses the expression in the paragraph.

Level 2. Standard Dictionary English Vocabulary and Cultural References

The term "Standard Dictionary English Vocabulary" refers to words that students at the 12th grade to college level and above are expected to know. Native English speakers with limited vocabulary and reading skills must look them up in a dictionary. Here are some sample words that are used in the text book. How many of them do you know?

- advent
- allegedly
- alluded
- anarchist
- ascertain
- aspire
- conceal
- deception
- detour

- emerge
- eminent
- exaggerate
- gullibility
- inadvertent
- pertinent
- pharmacological
- phenomenon
- presume

- prolific
- prone
- refute
- scrutinize
- stratagem
- subtly
- syndrome
- skeptical

At the level of Standard English, you can find the various meanings and pronunciation of each word in a "general" dictionary. A "general" dictionary is a very useful tool to find out the meanings of new words that are used by educated people as they speak and write in magazines, newspapers, novels, TV and textbooks like Rod Plotnik's *Introduction to Psychology*.

Plotnik's textbook makes use of many Standard Dictionary English Level words. If you do not have a vocabulary at least at the 12th grade level, you may not be able to understand much of the text, tests and lecture. Fortunately, the text and your instructor use many of these college level vocabulary words over and over in the book and in the lectures. Once you learn these words, your understanding of the text and the lecture will get easier. This study guide will provide you with a variety of exercises in each module to help you learn the words.

Cultural References. These are names of people, places, objects and historical events that may not be familiar to non-native speakers. Even native speakers may not be familiar with historical events and people. For example, the following Cultural References Terms are used in the first two modules. How many of them do you know?

- marathon runners
- the Super Bowl
- a class action suit

- Jell-O
- a switch hitter, a batter
- a line up

- Ellis Island
- an over-the-counter drug
- a prom queen

The first study aid, **Idiomatic Expressions and Cultural Terms**, will present and define the meaning of these expressions.

Level 3. Technical Professional Vocabulary

Scientists and professionals need words that have precise and exact definitions to be used without vagueness or ambiguity. The Professional Level includes the language of scientists, philosophers, language specialists, medical doctors, college professors, lawyers, engineers and other professionals. Technical Professional words are used to deal with the subject specialties such as economics, psychology, physics, engineering, law, medicine, etc. Every occupation and profession has its own special vocabulary. Many textbooks and professional books provide a glossary with precise definitions for the technical words used.

You may be thinking, "Why do we need a glossary? Why not use a general dictionary?" The problem is that a general dictionary provides many brief definitions for thousands of common words but very little or nothing at all about very special words used by scientists and professionals. When used by professionals, some of the everyday and slang meanings of a word or even the standard dictionary meaning may be either stripped away or changed. This can be confusing at first to the nonprofessional. However, with the study of the definitions the confusion clears up. Therefore, if you want to improve the quality of your use of words and your ability to think critically, you must take the time to master the use of precisely defined professional terms. Let us now look at the ways that Plotnik helps you learn the meaning of new words.

As you read the first module did you notice that Plotnik defines all technical words that appear in boldface type in the sentence following the word? He then repeats that definition in the glossary in the back of the book. A **Glossary** is a dictionary of technical words with the author's definition. For example, find the first boldfaced word in the text on page 4. The word is **Psychology**. Notice that the word is followed by a definition. Plotnik then defines the word again in the Glossary. Look for the word **Psychology** in the glossary at the end of the book. If you see these words again and you forget their meaning you can look them up in the Glossary at the back of the textbook.

Appendix: Prefix, Suffix, and Root Dictionary

Many exercises in the Language Enhancement Guide sections refer you to a special Appendix that I prepared to help you improve your vocabulary. The Appendix begins on page 352 of this book. It might be a good idea to turn to that page now to learn how you can use the Appendix in your work.

A STRATEGY FOR USING THE LANGUAGE ENHANCEMENT GUIDE

Step 1: Do a quick review of the assigned chapter. Familiarize yourself with the contents by reading heads, subheads, picture captions, and marginal text.

Step 2: Read through the corresponding material in this Language Enhancement Guide in the **Idioms and Cultural Concepts** section; find items in your text using the page references and study their contexts. Then read the assigned page of the textbook. As you read the page, if you find a non-technical word that you do not understand try to figure out the meaning from the context. This study guide will provide many helpful ways to figure out the words from the context. If you still need help with the word, look it up in a college level dictionary.

Step 3: Now do a careful, word-for-word reading of the module.

Step 4: Read the text carefully a second time. During this reading, write definitions and notes on the Outline. Take the Self-tests a first time, if you wish.

Step 5: Complete the remaining exercises in the Language Enhancement Guide.

Discovering Psychology

An Explosion of Knowledge

One day I found a box of my old college textbooks. I was delighted to discover the textbook I used when I took my first psychology course, years ago. Would you believe I still remembered some of the pictures and lessons?

I was shocked, though, to see how slender a book it was. It had a chapter on the eye, another on the ear, and others on the rest of the senses. There was some material on Freud, but not much on anyone else. I was struck by how much less knowledge there was in the field of psychology back then.

The explosion of research and thinking in psychology has created a problem for teachers and students. Textbooks are four times as thick, and they apologize for leaving material out. In the newer textbooks, such as the one by Rod Plotnik that you are using, the writing is lively and the graphics are superb, but there still is much more material to cover. The problem is that colleges and universities, which change very slowly, still expect you to master it all in one semester!

How to Tell the Forest From the Trees

My experience as a teacher says the single greatest problem of introductory psychology is that the sheer mass of information thrown at students overwhelms them, no matter how diligently they study. What is really important? Where are the connections between all these facts and ideas and names? What must I remember for the tests? The study of introductory psychology presents a classic example of the old problem of not being able to see the forest for the trees.

The solution is to develop a conceptual framework for understanding psychology. If you have an overview of what questions psychology attempts to answer, how it goes about seeking answers, and what the dominant themes in the answers have been, you will be able to fit any new fact, idea, or name into a coherent picture.

That's where Module 1 comes in. In addition to describing the kinds of work psychologists do, Rod Plotnik gives you an important tool: the six major theoretical approaches to psychology. As a student and consumer of psychology, you need to know how the major pioneers in the field have tried to answer our most important questions about human behavior. Module 1 is the road map for an exciting journey.

Effective Student Tip 1

Take a Tip from Me

I have been teaching psychology for many years, but that's not what makes me so smart (ahem!). I have learned from experience. The next tip, for example, owes a lot to my own checkered past. Have you ever heard of the "reformed drunk syndrome"? Guess who you call on if you want a really convincing lecture about the evils of Demon Rum? When I talk about the importance of good attendance, do as I say, not as I did!

But there's more to it. Not only does my experience as both a student and a teacher tell me that every student wants and needs to be effective (I tell you what the professor wants and needs in Tip 18), but I think the psychology of motivation says we all desire effectiveness in every aspect of our lives.

Meanwhile, I hope you will read all these Effective Student Tips, even the ones in the modules your professor does not assign. Some will touch you personally, others may give you something to think about, and some you won't agree with at all. Writing your answers to the "Your response…" questions should help you think about yourself as a student.

Please read the next tip and the last one right now. Tip 2 is the simplest, and yet the most important. Tip 25 says more about the underlying theme of all these Effective Student Tips.

Your response…

Do you consider yourself an effective person? In what ways "yes" and in what ways "no"?

Key Terms

Forget how big the textbook seems. You are not starting at square one in psychology. So much of psychology is becoming general knowledge these days that you already know quite a bit about it. Rod Plotnik defined 24 terms in this module he thought were especially important to know. How many of the following terms mean something to you right now, even without intensive study of the module?

approaches to
understanding behavior

autism

behavioral approach

clinical psychologist

cognitive approach

cognitive psychology

cross-cultural approach

developmental psychology

experimental psychology

functionalism

Gestalt approach

humanistic approach

introspection

personality psychology

physiological psychology
[psychobiology]

psychiatrist

psychoanalytic approach

psychobiological approach

psychologist

psychology

psychometrics

social psychology

structuralism

test anxiety

Outline

Reminder: Topic outline follows textbook closely. Key terms in boldface. Outline most useful for learning and review when you add notes and definitions. Try my questions, too (in italics with checkbox).

- *INTRODUCTION*

  ☐ *Why do you think Rod Plotnik begins with one very rare and one quite common example?*

  1. **Autism** – an extreme problem that could not be understood without psychology

  2. **Test anxiety** – an everyday problem for which psychology presents practical solutions

A. *Definition and Goals*

  1. What is **psychology**?

     a. Behavior

     b. Mental processes

  2. What are the goals of psychology?

     a. Describe

     b. Explain causes

     c. Predict

     d. Control

B. *Modern Approaches*

☐ *Can you learn the six approaches? Well enough to understand and remember them all through the course? If so, you will possess a master plan into which almost everything in psychology will fit.*

1. **Psychobiological approach**

   a. Genes, hormones, and nervous system

   b. Solving puzzle of how mind, brain, and body interact

2. **Cognitive approach**

   a. Processing, storing, and using information

   b. How information influences what we attend to, perceive, learn, remember, believe, and feel

   c. Increased popularity in last ten years

3. **Behavioral approach**

   a. How organisms learn new behaviors or modify existing ones through reward and punishment

   b. B. F. Skinner and strict behaviorism

   c. Albert Bandura and the social learning approach

4. **Psychoanalytic approach**

   a. Influence of unconscious fears, desires, and motivations

   b. Importance of childhood and unconscious conflict

   c. Sigmund Freud and psychoanalytic techniques (dream interpretation)

5. **Humanistic approach**

   a. Freedom, choice, personal growth, intrinsic worth, potential for self-fulfillment

   b. Abraham Maslow

   c. Dissatisfaction with both psychoanalysis and behaviorism

6. **Cross-cultural approach**

   a. Influence of cultural and ethnic similarities and differences

   b. Newest approach to psychology

C. Historical Approaches

☐ *Have you noticed that there is some overlap between the modern approaches (above) and the historical approaches (below)? Do you see how it's all part of the same story?*

1. **Structuralism**

    a. Wilhelm Wundt

    b. **Introspection**

    c. Measuring conscious elements of the mind

2. **Functionalism**

    a. William James

    b. Continuous flow of mental activity

3. **Gestalt approach**

    a. Max Wertheimer, Wolfgang Köhler, Kurt Koffka

    b. Perception more than sum of its parts

    c. Apparent motion (phi phenomenon)

4. **Behavioral approach**

    a. John B. Watson

    b. Objective, scientific analysis of observable behaviors

5. Popularity of approaches

D. Cultural Diversity: Discrimination

1. Women in psychology

2. Minorities in psychology

3. Trying to right the wrongs

E. Research Focus: Taking Lecture Notes

1. What's the best strategy for taking lecture notes?

2. A research study of three techniques (which also illustrates the four goals of psychology)

☐ *Which technique worked best? Can you figure out why it was superior?*

F. Careers in Psychology

1. What are you planning to do in psychology?

   a. **Psychologist**

   b. **Clinical psychologist**

   c. **Psychiatrist**

2. Where do psychologists work?

G. Research Areas in Psychology

1. What should I specialize in?

   a. **Social psychology** and **personality psychology**

   b. **Developmental psychology**

   c. **Experimental psychology**

   d. **Physiological psychology (psychobiology)**

   e. Cognitive psychology

   f. Psychometrics

2. Decisions

H. Application: Study Skills

1. Preparing for an exam

2. Setting goals

   a. Time goal

   b. General goal

   c. Specific performance goal

3. Taking notes

   a. In your own words

   b. Outline format [like this one]

   c. Associate new material with old [Concept/Glossary section]

   d. Ask yourself questions as you study

4. Rewarding yourself (self-reinforcement)

5. Procrastinating

   a. Stop thinking or worrying about final goal

   b. Break overall task down into smaller goals

   c. Write down a realistic schedule

Language Enhancement Guide

IDIOMATIC EXPRESSIONS AND CULTURAL TERMS

1. Idioms and informal usage. An idiom consist of words or phrases that are not directly translatable into other languages. Native English speakers immediately know the meaning of these phrases. People who are not native speakers and even some who are native speakers are confused by them.

Many idiomatic expressions in English are actually phrasal verbs, verb phrases composed of one or more verbs and a preposition. An example is "to focus on," on page 5 of your text. As the author uses it in your text, it means to examine; to study.

It's not always easy to guess the meanings of phrasal verbs in context (that is, as a part of the whole sentence or paragraph in which they occur). There are many of these expressions throughout the text; the most difficult in each module are listed and defined in this section. Some idioms and expressions have more than one meaning; the definition given here corresponds to the way the author uses the expression in the module.

2. Cultural Terms. These are names of people, places, objects and historical events that may not be familiar to non-native speakers. Even native speakers may not be familiar with historical events and people. For example, the following Cultural References terms are used in the text. How many of them do you know?

- marathon runners
- Jell-O
- Ellis Island
- the Super Bowl
- a switch hitter, a batter
- an over-the-counter drug
- a class action suit
- a line up
- a prom queen

The following idiomatic expressions and cultural terms are found in Module 1. The numbers in parentheses ( ) refer to the pages on which the words can be found.

to figure out (3) = to solve, to determine

to get through (3) = to complete, to finish

to focus on (5) = to examine; to study

to channel (worry) (8) = to control or direct

free will concept (10) = freedom to choose

efforts paid off (11) = rewarded

positions open (14) = positions available

to keep track of (20) = to keep a record of

how long will it take (20) = how much time is needed

VOCABULARY BUILDING

Prefixes, Suffixes, and Roots

Many words in the English language are made up of separate parts that have been borrowed from other languages such as Latin, Greek, Spanish, German, French, etc. The process of breaking up something to study its parts and the relationship among the parts is called **analysis**. When you can analyze a word and you know the meaning of each part, you can then determine the possible meanings of the word. When you combine the possible meanings of a word with the way the word is used in the sentence, you can often determine the author's meaning. Each part of the word is given a name. The part of the word that you read first is called the **prefix**. The part that is at the end of the word is called the **suffix**. Words that can stand alone with prefixes or suffixes attached to them are called **roots**.

For example, the word psychology has two parts- "psych" and "ology." Words that begin with the prefix *psyche* have to do with the "soul" and "mind." The suffix *ology* comes from the Greek word "logos" that means "study" or "word." When you combine the prefix and suffix, the word can be translated to mean the study of the mind. This meaning comes close to Plotnik 's definition of psychology. Plotnik defines psychology as, "the systematic, scientific study of behavior and mental processes." Plotnik uses the term mental processes to refer to activities of the mind such as thinking, feeling, imagining and remembering, etc.

Why Must Word Structure and Context be Combined?

Did you notice with the word psychology that when you figure out the meaning of a word based on the prefix and suffix you only come close to the meaning that the author intends? For many words knowing the prefix and suffix is not enough. You must also know how the word is used in the sentence and how the sentence fits into the paragraph. However, knowing how to break up words into their parts can help you determine as well as help you remember their meaning. Examine the next box for another example of how knowledge of prefixes and suffixes can help you determine the meaning of words.

Suffix	Meaning
-ologist	one who studies
-ological	the adjective form of ology

psychologist = one who studies psychology

psychological research = research that focuses on topics that make up psychology

WORD FAMILIES

Knowledge of prefixes, suffixes, and roots can help you guess the meanings of new words in context. An additional related technique is to know word families. Word families are groups of words that come from the same root, but are different parts of speech. Examine the text glossary and you will find many word families. Studying word families will help you analyze and remember the word parts. In the following example taken from your text glossary, notice how a few roots, prefixes and suffixes can be used to figure out the meaning of over a dozen words in exercise one.

Prefix/Root	Meaning
analysis	breaking something down into its parts, stages, causes or categories
metric	measure, measurement
psyche	soul/mind.
soma	body
therap/therapy	treatment/cure

Suffix	Meaning
-al/ological	like/being/belonging/characterized by/process/conditions
-ic	characteristic/having to do with/having the power to/ belonging to
-ist	a person who practices and studies/a believer
-ology	the study of

Exercise 1. Word Family

Based on an analysis of the prefix and suffix, guess the meaning of each term in the table. Then look up the technical meaning of the terms in the "psych" word family marked with a G in the text glossary.

Word Family	Meaning
psychology (G)	
psychologist	
psychological	
psychotherapy (G)	
psychotherapist	
psychiatrist (G)	
psychiatric	
psychoanalysis (G)	
psychoanalyst	
psychoanalytical	
psychobiological (G)	
psychosomatic (G)	
psychometics (G)	

Exercise 2. Other Word Families

A word family can be based on a prefix, suffix or root. Look over the text glossary for other words that have many different variations. For example, as you look over the A words find the prefix "anti" word family that includes antidepressant, antisocial personality and antipsychotic drugs. Based on the definitions provided what do you think is the meaning of the prefix "anti?" Look up the prefix "anti" in appendix A. Appendix A contains a dictionary of many of the most common prefixes, suffixes and roots used in the text.

Find five more prefixes or roots and guess their meaning. Compare your answers with the word parts listed in appendix A . For words parts not in appendix A consult a college level dictionary. The first two word families are included in the following table for you to look up.

Root/Prefix	Meaning	Examples
auto		automatic
bio		biological factors, biofeedback, biological needs

True-False

_____ 1. The goals of psychology are to explain, describe, predict, and control behavior.

_____ 2. There are as many different approaches to psychology as there are psychologists writing about psychology.

_____ 3. Techniques like free association and dream interpretation are products of the psychoanalytic approach to psychology.

_____ 4. Abraham Maslow wanted humanistic psychology to be a new way of perceiving and thinking about the individual's capacity, freedom, and potential for growth.

_____ 5. It is best to pick one of the general approaches to psychology and organize your thinking and work around it exclusively.

_____ 6. There has been ethnic discrimination in psychology, but at least women have always been equally represented.

_____ 7. Modern scientific psychology began with Wilhelm Wundt's attempt to accurately measure the conscious elements of the mind.

_____ 8. The key idea of behaviorism is that perception is more than just the sum of its parts.

_____ 9. Not only do you have several career choices in psychology — whichever one you choose, you are almost certain to make big bucks!

_____ 10. There is no special program for overcoming procrastination: just get off your duff and get to work.

Flashcards _for psych majors only…_

Contributors to Psychology: A matching exercise based on important people in psychology.

_____ 1. Albert Bandura

_____ 2. Mary Calkins

_____ 3. Ruth Howard

_____ 4. William James

_____ 5. Abraham Maslow

_____ 6. Rod Plotnik

_____ 7. B. F. Skinner

_____ 8. John B. Watson

_____ 9. Max Wertheimer, Wolfgang Köhler, and Kurt Koffka

_____ 10. Wilhelm Wundt

a. humanistic psychology movement

b. author of your psychology textbook

c. denied a doctorate in psychology by Harvard

d. social learning theory

e. founders of Gestalt psychology movement

f. strict behaviorism

g. studied function of conscious activity

h. first laboratory for psychological research

i. "Give me a dozen healthy infants…"

j. first African-American Ph.D. in psychology

Flashcards

Match each key term to the definition given in the textbook.

b	1. autism	a. examines how genes, hormones, and nervous system interact with environments
r	2. behavioral approach	b. rare problem with severe impairments in communication, motor systems, socialization
p	3. clinical psychologist	c. study of function rather than structure of consciousness; how mind adapts to change
j	4. cognitive approach	d. focuses on measurement of abilities, skills, intelligence, personality, abnormal behaviors
t	5. cognitive psychology	e. medical doctor (M.D.) with additional years of clinical training in diagnosis, treatment
i	6. cross-cultural approach	f. includes areas of sensation, perception, learning, human performance, motivation
n	7. developmental psychology	g. systematic scientific study of behaviors and mental processes
f	8. experimental psychology	h. focuses on influence of unconscious fears, desires, and motivations on thoughts, behavior
c	9. functionalism	i. studies influence of cultural and ethnic similarities and differences on functioning
o	10. Gestalt approach	j. interested in how we process, store, and use information; how information influences us
l	11. humanistic approach	k. physiological, emotional, cognitive problems in thinking, reasoning caused by stress of exams
s	12. introspection	l. emphasizes individual freedom, capacity for personal growth, potential for self-fulfillment
e	13. psychiatrist	m. study of basic elements like perception which make up conscious mental processes
h	14. psychoanalytic approach	n. examines moral, social, emotional, cognitive development throughout a person's entire life
a	15. psychobiological approach	o. emphasized that perception is more than sum of its parts; how sensation becomes perception
q	16. psychologist	p. has Ph.D. plus specialization in clinical psychology and supervised work in therapy
g	17. psychology	q. has completed 4-5 years of postgraduate education; has obtained Ph.D. in psychology
d	18. psychometrics	r. analyzes how organisms learn new behaviors through reward, punishment from environment
m	19. structuralism	s. method of exploring conscious mental processes by asking subjects to look inward
k	20. test anxiety	t. research into information processing, storage, retrieval

Multiple-Choice

_____ 1. Rod Plotnik opens his textbook with the story of the parents who discover their child is autistic to make the point that psychology
  a. is the science that has the answers to problems like this one
  b. is a rather grim science — lots of pain and suffering
  c. can answer some questions but not others
  d. comes out of our human need for answers about our behavior

_____ 2. Which one of the following is not a goal of psychology?
  a. to explain the causes of behavior
  b. to predict behavior
  c. to judge behavior
  d. to control behavior

_____ 3. The psychobiological approach to psychology focuses on
  a. the workings of the brain, nervous system, genes, hormones, etc.
  b. conscious processes like perception and memory
  c. the effects of reward and punishment on behavior
  d. unconscious processes

_____ 4. The cognitive approach to psychology studies how we
  a. are motivated by unconscious processes
  b. are motivated by the need for self-fulfillment
  c. process, store, and use information
  d. program our behavior by seeking rewards and avoiding punishments

_____ 5. The major contributor to the behavioral approach to psychology was
  a. Sigmund Freud
  b. B. F. Skinner
  c. William James
  d. Abraham Maslow

_____ 6. The great importance of the unconscious is a key idea in the _____ approach
  a. psychoanalytic
  b. cognitive
  c. behavioral
  d. psychobiological

_____ 7. _____ was one of the major figures of the humanistic approach to psychology
  a. Sigmund Freud
  b. Abraham Maslow
  c. B. F. Skinner
  d. Erik Erikson

_____ 8. The cross-cultural approach adds a valuable dimension to psychology in suggesting that
  a. in order to be a fully developed person, you have to spend some time living with other groups
  b. anthropology explains behavior better than psychology does
  c. the culture in which you grow up affects your thoughts, feelings, and behaviors
  d. what psychology learns about one race is probably not true about other races

_____ 9. Once we understand the six approaches to psychology, Rod Plotnik advises us to
   a. make a personal decision about which approach is best
   b. use information from all six approaches
   c. place our trust in the approaches that have stood the test of time
   d. judge each approach by the famous people who have supported it

_____ 10. The difference between "structuralism" and "functionalism" in the early years of psychology concerned whether
   a. Germany or America would assume the leadership role
   b. Abraham Maslow or William James was right
   c. psychology should study the brain or the cultural setting of behavior
   d. psychology should study specific or general mental activity

_____ 11. By explaining perceptual phenomena like the phi phenomenon [apparent motion], Gestalt researchers gave psychology the idea that
   a. the whole is more than the sum of its parts
   b. research results could be profitable when applied to advertising
   c. Wundt and the structuralists had been right about the importance of the individual parts
   d. individual parts are more significant than resulting wholes

_____ 12. The early behaviorist John B. Watson wanted psychology to be
   a. an introspective investigation of how people understood the workings of their minds
   b. an objective, scientific study of observable behavior
   c. a philosophical study of the continuous flow of mental activity
   d. a program for "building" whatever kinds of people society needed

_____ 13. After much effort to overcome a long history of discrimination, American psychology
   a. still has too few women and minorities
   b. is a good cross-section of the United States in general
   c. finally has achieved fair percentages of both women and minorities
   d. is still discriminatory and doing very little about it

_____ 14. After reading the material on careers and research areas, it would be reasonable to conclude that psychology
   a. requires so much education that few students should consider it
   b. will have fewer job opportunities in coming years
   c. offers a great variety of intellectual challenges and kinds of work
   d. is one of the best paid professions today

_____ 15. Which one of the following is not a good strategy for overcoming procrastination?
   a. stop thinking or worrying about the final goal
   b. break the task down into smaller goals
   c. write down a realistic schedule for reaching the goals
   d. only begin working once you are confident you won't fail

Answers for Module 1

True-False
1. T
2. F
3. T
4. T
5. F
6. F
7. T
8. F
9. F
10. F

Flashcards
1. b
2. r
3. p
4. j
5. t
6. i
7. n
8. f
9. c
10. o
11. l
12. s
13. e
14. h
15. a
16. q
17. g
18. d
19. m
20. k

Multiple-Choice
1. d
2. c
3. a
4. c
5. b
6. a
7. b
8. c
9. b
10. d
11. a
12. b
13. a
14. c
15. d

"Contributors to Psychology" Quiz

1. d   2. c   3. j   4. g   5. a   6. b   7. f   8. i   9. e   10. h

Psychology & Science

Science and the Scientific Method

When we think of science, we imagine a person in a white lab coat working some kind of magic we can't understand. But that's not science. Science is a method of asking and answering questions about nature, including human nature. Science is only one of many ways of solving problems by answering questions through the analysis of gathered information. There are older and more widely used methods, such as reliance on tradition, custom, or authority. For much of our work, however, science is the most powerful intellectual tool yet invented.

Science offers a methodical procedure for the analysis of objective events. It is *not* simply the discoveries scientists make, or the techniques scientists use, or the beliefs that any scientists may hold. Instead, science is a way of approaching the task of gathering information and creating knowledge. It is a *method* of analysis.

Rules of Procedure and Basic Assumptions About Reality

Science consists of two related features: (1) a set of characteristics or rules of procedure, and (2) a set of basic assumptions about reality. The first feature constitutes the rules of the game that scientists follow in the laboratory. These rules require objectivity, freedom from bias, objective data collection, public procedures, precise definitions, careful measurements, logical reasoning, rigorous control of variables, systematic examination of relationships, and self-criticism. Through replication, scientists aim to create theories that allow prediction and control.

The second feature constitutes the starting point of science, what all scientists agree on about how nature works. These assumptions are that all events are naturally determined, that nature is orderly and regular, that truth is relative, and that knowledge is gained through empiricism, rationalism, and replication. Of course these basic assumptions about reality are assumptions rather than proven facts. Consequently, it is not necessary to believe that these assumptions are universally 'true' in order to use the scientific method.

Together the two features of the scientific method also serve as a checklist for the researcher. Any violation of or deviation from the rules of procedure or the basic assumptions about reality puts an investigation outside the realm of science and renders its results untrustworthy.

Effective Student Tip 2

Attend Every Class

I shudder when I hear college teachers advise, "Come to class if it helps, but attendance isn't required." That's such poor psychology and such destructive advice. Students should attend *every* class, even the dull ones, because regular attendance leads directly to involvement and commitment, the basic ingredients of effective college work.

We aren't talking morals here, we're talking the psychology of effectiveness. Here's why attendance is the basis of successful college work. (1) Good attendance makes you feel more confident, purposeful and in control. (2) Attendance is the one feature of college that is completely under your control. (3) The reason for an absence usually reveals some area in which you feel ineffective. (4) Whether they make a big deal of it or not, your professors want and need your good attendance. What if no one came? (5) There is more to a class than the lecture. Other good things happen when you attend class regularly. Your professor gets to know you. You become better acquainted with your classmates. You learn from them and you learn by helping them. (6) Most students can achieve perfect attendance if they try, and their professors will admire them for it. You can help make a good class a great one.

Your response...

What is your attendance history? (I confessed mine.) Do you have an attendance goal for this class?

Key Terms

How many of these key terms do you know something about already, without further study?

animal model

Attention-Deficit/Hyperactivity Disorder (ADHD)

case study

confounded causes

control group

correlation

correlation coefficient

debriefing

dependent variable

double-blind procedure

experiment

experimental group

hypothesis

independent variable

interview

laboratory experiment

laboratory setting

naturalistic setting

negative correlation coefficient

perfect negative correlation coefficient

perfect positive correlation coefficient

physiological/genetic techniques

placebo

placebo effect

positive correlation coefficient

questionnaire

random selection

scientific method

self-fulfilling prophecy

standardized test

statistical procedures

survey

testimonial

zero correlation

Outline

- *INTRODUCTION*

  ☐ *In what possible way could rhino horn and vitamin C be connected?*

  1. **Attention-Deficit/Hyperactivity Disorder (ADHD)**

  2. Rhino horn and vitamin C

  A. *Methods for Answering Questions*

  1. Why the controversies about ADHD?

  2. Three research strategies for scientific investigation

     a. **Survey**

     b. **Case study**

     c. **Experiment**

B. Surveys

☐ *What are the main* advantages *of the survey method?*

☐ *What are the main* disadvantages *of the survey method?*

1. What do we know about ADHD?

2. Survey method

C. Case Study: Testimonials

☐ *What are the main* advantages *of a testimonial?*

☐ *What are the main* disadvantages *of a testimonial?*

1. What substances trigger attention deficit disorder symptoms?

2. Sources of error and bias in a **testimonial**

   a. Personal beliefs

   b. **Self-fulfilling prophecy**

   c. **Confounded causes**

D. Cultural Diversity: Placebos

☐ *What beliefs and practices in the United States might be thought of as our own "rhino horn?"*

1. **Placebo**

2. **Placebo effect**

E. Correlation

1. What is a correlation?

   a. **Correlation**

   b. **Correlation coefficient**

2. Meaning of correlations

   a. **Perfect positive correlation**

   b. **Positive correlation**

   c. **Zero correlation**

   d. **Negative correlation**

   e. **Perfect negative correlation**

3. Correlation versus causation

4. Correlations as clues

5. Correlation and prediction

F. Decisions about Doing Research

1. How would a researcher study ADHD?

   a. Which technique should I use?

   b. Which setting should I use?

2. Choosing a research technique

   a. **Interview** and **questionnaire**

   b. **Standardized test**

   c. **Laboratory experiment**

   d. **Physiological/genetic techniques**

   e. **Animal model**

3. Choosing a research setting

   a. **Naturalistic setting** (case study)

   ☐ *What are the main* advantages *of the case study?*

   ☐ *What are the main* disadvantages *of the case study?*

   b. **Laboratory setting**

   ☐ *What are the main* advantages *of the laboratory experiment?*

   ☐ *What are the main* disadvantages *of the laboratory experiment?*

G. Scientific Method: Experiment

1. Does ritalin help children with ADHD?

   a. **Scientific method**

   b. **Experiment**

2. Conducting an experiment – seven steps

   a. State **hypothesis**

   b. Identify variables

      (1) **Independent variable** (treatment)

      (2) **Dependent variable** (resulting behavior)

   c. Choose subjects

      (1) Sample

      (2) **Random selection**

   d. Assign subjects randomly

      (1) **Experimental group**

      (2) **Control group**

   e. Manipulate independent variable (administer treatment)

❑ *Why is the* **double-blind procedure** *superior to the typical experiment?*

   f. Measure resulting behavior (dependent variable)

   g. Analyze data

❑ *What are the most common* **statistical procedures?** *[read Appendix in textbook]*

❑ *Why is a control group needed in a scientific experiment?*

H. Research Focus: ADHD Controversies

❑ *Do you know a child who is hyperactive? What is he or she like?*

1. Why is there controversy after 30 years of research on ADHD?

   a. First question: who has ADHD?

   b. Second question: how should ADHD be treated?

      (1) Stimulants – advantages

      (2) Stimulants – disadvantages

2. Conclusions

❑ *Do you have an opinion concerning the controversies surrounding ADHD?*

I. Application: Concerns about Research

☐ *Would you volunteer to be a subject in a psychological experiment?*

☐ *Do you believe animals should be used in research?*

1. Commonly asked questions about being a subject

    a. Deception and **debriefing**

    b. American Psychological Association ethical guidelines

2. Pros and cons of using animal subjects

Language Enhancement Guide

IDIOMATIC EXPRESSIONS AND CULTURAL TERMS

The following are idiomatic expressions and cultural terms found in the module. Some of them have more than one meaning; the definition given here on the right is for the way the author uses the expression in this module. Remember that these words, like all words, can have different meanings in other contexts.

throwing a fit (25) = to lose emotional control and behave with anger or in a wild way

(activity) went on (25) = continued

to make it happen (28) = to cause

trigger the development (31) = start the development

short term improvement (37) = temporary

keep subjects in the dark (38) = do not inform subjects

VOCABULARY BUILDING

Remember that we pointed out in the last module that many words in the English language are made up of separate word parts that have been borrowed from many other languages such as Latin, Greek, Spanish, German, French, etc. This can create a problem for word analysis when the same prefix or suffix is borrowed from different languages and has different meanings. The prefix "in" for example can mean either "in" or "to" or "not" or "without." Here is an example.

"The researchers admit that the previous research was <u>inconclusive</u> but claim that they now have a better procedure and better evidence."

When we break "inconclusive" into its parts we find the word following the prefix "in" is "conclude" (conclusive). Conclude means to come to an end or close or reach a decision. Which one of the several meanings that the prefix "in" can have is appropriate here? To figure this out we must look at the context of the sentence and the discussion. Based on the context the best guess as to the meaning of "in" is "not" or "without." So inconclusive means "no conclusion" or "without a conclusion." It does not mean "in conclusion" or "to conclude." In the context of the sentence it means no decision or conclusion can be made based on past research. This is the meaning given in a dictionary and the meaning required in the sentence. However, you must be cautious in your word analysis because as helpful as it is most of the time there will be times when you can and will make errors. With practice and by checking a dictionary when you are in doubt, your word analysis skill will improve.

Word Analysis

Instructions: Study the following table of common prefixes, suffixes, and roots and then guess the meanings of the terms in the table that follows. The number in parentheses ( ) refers to the page in the current module where you can find the word. You can find the definition for any word marked with a **G** in the textbook Glossary. Words that are not marked are used by the textbook author in other modules. Remember that these words, like all words, can have different meanings in other contexts.

Exercise 1. Misconception

Prefix/Root	Meaning
mis-	bad/wrong
-ion/tion	act/process/means/results of
-ive	tending to (be)/ having to (be)

Word	Definition
misconception	incorrect interpretation; misunderstanding
misestimate	to guess with an error
misinterpret (33)	to interpret or explain with errors, explain incorrectly
misperceive (33)	
mistreated (39)	
mistake	
mistrust	
misunderstand	
miscalculation	
mislabel	

Exercise 2. Insight

Prefix/Root	Meaning
in- (1)	in/into/within
in/im- (2)	not/without

Caution: Many prefixes have different meaning when combined with different word roots or other prefixes. The prefix "in" has at least two different meanings that are covered in this and the next exercise.

Word	Definition
incision	to cut into something
insight (G)	seeing into something; the sudden grasp of a solution after many incorrect attempts
innate (G)	inborn ability; genetically programmed abilities of the brain
instinct (G)	
internal (locus of control) (G)	
intrinsic (G)	
involuntary	

Exercise 3. Inability

Prefix/Root	Meaning
in- (1)	in/into/within
in/im- (2)	not/without

inability	not being able to do something
inadequate	not enough
inanimate objects	non-moving or non-living things
inappropriate	not acceptable
incapacitated	deprived of strength or ability; disabled
impossible	not possible, can't be done
impractical	not practical, not easily or conveniently done
inadequate (G)	
insanity (G)	
insomnia (G)	
immature	
inactive	
insensitive	
immobile (56)	
incredible (44)	

True-False

_____ 1. Rod Plotnik's definition of psychology as the "scientific study of behaviors and mental processes" means that psychology is strongly linked to the power of the scientific method.

_____ 2. The scientific technique with the lowest potential for error and bias is the survey method.

_____ 3. Testimonials have a high potential for error and bias.

_____ 4. Surveys like the famous Kinsey report are interesting but quite unscientific.

_____ 5. If it turns out that there is a *negative* correlation between studying the textbook and getting good grades, you just wasted a big chunk of money.

_____ 6. If you can establish a significant correlation between two variables, you have also determined the causal relationship between them.

_____ 7. Research in naturalistic settings has greater reality, but research in the laboratory has greater control.

_____ 8. What the experimenter manipulates is called the dependent variable; how the subjects react is called the independent variable.

_____ 9. Random selection is crucial in choosing subjects because you want them to accurately represent the larger population you are studying.

_____ 10. There is no way to justify doing research using animals.

Flashcards

Match each key term to the definition given in the textbook.

_d_   1. case study

_c_   2. control group

_t_   3. correlation

_r_   4. correlation coefficient

_l_   5. debriefing

_j_   6. dependent variable

_g_   7. double-blind procedure

_s_   8. experiment

_o_   9. experimental group

_a_   10. hypothesis

_b_   11. independent variable

_f_   12. laboratory setting

_k_   13. naturalistic setting

_i_   14. placebo

_m_   15. questionnaire

_p_   16. random selection

_q_   17. scientific method

_e_   18. self-fulfilling prophecy

_n_   19. survey

_h_   20. testimonial

a. educated guess about some phenomenon stated in precise, concrete language to rule out error

b. a treatment or something the researcher controls or manipulates

c. composed of subjects who undergo all the same procedures but do not receive the treatment

d. in depth analysis of the thoughts, feelings, beliefs, or behaviors of a single person

e. having a strong belief about a future behavior then acting to carry out the behavior

f. studying individuals under systematic controlled conditions, with real-world influences eliminated

g. neither subjects nor researchers know which group is receiving which treatment

h. a statement in support of a particular viewpoint based on one's personal experience

i. some supposed medical intervention (pill, injection) that has no actual medical effects

j. the subjects' behaviors that are used to measure the potential effect of the treatment

k. a relatively normal environment in which researchers observe behavior but don't control it

l. explaining purpose and method of experiment to subjects, helping them deal with doubts or guilt

m. a technique for obtaining information by asking subjects read written questions, check answers

n. a way to obtain information by asking many individuals to answer a fixed set of questions

o. composed of subjects who receive the special treatment

p. ensures each potential subject has equal chance of being chosen

q. a general approach to gathering information and answering questions so error, bias is minimized

r. a number that indicates the strength of a relationship between two or more events

s. method for identifying cause and effect relationships by following rules against bias

t. an association or relationship between the occurrence of two or more events

Multiple-Choice

_____ 1. Rod Plotnik begins this module with the example of Dusty, a hyperactive seven-year old, to show that
   a. often psychology must yield to medical science
   b. psychology needs accurate answers to highly complex problems
   c. science must recognize the problems for which it cannot find answers
   d. hyperactivity can be controlled by high doses of vitamin C

_____ 2. The scientific method is defined as
   a. a general approach to answering questions that minimizes errors
   b. a faith that precise equipment will produce accurate information
   c. all of the findings of science in the modern era
   d. a set of guidelines published by the American Academy of Science

_____ 3. Which one of the following has the *lowest* potential for error or bias?
   a. case study
   b. survey
   c. experiment
   d. testimonial

_____ 4. When you encounter a testimonial, you know that it is
   a. true, if enough other people also report it
   b. false, because it is only a personal belief
   c. true, if the person conveying it has a good reputation for honesty
   d. possibly true, but not proven by science

_____ 5. A good example of a self-fulfilling prophecy is the belief that
   a. there's no use studying for multiple-choice exams because the questions are tricky
   b. psychology requires more study than literature
   c. if you do all your studying the night before the exam you'll do better
   d. you don't have to take notes in class if you listen carefully

_____ 6. One of the main disadvantages of the survey method is that
   a. many people won't go to the trouble of filling out the survey
   b. the results will be biased if the sample is not representative
   c. it is difficult to survey enough subjects to make the results valid
   d. it takes so long to conduct a survey that the method is impractical for most purposes

_____ 7. When she wears her lucky socks, Gail wins three golf matches out of four, a _____ correlation between wearing the socks and winning
   a. perfect negative
   b. negative
   c. positive
   d. perfect positive

_____ 8. Does this prove that the socks are the cause of Gail's winning?
   a. yes
   b. no
   c. it would if she won *every* time she wore the socks
   d. which socks Gail wears cannot possibly have anything to do with the outcome of the matches she plays

_____ 9. You probably hope the correlation coefficient between using this Study Guide and getting an A in the course is
   a. +1.00
   b. -1.00
   c. 0.00
   d. +0.00

_____ 10. Whether to do research in a naturalistic or laboratory setting involves the issue of
   a. comprehensiveness versus cost
   b. testimonial versus science
   c. realism versus control
   d. objectivity versus subjectivity

_____ 11. The special treatment given to the subjects in the experimental group is called the
   a. hypothesis
   b. independent variable
   c. dependent variable
   d. control variable

_____ 12. Which one of the following is an example of random selection?
   a. winning numbers in the lottery
   b. annual National Football League player draft
   c. numbers people play in the lottery
   d. annual Miss America contest

_____ 13. The purpose of having a control group in an experiment is to
   a. show what results the opposite treatment would produce
   b. show how a different group would react to the treatment
   c. identify and rule out the behavior that results from simply participating in the experiment
   d. provide backup subjects in case any members of the experimental group are unable to continue

_____ 14. Should you volunteer to be a subject in a psychological experiment?
   a. no, because you are completely at the mercy of the researcher
   b. yes, because ethical guidelines protect subjects from danger or undue deception
   c. no, because they'll never tell you what the experiment was really about
   d. yes, because looking dumb or foolish occasionally makes us more humble

_____ 15. The attitude of most psychologists toward the use of animals in research is that
   a. scientists must have complete freedom to conduct their research however they see fit
   b. ethical concerns are involved in research on humans but not on animals
   c. animals have no rights
   d. the issue is complicated and calls for a balance between animal rights and research needs

Answers for Module 2

True-False	Flashcards	Multiple-Choice
1. T	1. d	1. b
2. F	2. c	2. a
3. T	3. t	3. c
4. F	4. r	4. d
5. T	5. l	5. a
6. F	6. j	6. b
7. T	7. g	7. c
8. F	8. s	8. b
9. T	9. o	9. a
10. F	10. a	10. c
	11. b	11. b
	12. f	12. a
	13. k	13. c
	14. i	14. b
	15. m	15. d
	16. p	
	17. q	
	18. e	
	19. n	
	20. h	

Brain's Building Blocks

Psychology as a Spectrum of Approaches

In the first module we got acquainted with psychology and learned some of its history. In the second module we saw how psychologists pursue knowledge. It is all interesting and important, yet you could say that psychology itself really begins in Module 3.

Remember the six approaches to psychology discussed in the first module? I find it useful to think of them as forming a spectrum, a rainbow of ideas. At one end there is the psychobiological approach — the brain and nervous system Rod Plotnik describes in this module and the next. At the other end is the cross-cultural approach — the social interactions he covers in the last module, which examines social psychology.

I put the brain and nervous system at the beginning of the spectrum because the brain seems like the most obvious, most elemental starting point in psychology. You could just as well put social interaction first, however, because we become experts about other people long before we know anything about the brain. It doesn't really matter; the point is that the psychobiological and cross-cultural approaches are polar opposites in how we think about psychology.

The other four approaches (psychoanalytic, cognitive, behavioral, and humanistic) fall somewhere within the spectrum. How you arrange them only reveals your biases about their relative importance. (Which process, for example, do you consider more dominant — thinking or feeling?)

Our Starting Point, Deep in the Fields of Biology and Chemistry

At the far extreme we are studying now, psychology is almost pure biology and chemistry. But when Rod Plotnik discusses social psychology in the last module, or whenever he brings in the cross-cultural approach on one of his Cultural Diversity explorations, you will see just how deeply psychology also reaches into the fields of anthropology and sociology.

Now you can appreciate why this module is not an easy one to master (and probably wasn't an easy one to write, either). It involves a mini-course in biology. You could easily get lost just trying to remember the key terms. My advice is to concentrate on the *processes* involved. Try to appreciate how the brain and nervous system stand between us and the rest of the world, helping us understand it and make the best use of it. I suppose loyal Trekkies could compare the brain to the Starship Enterprise, going bravely where no man has gone before, in the name of peace and the orderly regulation of our affairs.

Effective Student Tip 3

Meet Your New Friend, the Professor

Last semester it was Jason. Somewhat brash, but immediately likable, Jason came up to my desk after the first class and announced, "I'm getting an 'A' in your class!"

I like it when students make such pronouncements. For one thing, I learn their names right away. For another, we have the beginnings of a relationship. But most importantly, we have established a basis for working together. Now that I know Jason really wants an 'A,' I've got to pay attention to him and try to keep him on track. For his part, Jason has to make a genuine effort, unless he wants me to think he is just a blowhard. Some students may not have much of an investment in the class, but Jason and I know what we are doing. We're serious.

Meanwhile, that girl in the back who frowned all through the first lecture..., that guy who didn't take any notes..., and others who are just faces in the crowd for the first few weeks..., all these students could learn something useful from Jason.

Say hello to your professor right away. Let him or her get to know you. You need a friend in this new class, and what better person than the professor?

Your response...

What kind of relationship do you usually have with your teachers? Friendly? Formal? None at all?

Key Terms

Perhaps you know some of these terms from biology. Which will require the most study?

action potential

afferent [sensory] neurons

all-or-none law

Alzheimer's disease

axon

axon membrane

basal ganglia

cell body

central nervous system

curare

dendrites

efferent [motor] neurons

fertilized egg

glial cells

interneuron

ions

mescaline

mind-body question

myelin sheath

nerve impulse

nerves

neural plasticity

neuron

neurotransmitter

Parkinson's disease

peripheral nervous system

phantom limb

reflex

resting state

reuptake

sodium pump

stereotaxic procedure

synapse

terminal buttons

Outline

- *INTRODUCTION*

  ☐ *How does* **Alzheimer's disease** *illustrate the importance of the building blocks of the brain?*

A. *Overview: Human Brain*

  1. What is the brain made of?

     a. **Glial cells**

     b. **Neurons**

  2. How do brain cells develop?

     a. **Fertilized egg**

     b. Growth and development

  3. Can the brain repair its damaged cells?

  4. Is the brain the same as the mind? [the **mind-body question**]

     a. How mind influences brain

     b. How brain influences mind

B. *Neurons: Structure & Function*

    1. **Cell body**

    2. **Dendrites**

    3. **Axon**

    4. **Myelin sheath**

    5. **Terminal buttons**

    6. **Synapse**

C. *Neurons versus Nerves*

    1. Can arms be reattached?

       a. **Peripheral nervous system**

       b. **Nerves**

       c. **Central nervous system**

    2. Nerves and neurons

D. *Sending Information*

    1. **Axon membrane**

    2. **Ions**

    3. Resting state

       a. **Resting state**

       b. **Sodium pump**

    4. **Action potential**

    5. Nerve impulse

       a. **Nerve impulse**

       b. **All-or-none law**

E. *Neurotransmitters and Receptors*

    1. What is happening to Ina's neurons?

    2. How **neurotransmitters** work

       a. Chemical keys and locks

       b. Either excitatory or inhibitory

3. How many chemical keys and locks?

4. How does Alzheimer's affect neurotransmitters?

5. What are the new neurotransmitters?

F. Reflex Responses

1. How do you move your hand without thinking (a **reflex**)?

2. Four steps in a reflex response

   a. Receptors in skin

   b. **Afferent [sensory] neurons**

   c. **Interneuron**

   d. **Efferent [motor] neurons**

3. Functions of reflexes

G. Research Focus: Phantom Limb

1. What happens after amputation?

2. What is **phantom limb**?

3. What is **neural plasticity**?

H. Cultural Diversity: Drugs

☐ *If it is true that all human societies seem to discover or invent psychoactive drugs, what does this say about our species? Is there a lesson for psychology?*

1. Cocaine – blocking **reuptake**

2. **Curare** – blocking receptors

3. **Mescaline** – mimics neurotransmitters

I. Application: Fetal Tissue Transplant

1. **Parkinson's disease**

2. **Basal ganglia**

3. Issues surrounding fetal tissue transplantation

4. Fetal tissue transplant – **stereotaxic procedure**

Language Enhancement Guide

IDIOMATIC EXPRESSIONS AND CULTURAL TERMS

The following are idiomatic expressions and cultural terms found in the module. Some of them have more than one meaning; the definition given here on the right is for the way the author uses the expression in this module. Remember that these words, like all words, can have different meanings in other contexts.

breaks down (43) = stops working

jerk away (52) = to quickly move away

VOCABULARY BUILDING: Word Analysis

Instructions: Study the following table of common prefixes, suffixes, and roots and then guess the meanings of the terms in the table that follows. The number in parentheses ( ) refers to the page in the current module where you can find the word. You can find the definition for any word marked with a **G** in the textbook Glossary. Words that are not marked are used by the textbook author in other modules. Remember that these words, like all words, can have different meanings in other contexts.

Exercise 1: Prefix

Prefix/Root	Meaning
pre-	before
un-	not
re-	again
flex	bend
natal	birth

Word	Definition
prefix	
prejudice (G)	
prenatal (G)	
prewired (46)	
reanalyzed	
recall (G)	
reflex (G)	
regrow (57)	
reuptake (55)	
unconscious (G)	
unaware (52)	

Exercise 2: Neurotransmitter

Word/Prefix/Suffix	Definition
inter-	between
neuro-	nerve
trans -	carry
plant	place, put
dis-	not
port	carry
-ion	the process of/the act of
-er	one who, that which
duc/duct/duce	lead/take/bend

Word	Definition
neurotransmitter (51)	
interneuron (54)	
transplant (56)	
transplantation (56)	
interconnect	
interaction	
disconnect	
motion	the process or act of moving
transportation	
transmit	
transmission	
transduction (85)	
transforms (90)	

True-False

_____ 1. Science has determined that the mind is a separate entity from the brain.

_____ 2. If that ad "this is your brain on drugs" isn't scary enough, you can add the fact that damaged neurons are not regrown or replaced.

_____ 3. Most neurons have a cell body, dentrites, and an axon.

_____ 4. A reflex is an action you have learned to execute so fast you don't think about it.

_____ 5. The "all-or-none law" refers to the fact that ions are either positively or negatively charged.

_____ 6. Neurotransmitters are the keys that unlock the receptors of dentrites, cell bodies, muscles, and organs.

_____ 7. The steady reduction in an important neurotransmitter in the brain is part of the cause of Alzheimer's disease.

_____ 8. Nerves are located in the central nervous system; neurons are in the peripheral nervous system.

_____ 9. Drugs like cocaine and mescaline achieve their effects by interfering with the normal workings of neurotransmitters.

_____ 10. The stereotaxic procedure is the treatment of Parkinson's disease with a drug called L-dopa.

Test-Taking Tips

You don't always have to remember _everything_ in order to get the question right. A combination of careful reading of the question and answers, plus reliance on your own general knowledge and intelligence, often reveals the correct answer. Here are some hints:

- Be wary of answers stated in extreme terms like "always," "never," or "100 percent."

- Be wary of answers that defy all common sense.

- Be wary of answers that appear to be way off the point.

- Be wary of answers that contain nonsense statements or that do not make sense.

- Be wary of answers that seem way out of keeping for the subject involved.

- Be wary of answers that don't fit in with everything else you know about the subject.

Flashcards

Match each key term to the definition given in the textbook.

_____ 1. action potential

_____ 2. all-or-none law

_____ 3. Alzheimer's disease

_____ 4. central nervous system

_____ 5. curare

_____ 6. dendrites

_____ 7. glial cells

_____ 8. ions

_____ 9. mind-body question

_____ 10. nerve impulse

_____ 11. neuron

_____ 12. neurotransmitter

_____ 13. Parkinson's disease

_____ 14. peripheral nervous system

_____ 15. phantom limb

_____ 16. reflex

_____ 17. reuptake

_____ 18. sodium pump

_____ 19. synapse

_____ 20. terminal buttons

a. process of removing neurotransmitters from synapse by reabsorbtion into terminal buttons

b. a chemical process responsible for keeping axon charged by returning sodium ions outside axon

c. vivid experience of sensations and feelings coming from a limb that has been amputated

d. branchlike extensions that arise from cell body and receive and pass signals to cell body

e. bulblike swellings at end of axon's branches that store neurotransmitters

f. if an action potential starts at the beginning of an axon, it will continue to the end of the axon

g. brain cell with specialized extensions for receiving and transmitting electrical signals

h. brain cells that provide scaffolding, insulation, chemicals to protect and support neuron growth

i. very small space between terminal button and adjacent dendrite, muscle fiber, or body organ

j. tiny electrical current that is generated when positive sodium ions rush inside the axon

k. tremors, shakes, progressive slowing of voluntary movements with feelings of depression

l. incurable, fatal disease involving brain damage, with memory loss, deterioration of personality

m. chemical particles that have electrical charges; opposite charges attract and like charges repel

n. system of neurons located in brain and spinal cord; limited capacity to regrow or regenerate

o. series of separate action potentials that take place segment by segment down length of axon

p. includes all the nerves that extend from spinal cord and carry messages to and from organs

q. chemical key with a particular shape that only fits a similarly shaped chemical lock or receptor

r. a drug that enters bloodstream and blocks receptors on muscles, causing paralysis

s. asks how complex mental activities can be generated by physical properties of the brain

t. an unlearned, involuntary reaction to some stimulus; prewired by genetic instructions

Multiple-Choice

_____ 1. Rod Plotnik begins with the example of Alzheimer's disease to illustrate the
   a. sad fact that the brain inevitably wears out
   b. hope offered by a new operation for those afflicted with the disease
   c. type of disease that could be prevented if people would take care of themselves
   d. key importance of the building blocks that make up the brain's informational network

_____ 2. Is the mind the same as the brain? Rod Plotnik says that
   a. the mind must be separate — otherwise there would be no soul
   b. brain and mind are closely linked, but exactly how remains a mystery
   c. the physical brain is the only thing — there is no actual "mind"
   d. questions like this are best left to philosophers

_____ 3. The human brain contains about _____ neurons and glial cells
   a. one thousand
   b. 100 thousand
   c. one trillion
   d. a zillion

_____ 4. Unlike nerves, neurons
   a. are not replaced or regrown
   b. have the ability to regrow or reattach
   c. are located outside the brain and spinal cord
   d. have no dendrites or axons

_____ 5. The purpose of the myelin sheath is to
   a. receive signals from neurons, muscles, or sense organs
   b. wrap around and insulate an axon
   c. protect the nucleus of the cell body
   d. drain dangerous electricity away from the brain

_____ 6. An unlearned, involuntary reaction to a stimulus is called a/n
   a. explosion
   b. electrical burst
   c. conditioned reflex
   d. reflex

_____ 7. The purpose of the ions in the axon's membrane is to
   a. generate a miniature electrical current
   b. plug up the tiny holes in the membrane's semipermeable skin
   c. pump excess sodium out of the neuron
   d. dry up the watery fluid that collects in the membrane

_____ 8. The axon is insulated and protected by the
   a. synapse
   b. terminal button
   c. myelin sheath
   d. sodium pump

_____ 9. John Thomas' arms could be reattached because
   a. neurons have the ability to regrow, regenerate, or reattach
   b. neurons are part of the peripheral nervous system
   c. nerves have the ability to regrow, regenerate, or reattach
   d. nerves are part of the central nervous system

_____ 10. The "all-or-none law" explains what happens when
   a. positively and negatively charged ions meet
   b. an impulse starts at the beginning of an axon
   c. electrical impulses spread throughout the body
   d. your brain gets the idea of a six-pack

_____ 11. If receptors in muscle fibers are thought of as locks, the keys are
   a. the action potential of the axon
   b. synapses
   c. the resting state of the axon
   d. neurotransmitters

_____ 12. The effect of a neurotransmitter on an adjacent neuron, muscle, or organ is
   a. excitatory
   b. inhibitory
   c. either excitatory or inhibitory
   d. determined by the all-or-none law

_____ 13. Endorphin, a natural pain killer in the brain, offers an example of
   a. the key role that neurotransmitters play in regulating our lives
   b. the way neurotransmitters out of control can cause diseases like Alzheimer's
   c. hope for finding a cure for Parkinson's disease
   d. left-over entities in the brain (like the appendix in the body)

_____ 14. The process of neural plasticity was discovered through research on
   a. Parkinson's disease
   b. phantom limb
   c. Alzheimer's disease
   d. reattachment of severed limbs

_____ 15. The newest hope for sufferers of Parkinson's disease is treating damaged cells with
   a. a new drug called L-dopa
   b. massive injections of dopamine
   c. genetically engineered cells grown in the laboratory
   d. transplanted human fetal brain tissue

Answers for Module 3

True-False	Flashcards	Multiple-Choice
1. F	1. j	1. d
2. T	2. f	2. b
3. T	3. l	3. c
4. F	4. n	4. a
5. F	5. r	5. b
6. T	6. d	6. d
7. T	7. h	7. a
8. F	8. m	8. c
9. T	9. s	9. c
10. F	10. o	10. b
	11. g	11. d
	12. q	12. c
	13. k	13. a
	14. p	14. b
	15. c	15. d
	16. t	
	17. a	
	18. b	
	19. i	
	20. e	

Incredible Nervous System

A Golden Age of Biology

Not long ago a researcher commenting on a startling and provocative new idea about human functioning remarked that we are living in "a Golden Age of biology." Hardly a week goes by without the media reporting a new breakthrough in genetics, evolutionary science, or human health. When early nineteenth-century scientists discovered the Rosetta Stone, they suddenly had a blueprint that unlocked the secrets of ancient Egypt. Today's scientists are mapping the genes and discovering the blueprint for how we humans are constructed.

Progress in psychology has been no less dramatic. Neuroscientists, who study the brain and nervous system, are coming closer and closer to explaining human consciousness, perhaps the greatest mystery of all.

In the previous module, Rod Plotnik asked the question, "are mind and brain two things, or the same thing?" This is an old argument in psychology and philosophy. Plotnik gave you some of the reasoning on both sides. This debate is rapidly changing, however. For one thing, it is becoming less the province of philosophy and more the property of neuroscience. Philosophers continue to attempt to use logic and reason to find an answer, but for the first time neuroscientists are able to look into the functioning brain (Plotnik tells how) and conduct laboratory experiments on thinking in action.

The Psychobiological Approach to Psychology

In the first module, Rod Plotnik carefully laid out six major approaches to psychology. It is hard to overstress the importance of becoming familiar with these six approaches. If you can learn them, and begin to see their reflections in all the facts and ideas you encounter in the textbook, you will be well on your way to having an overall view of the structure of the field of psychology and a real grasp of its organization.

The previous module, on the workings of the brain, and this one, on the functioning of the nervous system, contain the heart of the psychobiological approach to psychology. Understand that the six approaches are not simply matters of the personal interests of researchers and practicing psychologists. They are bold claims to explain *everything* in psychology, and to have the best answers to our needs for specific health and therapeutic applications. Right now, the psychobiological approach seems to be winning the debate. We live in an exciting time.

Effective Student Tip 4

Why You Must Be Effective in College

Effectiveness comes into play in all our endeavors, the most trivial as well as the most crucial. Consider a systems analyst, triumphant in the solution of a tricky problem (effectiveness confirmed), who then wheels around and fires a paper ball in a perfect jump shot into the wastebasket across the room (effective again). The urge behind each effort was effectiveness, but realistically it's more important that our systems analyst solve the problem than make the imaginary buzzer-beating shot.

If we were only dealing with office wastebasketball, we could afford to ignore the psychological factor of effectiveness. The stakes aren't very high. College is a different matter — probably the highest stakes in your life so far.

College is an essential rite of passage in our society, a critical bridge over which you cross into adulthood. College is more important today than ever, with at least two outcomes of great consequence: (1) College may determine whether you gain admittance to a technologically sophisticated world of commerce, industry, and the professions. (2) College helps shape your self-esteem and psychological health.

That's why you must handle your college experience effectively. Your future depends on it.

Your response...

Realistically, and aside from your "official" goals, what do you hope to get out of going to college?

Key Terms

There are more than the usual number of Key Terms in this module because it relies so heavily on biological concepts and ideas. If you have taken some biology, these terms will come fairly easily. If not, you will have to work harder on this module than on many others. Remind yourself that psychology is becoming an increasingly biological discipline. The work is difficult, but the rewards are great.

adrenal glands

amygdala

anterior pituitary

auditory association area

autonomic nervous system

Broca's area and Broca's aphasia

central nervous system

cerebellum

chromosome

computerized axial tomography (CAT scan)

cortex

endocrine system

fight-flight response

forebrain

fragile X syndrome

frontal lobe

frontal lobotomy

gene

gonads

hippocampus

homeostasis

hypothalamus

limbic system

magnetic resonance imaging (MRI scan)

medulla

midbrain

motor cortex

neglect syndrome

occipital lobes

pancreas

parasympathetic division

parietal lobe

peripheral nervous system

pons

positron emission tomography (PET scan)

posterior pituitary

primary auditory cortex

primary visual cortex

sex differences in the brain

somatic nervous system

somatosensory cortex

split-brain operation

sympathetic division

temporal lobe

thalamus

theory of evolution

thyroid

visual agnosia

visual association area

Wernicke's area and Wernicke's aphasia

zygote

Outline

- *INTRODUCTION*

  □ *What do Rod Plotnik's wildly different examples of unusual brains — Jason, Lucy, Steve, and baby Theresa — tell us about the development and functioning of our own brains?*

A. Genes & Evolution

    1. Genetic instructions

        a. Fertilization

        b. **Zygote**

        c. **Chromosome**

        d. Chemical alphabet (DNA)

        e. **Genes** and proteins

        f. **Fragile X syndrome**

    2. Evolution and the human brain

        a. **Theory of evolution**

        b. Human ancestors

B. Studying the Living Brain

    1. Scanning the *structure* of the brain

        a. **Computerized axial tomography (CAT scan)**

        b. **Magnetic resonance imaging (MRI scan)**

    2. Scanning the *function* of thebrain

        a. **Positron emission tomography (PET scan)**

        b. Identifying which areas of brain are involved in which mental activities

C. Organization of the Brain

    1. Two divisions of nervous system

        a. **Central nervous system**

            (1) Brain

            (2) Spinal cord

        b. **Peripheral nervous system**

2. Two subdivisions of peripheral nervous system

    a. **Somatic nervous system**

        (1) Afferent (sensory) fibers

        (2) Efferent (motor) fibers

    b. **Autonomic nervous system** [also see Limbic System]

3. Two subdivisions of autonomic nervous system

    a. **Sympathetic division**

    b. **Parasympathetic division**

    c. **Homeostasis**

4. What are the three major parts of the brain?

    a. **Forebrain**

    b. **Midbrain**

    c. Hindbrain

        (1) **Pons**

        (2) **Medulla**

        (3) **Cerebellum**

D. Control Centers: Four Lobes

☐ *What is the anatomical problem for which Plotnik describes the **cortex** as a "clever solution"?*

☐ *Why did baby Theresa live only nine days?*

1. **Frontal lobe** and frontal lobotomy

    a. First frontal lobotomy: an accident (amazing story of Phineas Gage)

    b. What is a **frontal lobotomy**?

    c. What did lobotomies do?

    d. Frontal lobe functions

        (1) **Motor cortex**

        (2) Motor cortex organization

        (3) Frontal lobe: cognitive functions

2. **Parietal lobe**: functions

    a. **Somatosensory cortex**

    b. Somatosensory cortex organization

    c. Parietal lobe: cognitive functions

3. **Temporal lobe**: functions

    a. **Primary auditory cortex** and **auditory association area**

    b. **Wernicke's area** and **Wernicke's aphasia**

    c. **Broca's area** and **Broca's aphasia**

4. **Occipital lobes**: functions

    a. **Primary visual cortex** and **visual association area**

    b. **Visual agnosia**

    c. **Neglect syndrome**

E. Limbic System: Old Brain

☐ *Why is the limbic system often called our "old brain" or our "animal brain"?*

☐ *What is the function of each of its four parts?*

1. Structures and functions of **limbic system**

    a. **Hypothalamus**

    b. **Amygdala**

    c. **Hippocampus**

    d. **Thalamus**

2. Autonomic nervous system

    a. **Sympathetic division** and the **flight-fight response**

    b. **Parasympathetic division**

    c. **Homeostasis**

F. Endocrine System

☐ *In what way is the **endocrine system** similar to the nervous system?*

1. A hormonal system – **hypothalamus**

2. Endocrine system's glands

   a. **Posterior pituitary**

   b. **Anterior pituitary**

   c. **Pancreas**

   d. **Thyroid**

   e. **Adrenal glands**

   f. **Gonads**

G. Research Focus: Sexual Differences

☐ *What factors might explain the existence of **sex differences in the brain**?*

☐ *How important do you think these differences are in everyday life?*

H. Cultural Diversity: Racial Myths

1. Skull size and intelligence

2. Brain size and intelligence

I. Application: Split-Brain

☐ *What does the **split-brain operation** reveal about how the brain works?*

1. Do the hemispheres have special tasks?

   a. Left hemisphere

      (1) Verbal

      (2) Mathematical

      (3) Analytical

   b. Right hemisphere

      (1) Nonverbal

      (2) Spatial

      (3) Holistic

2. How do brain parts interact?

Language Enhancement Guide

IDIOMATIC EXPRESSIONS AND CULTURAL TERMS

The following are idiomatic expressions and cultural terms found in the module. Some of them have more than one meaning; the definition given here on the right is for the way the author uses the expression in this module. Remember that these words, like all words, can have different meanings in other contexts.

slightly built (61) = very thin

barely talk (61) = have difficulty talking

cut away (61) = removed

triggered (by) (66) = started, stimulated

knocked (unconscious) (67) = hit, struck

Jell-O (67) = the trade name of a gelatin dessert; the trade name has become generic (or general) name for any product like it

to carry out (68) = to do

to make good on (69) = to deliver, to carry out, to meet

cope with (75) = adapt to, solve, manage

child-rearing (78) = taking care of a child

a well known (person) (79) = famous, prominent

promote (brain growth) (79) = stimulate

at this point in time (79) = at this time

VOCABULARY BUILDING: Word Analysis

Instructions: Study the following table of common prefixes, suffixes, and roots and then guess the meanings of the terms in the table that follows. The number in parentheses ( ) refers to the page in the current module where you can find the word. You can find the definition for any word marked with a **G** in the textbook Glossary. Words that are not marked are used by the textbook author in other modules. Remember that these words, like all words, can have different meanings in other contexts.

Exercise 1. Parasympathetic

Prefix/Root/Suffix	Meaning
para-	beside/resembling
sym-	with/together
gen-	become/produce/bear
soma / physio	body
-ic	characterized by/having the nature of/like/belonging to
pathy	feeling/sorrow/suffering
ogical/al	like/being/belonging/characterized by/ process/conditions
med	medicine, medical doctor

Word	Meaning
parasympathetic (66)	
sympathetic (66)	
sympathy	
paramedic	
physiological (G)	
genetic (62)	
somatic (66)	

STRUCTURAL CLUES: Transitions

Transitions are words (or phrases) that show a relationship between two ideas in a text. Transitions prepare you for information that is about to come; they let you know that the next idea may be a contrast, a conclusion, or an example of the previous idea. They appear between two parts of the same sentence, between two sentences, or between two paragraphs. Being able to recognize and understand transitional words and phrases will increase your reading speed and comprehension. Take a look at this example.

"If you went to work everyday and were exposed only to regular indoor lighting, your biological clock would take ten days to fully adapt. If, however, ..."

Without reading on, if you understand the function of the word however, you know that a contrasting idea is about to be presented. You can almost guess that the contrasting idea will have something to do with lighting. Now read the rest of the sentence.

"...you spent 6 to 8 hours of the first two days outside in bright sunlight, you would reset your biological clock and cause your circadian rhythm to be on local clock time."

The following table lists some common transitions and their functions:

Transition	Function
however, but, on the hand, rather, by contrast	present a contrasting idea
for example, for instance, similarly, another example, to illustrate	present an example to illustrate the preceding idea
in addition, additionally	present another idea, similar to the preceding one
as a result, therefore, consequently	present a result or conclusion
in other words	present the same idea in fresh new words
besides	in addition

Exercise 2

Instructions: Find the following sentences in Module 4. Read the first sentence or paragraph. As soon as you come to the transition at the beginning of the following sentence or paragraph, stop and guess what will come next. Then read on to see if you were correct.

p. 72, heading, Wernicke's Area, par. 1, "In almost all right-handed and left-handed people..." ("Curiously...")

p. 72, heading, Wernicke's Area, par. 3, "For example, a patient with..." ("Surprisingly...")

p. 72, heading, Audition or Hearing, par. 4, "The auditory association area..." ("Besides...")

p. 80, heading, What is a Split Brain, par 1, "When she was six years old..." ("In addition to...")

True-False

_____ 1. The brain and the spinal cord make up the central nervous system.

_____ 2. The right and left hemispheres of the brain make up the peripheral nervous system.

_____ 3. More than any other part, it is the operation of the hindbrain that makes you a person.

_____ 4. When Igor hands Dr. Frankenstein a fresh brain, what we see quivering in his hands is the cortex.

_____ 5. As human society evolves, the limbic system incorporates cooperative and positive tendencies and feelings into the brain.

_____ 6. The general tendency of the autonomic nervous system is homeostasis.

_____ 7. In the endocrine system, glands secrete hormones that affect many important bodily processes.

_____ 8. Psychologists now know that human intelligence is determined by both skull size and brain size.

_____ 9. The need to perform split-brain operations for medical purposes gives science a rare look at the degree of specialization in the brain's two hemispheres.

_____ 10. Science has finally explained why people are so different: each human being is either left-brained or right-brained.

Flashcards _for psych majors only..._

The Brain and Nervous System: Match each system or structure to its main components or functions.

_____ 1. central nervous system	a. sympathetic and parasympathetic divisions
_____ 2. peripheral nervous system	b. verbal, mathematical, analytical
_____ 3. somatic nervous system	c. motor cortex
_____ 4. autonomic nervous system	d. brain and spinal cord
_____ 5. frontal lobe	e. primary auditory cortex
_____ 6. parietal lobe	f. primary visual cortex
_____ 7. temporal lobe	g. somatic and autonomic nervous systems
_____ 8. occipital lobe	h. afferent (sensory) and efferent (motor) fibers
_____ 9. left hemisphere	i. nonverbal, spatial, holistic
_____ 10. right hemisphere	j. somatosensory cortex

Flashcards

Match each key term to the definition given in the textbook.

_____ 1. autonomic nervous system

_____ 2. central nervous system

_____ 3. cerebellum

_____ 4. computerized axial tomography (CAT scan)

_____ 5. cortex

_____ 6. endocrine system

_____ 7. fight-flight response

_____ 8. forebrain

_____ 9. frontal lobe

_____ 10. gene

_____ 11. gonads

_____ 12. homeostasis

_____ 13. hypothalamus

_____ 14. limbic system

_____ 15. magnetic resonance imaging (MRI scan)

_____ 16. occipital lobes

_____ 17. parietal lobe

_____ 18. peripheral nervous system

_____ 19. somatic nervous system

_____ 20. temporal lobe

a. all the nerves that extend from the spinal cord and carry messages to and from muscles, glands

b. tendency of autonomic nervous system to maintain balanced state of optimum functioning

c. passing low levels of X rays through brain and measuring radiation absorbed by brain cells

d. located directly in back of frontal lobe; functions include sense of touch, temperature, pain

e. glands (ovaries in females, testes in males) that regulate sexual development and reproduction

f. passing nonharmful radio frequencies though brain, measuring how signals and cells interact

g. system of glands which secrete hormones that affect organs, muscles, other glands in the body

h. located at back of brain; involved in coordinating but not initiating voluntary movements

i. part of limbic system; controls much of the endocrine system by regulating pituitary gland

j. a network of nerves that connect to sensory receptors or muscles you can move voluntarily

k. regulates heart rate, breathing, blood pressure, other mainly involuntary movements

l. a relatively large cortical area at the front part of the brain; involved in many functions

m. core of forebrain; involved in many motivational behaviors and organizing emotional behaviors

n. involved in hearing, speaking coherently, understanding verbal and written material

o. a thin layer of cells covering entire surface of forebrain; folds over on itself to form large area

p. involved in seeing, perceiving and recognizing visual objects

q. largest part of brain; has right and left sides (hemispheres) responsible for many functions

r. state of increased physiological arousal allowing for coping with threatening situations

s. made up of brain and spinal cord; carries information between brain and body

t. specific segment on strand of DNA containing instructions for building brain and body

Multiple-Choice

_____ 1. Rod Plotnik introduces us to four very different persons — Jason, Lucy, Steve, and baby Theresa — to show that
   a. one side of the brain controls most human behavior
   b. brain damage can strike almost anyone at any time
   c. the human nervous system is incredibly complex
   d. the brain will never be fully understood

_____ 2. The behavioral problems plaguing Jason, the child who had inherited fragile X syndrome, illustrate the role of _____ in human development
   a. evolution
   b. genetic instructions
   c. fertilization
   d. skull size

_____ 3. The new techniques of brain scans have a great advantage:
   a. they permit a look inside the living, functioning brain
   b. they are 100 percent harmless to the brain
   c. it is no longer necessary to perform frontal lobotomies in mental hospitals
   d. it's so hard to find volunteers for experimental brain surgery

_____ 4. Which one of the following is _not_ included in the peripheral nervous system?
   a. somatic nervous system
   b. autonomic nervous system
   c. limbic nervous system
   d. sympathetic nervous system

_____ 5. Which one of the following is _not_ one of the three main parts of the human brain?
   a. forebrain
   b. midbrain
   c. hindbrain
   d. topbrain

_____ 6. The cerebellum is an important part of the hindbrain that
   a. initiates voluntary movements
   b. influences social-emotional behavior
   c. coordinates voluntary movements and makes them graceful
   d. makes humans distinct from all other animals

_____ 7. The cortex is all folded and crinkled up because the human brain
   a. grows so fast during the first three years of life
   b. is divided into four separate lobes
   c. is protected by the skull
   d. evolved faster than the human skull that holds it

_____ 8. The incredible story of Phineas Gage's accident shows that
   a. the frontal lobe is critical to personality
   b. a person lives at best in a vegetative state after a frontal lobotomy
   c. the frontal lobe is wired to the opposite side of the body
   d. the frontal lobe receives sensory information from the body

_____ 9. Wernicke's aphasia and Broca's aphasia are evidence that
   a. language abilities are more inherited than acquired
   b. special areas of the lobes of the cortex control language abilities
   c. if one area is damaged, the other takes over for it
   d. human language is so complex that a number of things can go wrong with it

_____ 10. When you understand the limbic system, you understand why
   a. modern humans are so far advanced over their prehistoric ancestors
   b. a human can do so much more than an alligator
   c. modern society is still plagued by so many primitive behaviors
   d. the social life of human beings is so much more complex than that of alligators

_____ 11. If you saw a snake crawling out from under your car, what would happen next is an example of the
   a. fight-flight response
   b. homeostatic reaction
   c. parasympathetic push
   d. arouse-or-die response

_____ 12. Me Tarzan, you Jane. Therefore, according to research on sex differences in the brain:
   a. me spatial, you verbal
   b. me verbal, you spatial
   c. me emotional, you logical
   d. me lusty, you cold

_____ 13. The sad history of research on the relationship between intelligence and skull and brain size shows that
   a. when a Nobel Prize is involved, some scientists will fudge their data
   b. science can be influenced by the prejudices of the times
   c. science is not always the best way to answer a question about human behavior
   d. sloppy measurement can undercut a sound hypothesis

_____ 14. Which one of the following is _not_ true about hemispheric specializations?
   a. left hemisphere – verbal
   b. right hemisphere – holistic
   c. left hemisphere – mathematical
   d. right hemisphere – analytic

_____ 15. Are you left-brained or right-brained? The best answer is that you are probably
   a. left-brained, since you are a college student
   b. constantly using both hemispheres
   c. right-brained if you are female and left-brained if you are male
   d. left-brained, since most people are

Answers for Module 4

True-False	Flashcards	Multiple-Choice
1. T	1. k	1. c
2. F	2. s	2. b
3. F	3. h	3. a
4. T	4. c	4. c
5. F	5. o	5. d
6. T	6. g	6. c
7. T	7. r	7. d
8. F	8. q	8. a
9. T	9. l	9. b
10. F	10. t	10. c
	11. e	11. a
	12. b	12. a
	13. i	13. b
	14. m	14. d
	15. f	15. b
	16. p	
	17. d	
	18. a	
	19. j	
	20. n	

"The Brain and Nervous System" Quiz

1. d   2. g   3. h   4. a   5. c   6. j   7. e   8. f   9. b   10. i

Module 5

Sensation

What is Real?

Back in the happy days before I studied psychology, I simply "knew" that there was a real world out there and that it came straight into my mind (I never thought to wonder how, or what "mind" is). When you study sensation (Module 5), perception (Module 6), and consciousness (Module 7), however, it gets confusing. If you don't watch out, you could find yourself in the predicament of poor Descartes, whose search for a proof of existence had him doubting his own existence, until he decided that just thinking about the problem must prove he was there to do it.

The story begins in this module, with the mechanisms of the sense organs (eye, ear, nose, tongue, and skin) and the processes by which they receive stimuli (light and sound waves, chemicals, and pressures) from the environment. But be prepared for a disappointment: it doesn't mean a thing.

How We Relate to the World

Suppose that right in the middle of writing a great paper your computer suddenly crashed and all you could recover was a data dump of everything it "knew" about your paper. You would experience a similar disappointment. All you would see on the print-out would be a long succession of ones and zeros, the binary code in which computers work. It wouldn't mean a thing.

The processes of perception transform meaningless sensations into useful information. It's sort of like the word processing software that turns those ones and zeros in your paper into (hopefully) great prose. Now the raw sensations begin to take on meaning, as they are interpreted by the perceptual processes involved.

Are we finally in contact with the real world? In a way, but notice that we are also one step removed from that world, apprehending it second-hand through the possibly distorted mechanisms of perception. Even then, exactly *what* do the perceptions mean? The researchers in neuroscience we mentioned in the previous module are trying to find out. We could guess that the answer will involve a complex interaction of cognition and emotion, each enriching the information and making it more useful to us.

We could say that at last we have the real world, but now it is at least three steps removed, as we experience it in our conscious (and unconscious?) mind. How real is it anymore? Perhaps psychology must leave the question of reality to philosophers and theologians. I still believe it's out there, but now I know that what is in my mind is constructed, not real.

Effective Student Tip 5

Go Ahead, Ask Me

I am always astounded when I review my class lists early in the new semester. There are more than a few students who have not yet said a word in class.

For some, it is politeness. Heaven knows, I am flying, and they hesitate to interrupt. For others, it is modesty. Maybe the point they would make isn't all that brilliant. For others it is excruciating shyness. If they did speak up, they know the class would turn as one and sneer, "You idiot!"

For each of these students, an effective strategy would be to ask a simple question. A good question can be just the thing to begin your involvement in the class.

As you prepare for the next class, find something in the textbook or your lecture notes that really interests you. What more would you like to know? Think how you could ask about it in a short, clear question. Pick a moment when your question is relevant, then ask away. (If you feel you can't do it, ask your first question either before or after class. It's a start.)

What do you get out of it? Aside from the information you wanted, you have made contact with the professor and your fellow students. You have demonstrated to yourself that you can talk in class. And the class is more fun now.

Your response…

How comfortable do you feel in class? Do you talk? Is talking something you enjoy, or dread?

Key Terms

There are so many key terms in the module because it covers all of the senses. The terms may be easier to learn if you organize them by the senses they help explain.

---

acupuncture	frequency theory	placebo
adaptation	gate control theory of pain	placebo effect
afterimage	hair cells	primary auditory cortex
auditory association area	iris	pupil
auditory canal	lens	retina
auditory nerve	loudness	rods
cochlea	Meniere's disease	sensations
cochlear implant	middle ear	somatosensory cortex
conduction deafness	monochromats	sound waves
cones	motion sickness	taste
cornea	nearsightedness	taste buds
decibel	neural deafness	touch
dichromats	olfaction	transduction
direction of a sound	olfactory cells	trichromatic theory
disgust	opponent-process theory	tympanic membrane
double-blind design	outer ear	vertigo
endorphins	pain	vestibular system
external ear	pitch	visible spectrum
farsightedness	place theory	

Outline

- **INTRODUCTION**

    ☐ *How would you answer Rod Plotnik's question: "Do you see with your eyes or with your brain?"*

    ☐ *Can you explain how the three characteristics of all senses (below) produce the experiences of seeing, hearing, smelling, touching, tasting, and position?*

    1. **Transduction**

    2. **Adaptation**

    3. **Sensations**

A. *Eye: Stimulus, Structure, & Function*

1. Why can't you see radio waves?

☐ *What is the **visible spectrum** and what makes it visible?*

☐ *What happens when you look at something? Can you explain the process of looking?*

   a. Light waves

   b. Image reversed

   c. **Cornea**

   d. **Pupil**

   e. **Iris**

   f. **Lens**

   g. **Retina**

   h. Eyeball

      (1) Normal vision

      (2) **Nearsightedness**

      (3) **Farsightedness**

2. Retina: a mineature computer

   a. Photoreceptors

   b. **Rods**

   c. **Cones**

   d. Transduction

   e. Optic nerve and blind spot

3. Visual pathway: eye to brain

   a. Retina

   b. Optic nerve

   c. Primary visual cortex

   d. Association area and visual agnosia

   e. Information processing

   f. Stimulation or blindness

4. How do you see color?

   a. Wave lengths

   b. Theories of color vision

     (1) **Trichromatic theory**

     (2) **Opponent-process theory** based on **afterimage**

   c. Color blindness

     (1) **Monochromats**

     (2) **Dichromats**

B. Ear: Stimulus, Structure, & Function

1. Stimulus: **sound waves**

   a. Amplitude and **loudness**

   b. Frequency and **pitch**

2. How loud is the library?

   a. **Decibel**

   b. Why be concerned about decibels?

3. Hearing or auditory system

   a. **Outer ear**

     (1) **External ear**

     (2) **Auditory canal**

     (3) **Tympanic membrane**

   b. **Middle ear**

     (1) Ossicles

     (2) Oval window

   c. Inner ear

     (1) **Cochlea**

     (2) **Hair cells** and basilar membrane

     (3) **Auditory nerve**

d. Brain: auditory areas

    (1) **Primary auditory cortex**

    (2) **Auditory association area**

4. Information from sound waves

    a. Judging **direction of a sound**

    b. Judging pitch

        (1) **Frequency theory**

        (2) **Place theory**

    c. Judging **loudness**

C. Vestibular System

1. **Vestibular system**

    a. Semicircular canals

    b. Sense of position

2. **Motion sickness**

3. **Meniere's disease** and **vertigo**

D. Chemical Senses: Taste & Smell

1. **Taste**

    a. Four basic tastes

    b. Surface of the tongue

    c. **Taste buds**

    d. All tongues are not the same

    e. Taste and smell (flavor)

2. Smell or **olfaction**

☐ *What are the three functions of olfaction?*

    a. Stimulus

    b. **Olfactory cells**

    c. Sensations

    d. Functions of olfaction

E. Touch: Stimulus, Structure, & Function

   1. Sense of **touch**

      a. Skin

      b. Hair receptors

      c. Free nerve endings

      d. Pacinian corpuscle

   2. Brain areas – **somatosensory cortex**

F. Cultural Diversity: Different Tastes

   ☐ *Although most foods cause delight, some cause* **disgust**. *Why?*

   ☐ *Why is this experience automatically translated into a facial expression?*

G. Research Focus: Pain & Placebos

   1. Does the mind make pain go away?

      a. **Placebo**

      b. **Placebo effect**

   2. Research findings on the placebo effect

      a. **Double-blind design**

      b. Medical treatment or placebo effect?

H. Pain: A Different Sense

   1. **Pain** sensations

      a. Localized

      b. Generalized

   3. **Gate control theory of pain**

   3. **Endorphins**

   4. **Acupuncture** explained

      a. Competing stimuli

      b. Psychological factors

I. Application: Artificial Senses

1. Artificial visual system

   a. Eye and retina

   b. Brain implant

   c. Functional vision

2. Artificial hearing system

   a. **Conduction deafness**

   b. **Neural deafness**

   c. **Cochlear implant**

   d. How well do cochlear implants work?

Language Enhancement Guide

IDIOMATIC EXPRESSIONS AND CULTURAL TERMS

The following are idiomatic expressions and cultural terms found in the module. Some of them have more than one meaning; the definition given here on the right is for the way the author uses the expression in this module. Remember that these words, like all words, can have different meanings in other contexts.

billboards (85) =

breakdown (88) = stop working, stop functioning

The Nobel Prize (89) = A million dollar prize awarded each year by the Swedish Academy to people who have made major contributions to the world in such fields as medicine, biology, chemistry, economics, literature and world peace. The Nobel Prize is considered to be the highest academic honor a person can achieve.

Rolling Stones (94) = the name of a famous Rock and Roll music group

pick up (vibrations) (94) = respond to

jugular vein (102) = a large vein on the side of the neck

primary (95) = the first most important person, thing or process

secondary = the second most important person, thing or process

VOCABULARY BUILDING: Word Analysis

Instructions: Study the following table of common prefixes, suffixes, and roots and then guess the meanings of the terms in the table that follows. The number in parentheses ( ) refers to the page in the current module where you can find the word. You can find the definition for any word marked with a **G** in the textbook Glossary. Words that are not marked are used by the textbook author in other modules. Remember that these words, like all words, can have different meanings in other contexts.

Exercise 1: Visible

Prefix/Root/Suffix	Meaning
visi/vis/visual-	see
trans-	to send/carry across
-ion/tion	the process of/ the act of
spect-	to look/appearance

Word	Meaning
visible (86)	
vision	
spectrum (86)	
transparent (87)	
adaptation (85)	

Exercise 2: Periphery

Prefix/Root/Suffix	Meaning
peri-	around/about/surrounding/near
meter/metr	measure

Word	Meaning
periphery (88)	
peripheral (89)	
perimeter	
speedometer	

Exercise 3. Invisible

Prefix/Root/Suffix	Meaning
in/im -	not/without
audio	sound, hearing
-ive	tending to (be)/having to (be)
-ible/able	sensible, visible, readable
-ity	act of being
-al	like, being, belonging

Word	Meaning
invisible (86)	
inhibited (91)	
inactive	
imperfect	
incompetent	
immoral	
incompatible	
insensitivity	
audition (92)	
inaudible	
auditory	

True-False

_____ 1. All of the senses share three characteristics: transduction, adaptation, and the experience of "sensing" something.

_____ 2. The reason you can "see" a giraffe is that the animal emits light waves which humans can detect.

_____ 3. The retina performs the work called transduction.

_____ 4. The images you "see" are created by the primary visual cortex and related association area of the brain.

_____ 5. _All you baseball players, listen up!_ If your preferred eye is the left eye, you should bat left-handed.

_____ 6. Sound waves vary in amplitude and frequency.

_____ 7. The vestibular system provides feedback on your body's position in space by interpreting sound waves from your environment.

_____ 8. The tongue has receptors for only four basic tastes.

_____ 9. Humans won't eat just anything — we have biologically determined preferences for some foods and feelings of disgust at the thought of others.

_____ 10. Acupuncture often produces pain relief — probably by causing secretion of endorphins in the brain.

Flashcards

Match each key term to the definition given in the textbook.

_____ 1. acupuncture

a. a universal facial expression (eyes closed, lips curled downward) indicating rejection of foods

_____ 2. adaptation

b. says rubbing an injured area or becoming involved in other activities blocks pain impulses

_____ 3. disgust

c. thin film with three layers of cells located at back of eyeball; includes photoreceptor cells

_____ 4. endorphins

d. may result when eyeball is too long; result is that near objects are clear but distant are blurry

_____ 5. frequency theory

e. smell receptors located in nasal passages; use mucus into which volatile molecules dissolve

_____ 6. gate control theory of pain

f. says color vision is due to eye and brain responding to either red-green or blue-yellow

_____ 7. nearsightedness

g. a sense organ changes physical energy into electrical signals that become neural impulses

_____ 8. olfactory cells

h. says color vision is due to three kinds of cones in retina sensitive to blue, green, or red

_____ 9. opponent-process theory

i. includes pressure, temperature, and pain; from miniature sensors beneath outer layer of skin

_____ 10. place theory

j. inserting thin needles into various points on the body's surface and twirling them to relieve pain

_____ 11. placebo effect

k. stimulus activates sensory receptors, producing electrical signals that are processed by the brain

_____ 12. retina

l. one particular segment of electromagnetic energy whose waves can be seen by human eye

_____ 13. sensations

m. three semicircular canals in inner ear determination our sense of balance and position

_____ 14. sound waves

n. chemicals produced by the brain and secreted in response to injury or stress cause reduced pain

_____ 15. touch

o. says rate at which nerve impulses reach brain determine how low a sound is

_____ 16. transduction

p. change in patient's illness attributable to an imagined treatment rather than to a medical one

_____ 17. trichromatic theory

q. dizziness and nausea resulting from malfunction of semicircular canals of vestibular system

_____ 18. vertigo

r. prolonged or continuous stimulation results in a decreases responding by the sense organs

_____ 19. vestibular system

s. location of basilar membrane vibrations determines medium and higher sounds

_____ 20. visible spectrum

t. stimuli for audition; resemble ripples on pond; have height (amplitude) and speed (frequency)

Multiple-Choice

_____ 1. Rod Plotnik says the experience of Katie, a blind woman who had tiny gold wires implanted into the back of her brain, raises the question
    a. are some cases of blindness actually hysterical?
    b. can blind persons regain their sight through intense practice?
    c. do you see with your eyes or with your brain?
    d. can science go too far in tampering with human capabilities?

_____ 2. The process by which a sense organ changes physical stimuli into impulses is termed
    a. transduction
    b. adaptation
    c. sensing
    d. experiencing

_____ 3. A decline in responding with prolonged or continuous stimulation is called
    a. transduction
    b. adaptation
    c. sensing
    d. experiencing

_____ 4. When you get that new road rocket for graduation, you may want a radar detector, too, because those things
    a. see the pulses of light that radar guns use
    b. hear the faint vibrations of radar guns
    c. see long wave lengths you can't
    d. make your car look cool

_____ 5. The function of the cornea is to
    a. bend and focus light waves into a narrower beam of light
    b. screen out irrelevant light waves
    c. prevent convergence from occurring too soon
    d. add color to light waves entering the eye

_____ 6. If you see close objects clearly but distant objects appear blurry, you are
    a. nearsighted
    b. farsighted
    c. normal
    d. abnormal

_____ 7. The work of the retina is to
    a. add sharp focus to what you are seeing
    b. transform light waves into impulses
    c. turn the inverted image we see right side up
    d. change impulses into light waves we can see

_____ 8. How loud a sound seems is determined by the _____ of the sound waves
    a. amplitude
    b. frequency
    c. pitch
    d. cycle

_____ 9. If a tree falls in an uninhabited forest, does it make any sound?
  a. obviously, it does
  b. not if there is no human there to "hear" it
  c. it depends on whether we define "sound" as the waves of air or the subjective experience of hearing
  d. I thought this was psychology, not philosophy

_____ 10. Infants have the widest range of human hearing because
  a. babies need to keep track of where their mothers are at all times
  b. hearing is an important part of language acquisition
  c. they're brand new
  d. science has not determined the reason

_____ 11. The function of the cochlea is to
  a. turn vibrations into nerve impulses
  b. move fluid forward toward the oval window
  c. house the hammer, anvil, and stirrup
  d. house the band of fibers called the auditory nerve

_____ 12. Our sense of movement and position in space is determined by
  a. movement of fluid in the three semicircular canals of the vestibular system
  b. the primary visual cortex and related association areas
  c. faint echoes from surrounding objects that the brain can decode
  d. the movement of fluid in the eardrum

_____ 13. Which one of the following is _not_ one of the four basic tastes?
  a. sweet
  b. sharp
  c. salty
  d. sour

_____ 14. Our sense of touch comes from
  a. a half-dozen miniature sensors located in the skin
  b. millions of tiny nerves on the surface of the skin
  c. special glands for pressure, temperature, and pain
  d. stimulation of the tiny hairs that cover the body

_____ 15. Can the ancient Oriental procedure called acupuncture actually relieve pain? Modern science says
  a. yes, because there are some mysteries Western science is not equipped to explain
  b. perhaps, because stimulation of certain points may cause the secretion of endorphins
  c. no, because there cannot be a relationship between twirling needles in the skin and pain caused by the nervous system
  d. no, because there is no research to date that supports acupuncture

Answers for Module 5

True-False	Flashcards	Multiple-Choice
1. T	1. j	1. c
2. F	2. r	2. a
3. T	3. a	3. b
4. T	4. n	4. c
5. F	5. o	5. a
6. T	6. b	6. a
7. F	7. d	7. b
8. T	8. e	8. a
9. F	9. f	9. c
10. T	10. s	10. c
	11. p	11. a
	12. c	12. a
	13. k	13. b
	14. t	14. a
	15. i	15. b
	16. g	
	17. h	
	18. q	
	19. m	
	20. l	

Module 6

Perception

How to Ruin a Professor's Day

When I took experimental psychology, years ago, our professor enjoyed bedeviling us with the same classic perceptual illusions that Rod Plotnik discusses in Module 6. The one that really got us was the famous Müller-Lyer illusion. It is so powerful that it fooled us every time, even after we already knew the lines were the same length. One day a troublemaker in the back row asked, "But *why* does it work?" Our professor hung his head and had to admit, "I don't know."

Today, cognitive psychology has an intriguing answer (it's in Module 6). Besides the fascination of discovering how sensing and perceiving work, understanding these processes can be personally liberating. Here's why.

The Task of Self-Management

Step on a rattlesnake and it whirls and strikes. Step on a human and... a hundred different things could happen. Instinct governs much of the snake's behavior, but almost none of the human's. That's why we humans constantly face the task of self-management, or self-regulation. We also face parallel tasks of managing physical objects and other people, but self-management is the most difficult because it's so subjective. As you will see in the modules on mental disorders, it's easy for things to get out of whack. Normally, the activity of self-management goes on so automatically it seems unconscious, but we are constantly working at it.

That's what I like about the module on perception. It helps us appreciate the incredibly complex processes of apprehending and interpreting reality, and in so doing can help us be more realistic about ourselves. There are many things in life to worry about and to fear. An important part of self-management is deciding which stimuli represent real threats and which do not. The disadvantage of our limitless freedom to create wonderful new things is our equally great ability to create fears where they are not appropriate. When we get a better handle on our processes of self-management, however, we begin to appreciate that some apparent perceptions are really glitches in the self-managing process, and we realize that we are scaring ourselves needlessly.

The modules on sensation and perception remind us that we are constantly creating our own reality. Just as illusions can fool us, we can torment ourselves with worries and fears about dangers that are illusory, not real.

Effective Student Tip 6

When You Participate, You Practice

My heart goes out to students who say "I would rather listen than talk...." They are invariably the quiet, supportive type of person the world needs a whole lot more of. (For a teacher, Hell would be a perpetual talk show, with everyone shouting at each other for all eternity and no one listening!) Yet I know that only listening is not really good for them.

Taking part in class discussion binds us to the group, satisfies deep social needs, and increases our sense of effectiveness. But it has a purely academic payoff as well. When you participate, you are practicing the facts and ideas of the course.

In class, you may have the strong feeling that you understand a point better than the student who is talking, maybe even better than the professor. When it's your turn to talk, you find out just how well you do understand it. As you struggle to put your ideas into words, you come to appreciate both what you have right and what you don't. The reactions of your professor and classmates further inform you how well you have grasped the material. Next time, you reword it, rework it, and begin to master it. The facts and ideas of the course are becoming more personal and more real. You aren't just sitting there waiting for the end of the period. You're really learning.

Your response...

Are you a talker or a listener in your classes? Is class discussion valuable, or a waste of time?

Key Terms

Many of these key terms open up a whole new world. You'll never see things quite the same way after you learn the principles explained by these terms. This module can be fun.

absolute threshold (Gustav Fechner)

Ames room

apparent motion

atmospheric perspective

brightness constancy

clairvoyance

closure principle

color constancy

continuity principle

convergence

cultural influences

depth perception

extrasensory perception (ESP)

figure-ground principle

Ganzfeld procedure

Gestalt approach

illusion

impossible figure

interposition

just noticeable difference (JND)

light and shadow

linear perspective

monocular depth cues

motion parallax

perception

perceptual constancy

perceptual sets

phi movement

precognition

principles of organization

proximity principle

psi

psychokinesis

real motion

relative size

retinal disparity

self-fulfilling prophecies

sensation

shape constancy

similarity principle

simplicity principle

size constancy

structuralism

subliminal messages

subliminal stimulus

telepathy

texture gradient

threshold

virtual reality

Weber's law

Outline

- *INTRODUCTION*

  ☐ *What are the three basic questions about perception Rod Plotnik says psychology tries to answer?*

A. *Perceptual Thresholds*

1. First question: at what point do we become aware of a stimulus?

   a. **Threshold**

   b. **Absolute threshold (Gustav Fechner)**

   c. **Subliminal stimulus**

2. Second question: at what point do we know if a stimulus has increased or decreased in intensity?

    a. **Just noticeable difference** (E. H. Weber)

    b. **Weber's law**

3. Importance of just noticeable differences (JNDs) in industry

B. Sensation versus Perception

1. Seeing and perceiving

    a. **Sensation**

    b. **Perception**

2. Third question: how do sensations become perceptions?

    a. Stimulus

    b. Sense organs

    c. Brain

    d. Sensations

    e. Experience

    f. Perception

C. Principles of Perceptual Organization

1. Great debate: how are perceptions formed?

    a. **Structuralists**

    b. **Gestalt psychologists**

    c. **Principles of organization**

2. Principles of organization

    a. **Figure-ground principle**

    b. **Similarity principle**

    c. **Closure principle**

    d. **Proximity principle**

    e. **Simplicity principle**

    f. **Continuity principle**

D. Perceptual Constancy

1. Size, shape, brightness, and color constancy

2. **Perceptual constancy** in a potentially chaotic world

☐ *How does perceptual constancy make our world understandable?*

   a. **Size constancy**

   b. **Shape constancy**

   c. **Brightness constancy**

   d. **Color constancy**

E. Depth Perception

1. How we look at two-dimensional images and create a three-dimensional world (**depth perception**)

2. Binocular depth cues (**convergence**)

3. **Retinal disparity** and the cyclops

4. **Monocular depth cues** for depth perception

   a. **Linear perspective**

   b. **Interposition**

   c. **Relative size**

   d. **Light and shadow**

   e. **Atmospheric perspective**

   f. **Texture gradient**

   g. **Motion parallax**

F. Illusions

1. Seeing versus believing

☐ *How can an* **illusion** *help us understand the process of perception?*

   a. **Ames room**

   b. **Impossible figures**

   c. Moon illusion

    d. Ponzo illusion

    e. Müller-Lyer illusion

  2. What do we learn from illusions?

G. Research Focus: Subliminal Perception

  1. Popcorn controversy

  2. Research question: Do subliminal messages change specific behaviors?

    a. **Subliminal messages**

    b. **Self-fulfilling prophecies**

  3. Research question: Do subliminal emotions affect behavior?

H. Cultural Diversity: Changing Perceptions

  ☐ How do **cultural influences** affect perception?

  1. Perception of images

  2. Perception of constancy and depth

  3. Perception of motion

  4. **Perceptual sets**

I. ESP: Extrasensory Perception

  ☐ Tell the truth — do you believe that at least a few people possess the special power of perception we call ESP? If you answered "yes," doesn't that create a problem with psychology as a science? Can a science of behavior be valid if some human abilities may sometimes fall outside its scope?

  1. Controversy (over claimed **psi** abilities)

    a. Problem: trickery

    b. Problem: questionable methodology

  2. ESP (**extrasensory perception**) abilities

    a. **Telepathy**

    b. **Precognition**

    c. **Clairvoyance**

    d. **Psychokinesis**

  3. ESP experiment: **Ganzfeld procedure**

  4. Current status of ESP

J. Application: Creating Perceptions

    1. Creating movies

        a. **Real motion**

        b. **Apparent motion**

    2. Creating reality (**virtual reality**)

    3. Creating moving lights (**phi movement**)

    4. Creating impressions

Language Enhancement Guide

IDIOMATIC EXPRESSIONS AND CULTURAL TERMS

The following are idiomatic expressions and cultural terms found in the module. Some of them have more than one meaning; the definition given here on the right is for the way the author uses the expression in this module. Remember that these words, like all words, can have different meanings in other contexts.

relatively normal (111) = normal compared to other behavior, situations or events

to get back (111) = to reclaim

took her breath away (111) = surprised her

at what point (112) = at what place, position or time

turned down a great deal (113) = lowered or decreased (the volume of the stereo)

personalized interpretations (115) = based on a person's own experience

principle (of science) (116) = results can be replicated

standing out against (117) = to be easily seen

to draw on (126) = to use

out of nowhere (127) = mysteriously appear

take for granted (129) = to accept something without any questions or doubts

VOCABULARY BUILDING: Word Analysis

Instructions: Study the following table of common prefixes, suffixes, and roots and then guess the meanings of the terms in the table that follows. The number in parentheses ( ) refers to the page in the current module where you can find the word. You can find the definition for any word marked with a **G** in the textbook Glossary. Words that are not marked are used by the textbook author in other modules. Remember that these words, like all words, can have different meanings in other contexts.

Exercise 1. Perception

Prefix/Root/Suffix	Meaning
per-	through/throughout
-fect	making/doing
-ceptive	aware/see
im/in -	not/without
-ible/able	able to/able to make
-ive	tending to (be)/having to
-ion	the process of/the act of
spect	to look/to see
trans-	to send/carry across/beyond
lucent	clear/shine/bright

Word	Meaning
perception	
perceptive	
perceptible	
imperceptible	
perfect	
imperfect	
imperfection	
perspective	
translucent (129)	

Exercise 2. Subliminal

Prefix/Root/Suffix	Meaning
sub	under
auto	self
-mobile	move/change position/ to affect emotions
sequ/secu	follow
tech	skill
ence	quality/state/condition/act/means/results
-ly	in the manner of/to the degree/in the direction
vary	change
-ity	being/ characterized by
limen	threshold
-al	relating to/ belonging to/characterized by

Word	Meaning
subliminal (125)	
automatically (111)	
variability (112)	
automobile	
automatic	
sequence	
sequential (138)	
consecutive	
technique	
substandard	

Guessing From Context

You won't find the following words and expressions from this Module in the Concept/Glossary in the Appendix. These words are used by the author as part of his extensive college level vocabulary.

Mastery of these words is useful in reading, writing, and talking about psychology and other academic subjects. See if you can guess their meanings by studying their contexts (their relationship to the words around them). To do this, first find the word or expression in your text and guess its meaning using the clues in the context. You may find clues in an explanation that immediately follows the word, in a synonym that appears nearby, or in the form of examples. Try to use your knowledge of prefixes, suffixes and roots to analyze the word. If you do not remember or know the meaning of these parts of the word look it up in the Appendix. However, you must remember that the same part of the word may have different meanings in different contexts or may not be listed.

Sometimes, this is easy. Scrutiny (p. 128) is an example — when you first see the term, you may not know what it means. But if you reread the sentence you will notice that the word is followed by the phrase "of scientific investigation." In Modules 1 and 2 you have learned that "scientific investigation" requires systematic study, observation, questioning and experimentation. Based on this knowledge, the term "scrutiny" seems to mean "a systematic study, observation and questioning." A dictionary might define the word this way, "a close examination and critical questioning." Notice that this is very close to the meaning that can be inferred from context of the sentence.

Now, write down your own definitions of the following words. Then ask a native speaker what they mean, or look them up in a dictionary to see if your guesses were correct.

instantaneously (114)

perplexed (126)

anomalous (129)

ingenious (130)

True-False

_____ 1. A threshold is a point above which we are aware of a stimulus.

_____ 2. A physiologist calls it "sensation" and a psychologist calls it "perception," but they are both talking about the same thing.

_____ 3. The brain follows a number of perceptual rules to make sense out of the mass of visual stimuli it receives.

_____ 4. If it were not for perceptual constancies, the world would seem ever-changing and chaotic.

_____ 5. In the Müller-Lyer illusion, one boy looks like a giant and the other like a midget.

_____ 6. Illusions are interesting because they remind us that perception is an active process.

_____ 7. Horses at the track, real motion; movie replay of the race, apparent motion.

_____ 8. A perceptual set is a kind of stubbornness that makes subjects stick to the first answer they give even if they realize they were wrong.

_____ 9. Anthropologists have discovered that how you see things depends at least in part on the culture in which you were raised.

_____ 10. There is a large body of accepted scientific evidence that supports the existence of ESP.

More Test-Taking Tips

Remember that a combination of careful reading of the question and answers, plus reliance on your own general knowledge and intelligence, often reveals the correct answer. Here are more hints:

- Be on the lookout for any *part* of an answer that makes the *whole* answer untrue.

- When you find an answer that sounds correct, you must check to make sure there isn't another answer that is even *more* true.

- Trust your common knowledge and don't choose an answer that is obviously not the way the world really works.

- Often the question itself contains a strong hint about the right answer.

- Use everything you know. Even if you can't recall the specific information needed, think about what you *do* remember concerning the subject.

- Don't jump to the conclusion that an answer is correct just because it uses the right word. The entire statement must be true.

Flashcards

Match each key term to the definition given in the textbook.

_____ 1. Ames room

a. point above which a stimulus is perceived and below which it is not perceived

_____ 2. apparent motion

b. tendency to automatically identify element of more detail which then stands out

_____ 3. clairvoyance

c. group of presumed psychic experiences that lie outside normal sensory processes or channels

_____ 4. convergence

d. tendency to see object as keeping its same form in spite of viewing it from different angles

_____ 5. extrasensory perception (ESP)

e. illusion that a stimulus or object is moving in space when in fact it is stationary

_____ 6. Ganzfeld procedure

f. a controlled method for eliminating trickery, error, and bias while investigating ESP abilities

_____ 7. Gestalt psychologists

g. tendency to fill in missing parts in order to see a figure as complete

_____ 8. illusion

h. perceptual experience of perceiving an object as being so distorted that it could not really exist

_____ 9. impossible figure

i. binocular cues for depth that depend on signals from muscles as they move both eyes inward

_____ 10. phi movement

j. a demonstration that our perception of size can be distorted by manipulating our cues for depth

_____ 11. principle of closure

k. perceptual experience in which a drawing seems to defy basic geometric rules

_____ 12. principle of continuity

l. computer generated experience of a real feeling of being inside an object or environment

_____ 13. principle of figure-ground

m. tendency to perceive objects as remaining the same even when image on retina changes

_____ 14. psychokinesis

n. tendency to organize stimuli according to a series of points along a continuous path

_____ 15. self-fulfilling prophecies

o. unknowingly acting on a strong belief about some behavior so the belief is confirmed

_____ 16. shape constancy

p. illusion that stationary lights flashing at regular intervals seem to be moving

_____ 17. size constancy

q. presumed ability to exert mind over matter, such as moving an object without touching it

_____ 18. subliminal message

r. presumed ability to perceive events or objects that are out of sight

_____ 19. threshold

s. brief auditory or visual messages that are presented just below the absolute threshold

_____ 20. virtual reality

t. processes by which brain organizes stimuli into meaningful patterns or perceptions

Multiple-Choice

_____ 1. An absolute threshold is the intensity level that you
   a. can detect every time it is presented
   b. know is there, even if you can't quite detect it
   c. can just barely detect
   d. can detect 50 percent of the time

_____ 2. Weber's law of the just noticeable difference explains why
   a. your parents don't believe you really turned your stereo down
   b. kids like heavy metal and their parents like Montovani
   c. you study better if you have the radio on
   d. many teenagers knew Milli-Vanilli weren't really singing

_____ 3. Sensation is to perception as _____ is to _____
   a. a grownup ... a child
   b. complete ... unfinished
   c. a word ... a story
   d. a movie ... reality

_____ 4. The perceptual rule that makes important things stand out is called
   a. closure
   b. proximity
   c. figure dominance
   d. figure-ground

_____ 5. Thank goodness for size constancy — without it you would
   a. never know for sure how big or small anything really was
   b. immediately get bigger after a single large meal
   c. be overcome by grief when your honey walks farther and farther away from you
   d. see things change in size whenever the light changed in brightness

_____ 6. The advantage to the human species of having two eyes is
   a. figure-ground discrimination
   b. monocular cues
   c. retinal disparity
   d. glasses balance on the nose better

_____ 7. The reason people seem to change size as they change sides in the Ames room is that
   a. the room is not actually rectangular
   b. hidden mirrors distort the images you see as you look in
   c. a lens in the peephole forces you to view them upside down
   d. the subtle coloring of the walls creates a hypnotic trance in the viewer

_____ 8. The reason you couldn't figure out that two-pronged/three-pronged gadget in the textbook is that
   a. seeing it in a textbook aroused test anxiety and that threw you off
   b. you were attempting to see it as an object in the real world
   c. Westerners aren't as good at this kind of puzzle as Africans are
   d. it was just a joke

_____ 9. One explanation for why the arrows in the Müller-Lyer illusion don't appear to be the same length is that
   a. our previous experience with arrows tells us they *aren't* all the same
   b. they really aren't quite the same — there is a tiny difference in length
   c. your experience with the corners of rooms makes you see the arrows differently
   d. this famous illusion remains unexplained — even Professors Müller and Lyer couldn't explain it

_____ 10. Should you scrap this Study Guide and buy a subliminal message tape? Research suggests that any improvement you get with those tapes is probably due to
   a. a self-fulfilling prophecy
   b. turning the volume up too high
   c. the Ponzo illusion
   d. the effects of extra practice

_____ 11. Seeing water buffalo as "insects" shows that size constancy and depth perception are strongly affected by
   a. cultural beliefs about animals
   b. seeing a black-and-white photo for the first time
   c. previous visual experience
   d. racial inheritance

_____ 12. Tops on the list of people *not* to invite to an ESP demonstration:
   a. Gustav Fechner
   b. E. H. Weber
   c. Max Wertheimer
   d. Amazing Randi

_____ 13. Despite the fact that many people believe in it, convincing evidence of ESP has been undercut by the
   a. hocus-pocus that surrounds ESP demonstrations
   b. refusal of psychologists to investigate it seriously
   c. inability to repeat positive results
   d. fact that some people have it and others don't

_____ 14. When John Wayne grabs the reins on the stagecoach, we see the horses as really flying because our brains
   a. apply the principle of closure and fill in the blanks between frames of the movie
   b. "suspend doubt" as we get more and more involved in the movie
   c. accept the data coming in from the retina and optic nerve
   d. know that the horses in the movie really were moving as they were being filmed

_____ 15. *Special question for tech-heads:* when "virtual reality" becomes an accomplished fact, you will be able to
   a. watch Star Trek reruns in 3-D
   b. dial up famous psychologists on your computer at home
   c. learn all the facts you need in psych while you sleep
   d. trade in your psych textbook for a headset and a computer disk

Answers for Module 6

True-False	Flashcards	Multiple-Choice
1. T	1. j	1. d
2. F	2. e	2. a
3. T	3. r	3. c
4. T	4. i	4. d
5. F	5. c	5. c
6. T	6. f	6. c
7. T	7. t	7. a
8. F	8. h	8. b
9. T	9. k	9. c
10. F	10. p	10. a
	11. g	11. c
	12. n	12. d
	13. b	13. c
	14. q	14. a
	15. o	15. d
	16. d	
	17. m	
	18. s	
	19. a	
	20. l	

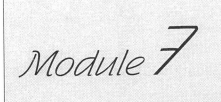

Module 7

Consciousness, Sleep, & Dreams

Do Dreams Have Meaning?

Freud is dead... Freud is dead... Freud is dead.... Keep repeating it long enough, and maybe Freud will go away. He has a way of coming back, though, no matter how often psychology pronounces him dead wrong.

One of Freud's most provocative ideas is the notion that all dreams have meaning. He thought it was his most important discovery, and wrote, "Insight such as this falls to one's lot but once in a lifetime." Dreams were important to Freud because they allowed the best look into the workings of the unconscious. When you learn more about Freud's theory of personality (in Module 19) and his technique of psychoanalysis (in Module 24), you will see that he thought of dreaming, with unconscious meanings hidden behind innocent sounding surface stories, as a model for all human psychic life.

The newer theories of dreaming discussed in Module 7 discount or reject Freud's theory, perhaps partly because — you knew this was coming — Freud says dreams represent sexual wishes. Building on research into sleep and brain biology, the new theories are filling in blanks Freud could only guess at. Still, these theories do not disprove Freud completely.

Turn Your Bed Into a Research Laboratory

The deciding evidence may be your own dreams. Why not use them as a research project? Many people find it useful to keep a dream journal, which helps them get down more details than we normally remember and also serves as a record that can be reviewed from time to time. The cares and worries of the day quickly chase dream details away, so try waking up slowly and peacefully. If you sense that you had a dream, keep your eyes closed and stay with it. Tell it to yourself a few times. Then get up (or grab your bedside pencil and pad if it is still night) and write down as much as you remember.

The hard part, of course, is trying to interpret the dream. Here's how. Review the story of the dream, then ask how it connects to your life. This is a process of indirection and confusion, and you have to go where the dream leads, no matter how apparently meaningless it seems. The *crucial clues* will be what Freudians call your *associations* to the dream, the things that come to mind as you think about each element of the dream. What feelings does it arouse? What thoughts (none sexual, of course) pop into your mind? How do the feelings and thoughts associated with the dream relate to issues in your psychological life? Is it possible that your dream does have meaning?

Effective Student Tip 7

Stay Focused

Everyone tells you how great it is that you are in college, but sometimes it seems like they don't really understand what you are up against. You may be away from home for the first time, trying to get along with your roommates, cheering on your college team, and worrying about how to get a date. Your parents and friends back home expect letters and phone calls. If you are a returning student, your children miss you, your spouse resents getting less attention, and your boss still asks you to stay late to finish that big project. In either case, you are discovering how easy it is to become distracted from your basic purpose for being in college.

No matter how important a party, your friend's need to talk all night, or extra work at the office may seem at the time, learning and succeeding are what college is really all about. The most important attributes of college are what happens in your classrooms and at your desk, when it's time to study.

Keep your emotional radar attuned to incoming distractions. When all you hear is the beep, beep, beep of threats to learning and succeeding, it's time to defend yourself. Remind yourself why you are in college. Then make the necessary adjustments to get back to the work you came to college to do.

Your response...

Think about a typical day in your college life. What distractions do you often face?

Key Terms

Everyone is fascinated by the topics in this module, especially sleep and dreaming. Learn these terms and you will be able to explain anything your friends want to know (well, enough to keep them listening).

activation-synthesis theory of dreams	dreaming	REM sleep
adaptive theory	entering spiritual world theory of dreams	repair theory
alpha stage	extension of waking life theory of dreams	reticular formation
altered states of consciousness	Freud's theory of dreams	seasonal affective disorder (SAD)
automatic processes	insomnia	sleep
benzodiazepines	jet lag	sleep apnea
biological clocks	light therapy	sleepwalking
circadian rhythm	melatonin	stage 1 sleep
cognitive unconscious	narcolepsy	stage 2 sleep
consciousness	night terrors	stage 4 sleep
continuum of consciousness	nightmares	stages of sleep
controlled processes	non-REM sleep	suprachiasmatic nucleus
daydreaming	questionnaire	theory of the unconscious (Freud)
	REM rebound	unconsciousness

Outline

- **INTRODUCTION**

  ☐ *What was the purpose of placing a person in a cave for four months?*

A. *Continuum of Consciousness*

  1. Is every moment different?

     a. **Consciousness**

     b. **Continuum of consciousness**

        (1) **Controlled processes**

        (2) **Automatic processes**

        (3) **Daydreaming**

        (4) **Altered states of consciousness**

        (5) **Sleep** and **dreaming**

(6) **Theory of the unconscious** (Freud) or **cognitive unconscious**?

(7) **Unconsciousness** [physical]

2. What is consciousness?

B. *Rhythms of Sleeping and Waking*

1. Cave time

   a. **Biological clocks**

   b. **Circadian rhythm**

2. Sleep-wake clock

   a. **Suprachiasmatic nucleus**

   b. Does the brain have a clock?

3. Circadian rhythms: problems and treatments

   a. Accidents

   b. **Jet lag**

   c. **Light therapy**

   d. **Melatonin**

C. *World of Sleep*

1. **Stages of sleep**

   a. **Alpha stage**

   b. **Non-REM sleep**

   (1) **Stage 1 sleep**

   (2) **Stage 2 sleep**

   (3) Stage 3 and **Stage 4 sleep**

   c. **REM sleep**

   (1) Characteristics of REM sleep (paradoxical sleep)

   (2) REM and dreaming (**REM rebound**)

   (3) REM versus non-REM sleep

2. Awake and alert

3. Passing through the sleep stages

D. Research Focus: Morning or Evening Person

☐ *Are you a morning person or an evening person?*

1. Question: are there morning and evening persons?

   a. **Questionnaire**

   b. Research finding

2. Clues to preferences

   a. Body temperature

   b. Behavioral differences

E. Questions about Sleep

☐ *What are your personal answers to questions 1 and 3 (below) about sleep?*

1. How much sleep do I need?

2. Why do I sleep?

   a. **Repair theory**

   b. **Adaptive theory**

3. What happens if I go without sleep?

   a. Effects on body

   b. Effects on brain

4. What causes sleep?

   a. Circadian rhythm

   b. **Reticular formation**

   c. Pons and sleep-related neurotransmitters

   d. Body temperature

F. Cultural Diversity: Incidence of SAD

1. Problem and treatment of **seasonal affective disorder (SAD)**

2. Frequency of SAD in the United States

3. Frequency of SAD in Iceland

4. Cultural differences

G. *World of Dreams*

❏ *How would you explain the "elevator dream" Rod Plotnik offers as a sample?*

1. Meaning of dreams (the elevator dream)

❏ *What are the key differences in the way the competing theories of dream interpretation explain the elevator dream?*

   1. **Freud's theory of dreams**

   3. **Extension of waking life theory of dreams** (Rosalind Cartwright)

   3. **Activation-synthesis theory of dreams** (J. Alan Hobson and Robert McCarley)

   4. **Entering spiritual world theory of dreams**

2. What are typical dreams?

H. *Application: Sleep Problems and Treatments*

❏ *Have you experienced a sleep problem? What was it like? What did you do about it?*

1. **Insomnia**

   a. Psychological causes

   b. Physiological causes

   c. Non-drug treatment for insomnia (behavioral)

   d. Drug treatment for insomnia (**benzodiazepines**)

2. **Sleep apnea**

3. **Sleepwalking**

4. **Night terrors** in children

5. **Nightmares**

6. **Narcolepsy**

Language Enhancement Guide

IDIOMATIC EXPRESSIONS AND CULTURAL TERMS

The following are idiomatic expressions and cultural terms found in the module. Some of them have more than one meaning; the definition given here on the right is for the way the author uses the expression in this module. Remember that these words, like all words, can have different meanings in other contexts.

to come and go (135) = not have it all the time

snapped at (135) = shouted in anger

keep track of (time) (135) = keep a record of the amount of time

in the absence of (135) = without

gives rise to (137) = to cause

to knock out (137) = to make a person unconscious by hitting them on the head

paradoxical (141) = a statement or claim that sounds contradictory or false but may be true

(serious) bouts (150) = experiences

relatively rare (151) = has a low rate of occurrence compared to other similar events

VOCABULARY BUILDING: Word Analysis

Instructions: Study the following table of common prefixes, suffixes, and roots and then guess the meanings of the terms in the table that follows. The number in parentheses ( ) refers to the page in the current module where you can find the word. You can find the definition for any word marked with a **G** in the textbook Glossary. Words that are not marked are used by the textbook author in other modules. Remember that these words, like all words, can have different meanings in other contexts.

Exercise 1. Repair

Prefix/Root/Suffix	Meaning
re-	back to a earlier condition/again/repeatedly
-tion/ion	the act/process/means/result of
flex	bend/curve
gress	to step/to walk/to go
duc/duct	to lead/to bring

Word	Meaning
repair (144)	
replenish (144)	
restorative (144)	
receive (145)	
recurrent (149)	
research (134)	
regress (158)	
reduce (158)	
resistance (160)	
resumed (160)	
reflex (181)	
reconstruction	
redraw	
reappear	
recall	
replace	
reaction	
reflex	
regression	

GUESSING FROM CONTEXT

You won't find the following words and expressions from this module in the textbook Glossary, but they are useful in reading, writing, and talking about psychology and other academic subjects. See if you can guess their meanings by studying their contexts (their relationship to the words around them).

To do this, find the word or expression in your textbook and guess its meaning using the clues in the context. You may find clues in an explanation that immediately follows the word, in a synonym that appears nearby, or in the form of examples. After you have defined the terms, ask a native speaker what they mean or look them up in a dictionary to see if your guesses were correct.

stamina (135)

continuum (136)

phase (140)

transition (140)

incidence (147)

optimal (150)

discrepancy (147)

traumatic (148)

True-False

_____ 1. Human beings are always in one of two distinct states: awake and conscious or asleep and unconscious.

_____ 2. One adjustment problem faced by humans is that the circadian rhythm of our biological clocks is set closer to 25 hours than to 24.

_____ 3. Exposure to bright light is a fast way to reset our biological clocks.

_____ 4. Researchers study sleep by measuring brain waves.

_____ 5. Once you sink into true sleep, your bodily activity remains constant until you awake in the morning.

_____ 6. The existence of the REM rebound effect suggests that dreaming must have some special importance to humans.

_____ 7. Research on sleep deprivation and performance proves that the "repair theory" of sleep is correct.

_____ 8. Everyone dreams.

_____ 9. As with everything else in his theories, Freud's explanation of dreams has a sexual twist.

_____ 10. The activation-synthesis theory of dreams places great importance on getting to the underlying meaning of each dream.

For Psych Majors Only. . .

How to Construct a Dream (Sigmund Freud): If every dream represents a secret wish disguised as a jumbled, apparently meaningless story, how is the disguise constructed? Freud describes the "dream work" as four processes:

1. **Condensation** is the compression of several thoughts into a single element, which has the effect of making the dream seem *incoherent*.

2. **Displacement** is the transfer of psychical intensity from the actual dream thoughts to other ideas, which has the effect of making the dream seem *meaningless*.

3. **Symbolism** is the transformation of the dream thoughts into apparently unconnected pictorial arrangements or scenes, which has the effect of making the dream seem *illogical*.

4. **Secondary elaboration** is the interpretative revision of the dream content or scenes into stories, however absurd, which has the effect of making the dream seem *strange*, perhaps ridiculous or frightening, but *not connected to dreamer*.

The next time you remember a dream fairly clearly, try using these ideas to take it apart. It's not easy, but you may gain insight into the meaning of your dreams, and also into the provocative genius of Sigmund Freud.

Flashcards

Match each key term to the definition given in the textbook.

_____ 1. activation-synthesis theory

_____ 2. adaptive theory

_____ 3. altered states of consciousness

_____ 4. automatic processes

_____ 5. circadian rhythm

_____ 6. continuum of consciousness

_____ 7. controlled processes

_____ 8. entering spiritual world theory of dreams

_____ 9. extension of waking life theory of dreams

_____ 10. Freud's theory of dreams

_____ 11. jet lag

_____ 12. light therapy

_____ 13. narcolepsy

_____ 14. night terrors

_____ 15. REM rebound

_____ 16. REM sleep

_____ 17. repair theory

_____ 18. seasonal affective disorder (SAD)

_____ 19. sleep apnea

_____ 20. unconscious (Freud)

a. sleep evolved to prevent energy waste and exposure to nocturnal predators

b. depressive symptoms beginning in fall and winter and going away in spring

c. activities that require full awareness, alertness, and concentration to reach some goal

d. wide range of experiences from being aware and alert to being unaware and unresponsive

e. irresistible attacks of suddenly falling asleep throughout the day

f. says sleep replenishes key factors in brain and body depleted by activities during day

g. using meditation, drugs, hypnosis to produce an awareness that differs from normal state

h. activities that require little awareness, take minimal attention, and do not interfere with life

i. when one's internal clock is out of step with the actual time

j. says dreams contain many thoughts, fears, and concerns as are present during waking hours

k. dreams result from random and meaningless activity of nerve cells in the brain

l. episodes during sleep when a person stops breathing for 10 seconds or longer

m. a mental place sealed off from voluntary recall where we place threatening wishes or desires

n. says dreams are wish fulfillments, satisfaction of unconscious sexual or aggressive desires

o. an increased percentage of time spent in REM sleep if deprived of REM sleep on previous night

p. frightening sleep experiences that suddenly wake children up, often with a scream

q. sleep during which eyes move rapidly back and forth behind closed eyelids

r. use of bright artificial light to reset circadian rhythms

s. says dreams are ways of contacting souls of animals, supernaturals, departed relatives

t. a biological clock genetically programmed to regulate physiological responses (24-25 hr day)

Multiple-Choice

_____ 1. Rod Plotnik opens the module on consciousness with the story of Stefania's three-month stay in a cave to illustrate the fact that
    a. body time runs slower than celestial time
    b. without sunlight, humans begin to lose their grip on reality
    c. without sunlight, Stefania's night vision became very acute
    d. we would all be much more cheerful if there were no clocks around

_____ 2. We naturally think in terms of the two states called "conscious" and "unconscious," but actually there
    a. are three states, including the "high" from drugs
    b. are four states: conscious, drowsy, dreaming, and unconscious
    c. is a continuum of consciousness
    d. is no measurable difference between consciousness and unconsciousness

_____ 3. Psychologists call activities that require full awareness, alertness, and concentration
    a. automatic processes
    b. altered states
    c. comas
    d. controlled processes

_____ 4. Have you noticed that you often wake up just before the alarm clock goes off? Credit it to the fact that we humans have a built-in
    a. aversion to jangling noise, which we try to avoid
    b. biological clock
    c. sense of responsibility
    d. brain mechanism that is always monitoring the external environment, even during sleep

_____ 5. If human beings were deprived of all mechanical means of telling time (like clocks), they would
    a. still follow schedules and be punctual, thanks to their biological clocks
    b. follow a natural clock with a day about 30 hours long
    c. not stick to strict schedules the way we do now
    d. lose all sense of when things should be done

_____ 6. The most promising new treatment for jet lag appears to be
    a. periods of bright light
    b. avoidance of food for 24 hours before a long flight
    c. surgical resetting of the biological clock
    d. drugs that induce sleep in the new time zone

_____ 7. Dreams are most likely to occur during
    a. stage 1 (theta waves)
    b. EEG sleep
    c. non-REM sleep
    d. REM sleep

_____ 8. REM sleep is often called "paradoxical sleep" because
   a. you appear to be looking around even though obviously you can't see anything
   b. you have dreams, but they don't make any sense
   c. although you are asleep, your body and brain are in a general state of arousal
   d. your muscles are tense and ready for action even though you are asleep

_____ 9. Modern research on sleep suggests that most of us need
   a. about 10 hours of sleep a night
   b. about 8 hours of sleep a night
   c. short naps every 4 hours rather than a long night of sleep
   d. varying amounts of sleep — there is no general pattern

_____ 10. Research in both Iceland and New York showed that seasonal affective disorder (SAD) is caused by
   a. an above average number of days of bright light
   b. a combination of diminished light and low temperature
   c. personal tragedy and family problems
   d. both amount of light and cultural factors

_____ 11. According to Freud's famous theory, at the heart of every dream is a
   a. hate-filled thought
   b. clue to the future
   c. shameful sexual memory
   d. disguised wish

_____ 12. The activation-synthesis theory says that dreams result from
   a. a biological need to pull together and make sense of the days' activities
   b. "batch processing" of all the information gathered during the day
   c. random and meaningless activity of nerve cells in the brain
   d. the need to express hidden sexual and aggressive impulses

_____ 13. Sleep and dream researchers point out that you may not always understand what your dreams mean because
   a. you only remember small fragments of them
   b. they are expressed in a code only an expert can understand
   c. they simply don't mean anything significant in your life
   d. you may be one of those people who don't dream every night

_____ 14. The best advice for combating insomnia is to
   a. get in bed at the same time every night and stay there no matter what happens
   b. get out of bed, go to another room, and do something relaxing if you can't fall asleep
   c. review the problems of the day as you lie in bed trying to go to sleep
   d. try sleeping in another room, or on the couch, if you can't fall asleep in your bed

_____ 15. Which one of the following is _not_ a sleep problem?
   a. night terrors
   b. sleepwalking
   c. narcolepsy
   d. oversleeping

Answers for Module 7

True-False	Flashcards	Multiple-Choice
1. F	1. k	1. a
2. T	2. a	2. c
3. T	3. g	3. d
4. T	4. h	4. b
5. F	5. t	5. c
6. T	6. d	6. a
7. F	7. c	7. d
8. T	8. s	8. c
9. T	9. j	9. b
10. F	10. n	10. d
	11. i	11. d
	12. r	12. c
	13. e	13. a
	14. p	14. b
	15. o	15. d
	16. q	
	17. f	
	18. b	
	19. l	
	20. m	

Hypnosis & Drugs

I'll Have Mine Straight

Being a nature lover gives you a warped view of life. In general, you prefer it straight. When you're outdoors, you don't wear a headset because you would rather listen to birds, waves and wind. When you're having fun, you would rather have all your senses set on normal, not excited or dulled by psychoactive agents, legal or otherwise.

For most humans, however, and apparently for most of human history, normal consciousness isn't quite satisfying. Sometimes we want it heightened, sometimes we need it muted. Hence the long history of human attempts to alter consciousness through self-medication. Almost all of us have found some technique, or substance, that adjusts our consciousness to the point where it feels just right.

This module discusses two methods of altering consciousness. Hypnosis is either a state of great suggestibility or an alternate route to deeper truths about ourselves. Rod Plotnik discusses the debate over what hypnosis is, how it works, and what it can do. But regardless of your position in this debate, hypnosis is different from ordinary consciousness. Psychoactive drugs are a mind-altering power of a different sort.

Why Do We Use Drugs?

In textbook after textbook I've seen, the section on drugs reads like something you would get in pharmacy school. Good, solid technical information on psychoactive drugs, including the most recent illegal drugs to hit the streets, but nothing on the really important issue — why we use psychoactive drugs at all, let alone to such excess.

Rod Plotnik raises that question, and provides provocative answers about the biology and history of drug use. Personally, I'm dead set against any use of psychoactive drugs [...says he, after gulping down a can of caffeine-laced cola!], but I don't think it does any good to tell you that. Rod has it right. Instead of moralizing, let's investigate the psychological processes by which almost all of us "self-medicate," in our continual attempt to manage our thoughts, feelings, and behavior. This is exciting stuff.

Effective Student Tip 8

People Power

One of my arguments for setting a goal of perfect attendance is that when you go to class every day the group takes over. It's not that you feel like a captive, but more like a member of a family that is determined not to let you fail. In a good class, I often notice that the regulars kind of take an informal attendance, not satisfied until all the other regulars have arrived, or pointedly worrying about the one who hasn't.

These friendships become the basis for study groups, which are invaluable for students who are struggling and even more valuable for the good students who are helping them. (Here is a paradox of instruction: the teacher always learns more than the student, because in order to teach something to someone else you first have to really understand it yourself). Study groups give their members ten times more opportunities to ask questions and talk (and therefore practice) than class time allows.

Another reason to get acquainted with your classmates is the opportunity to make new friends and expand your cultural horizons. Most colleges attract students from every part of the city and from all over the world. Finally, there is the fact that we humans may be the most social species on earth. Biologically speaking, other people replace our missing instincts. Practically speaking, friends make life fun.

Your response…

Do you ever feel lonely? How easily do you make new friends? Do you talk to your classmates?

Key Terms

Most of these key terms are as timely as today's news, where you are likely to find them. All you need to do is sharpen up your definitions.

addiction

age regression

alcohol

Alcoholics Anonymous (AA)
Narcotics Anonymous (NA)

alcoholism

caffeine

cocaine

cognitive-behavioral theory
of hypnosis

DARE (Drug Abuse
Resistance Program)

designer drugs

hallucinogens

hypnosis

hypnotic analgesia

hypnotic induction

imagined perception

LSD

marijuana

MDMA ("ecstasy")

mescaline

methamphetamine

nicotine

opiates

posthypnotic amnesia

posthypnotic suggestion

psilocybin

psychoactive drugs

psychological dependency

stimulants

substance abuse

tolerance

trance theory of hypnosis

withdrawal symptoms

Outline

- *INTRODUCTION*

  ☐ *How are hypnosis and drug use somewhat alike?*

A. *Hypnosis: Theory, Behavior, & Use*

  1. What is **hypnosis**?

  2. Common questions about hypnosis

      a. Can I be hypnotized?

      b. Are you susceptible?

      c. How is a person hypnotized?

          (1) **Hypnotic induction**

          (2) Method to induce hypnosis

  3. Trance theory of hypnosis

      a. **Trance theory of hypnosis** (Milton Erickson)

      b. Hidden observer explanation (Ernest Hilgard)

4. Cognitive-behavioral theory of hypnosis

    a. **Cognitive-behavioral theory of hypnosis**

    b. Social behaviors in conformity

5. Behaviors under hypnosis

    a. **Age regression**

    b. **Imagined perception**

    c. **Hypnotic analgesia**

    d. **Posthypnotic suggestion**

    e. **Posthypnotic amnesia**

6. Hypnosis: applications

    a. Medical and dental uses

    b. Therapeutic and behavioral uses

B. Drugs: Use and Effects

1. A case study

☐ *Why is it significant that Freud had a problem? What does it say about drugs? About psychology?*

2. Definition of terms

    a. **Tolerance**

    b. **Addiction**

    c. **Withdrawal symptoms**

    d. **Psychological dependency**

3. Why use drugs?

    a. Long human history of drug use

    b. **Psychoactive drugs**

4. Drug usage

5. Drug effects on the nervous system

    a. Drugs increase the release of neurotransmitters

    b. Drugs mimic the action of neurotransmitters

     c. Drugs block the locks of receptors

     d. Drugs block the removal of the neurotransmitter (reuptake)

C. *Stimulants*

   ☐ *Rod Plotnik quotes a great marketing slogan used to sell amphetamines in Sweden in the 1940s. When we look back on our own times, what ad campaigns may seem equally irresponsible?*

  1. Earlier use of **stimulants**

  2. Amphetamines

     a. **Methamphetamine**

     b. Effects on nervous system

     c. Dangers

  3. **Cocaine**

     a. Effects on nervous system

     b. Dangers

  4. **Caffeine**

     a. Effects on nervous system

     b. Dangers

  5. **Nicotine**

     a. Effects on nervous system

     b. Dangers

D. *Opiates*

  1. Early and current usage

  2. **Opiates** (opium poppy)

     a. Effects on nervous system

     b. Dangers

E. *Hallucinogens*

    1. Unusual perceptions (**hallucinogens**)

    2. **LSD**

        a. Effects on nervous system

        b. Dangers

    3. **Psilocybin** (magic mushrooms)

        a. Effects on nervous system

        b. Dangers

    3. **Mescaline** (peyote cactus)

        a. Effects on nervous system

        b. Dangers

    4. **Designer drugs (MDMA "ecstasy")**

        a. Effects on nervous system

        b. Dangers

F. *Alcohol*

    1. Alcohol: history and use

    2. What does **alcohol** do?

        a. Effects on nervous system

        b. Dangers

    3. Why is alcohol such a dangerous drug?

    4. Who's at risk for abusing alcohol

        a. Environmental risk factors

        b. Genetic/physiological risk factors

G. Cultural Diversity: Alcoholism

1. Do cultures differ in their physiological response to alcohol?

2. What is **alcoholism**?

3. Do cultures differ in rates of alcoholism?

4. Do cultures have a similar course of alcoholism?

H. Marijuana

1. Popularity and use

2. **Marijuana**

   a. Effects on nervous system

   b. Dangers

I. Research Focus: Drug Prevention

1. Research question: How effective is America's most popular drug prevention program?

2. **DARE (Drug Abuse Resistance Program)**

   a. Method

   b. Results and discussion

   b. Conclusion

J. Application: Treatment for Drug Abuse

1. Case history

2. What is **substance abuse**?

3. How is substance abuse treated?

   a. Step 1: Admitting that one has a drug problem

   b. Step 2: Entering a treatment program

   c. Step 3: Joining a support group

   d. Step 4: Remaining abstinent

Language Enhancement Guide

IDIOMATIC EXPRESSIONS AND CULTURAL TERMS

The following are idiomatic expressions and cultural terms found in the module. Some of them have more than one meaning; the definition given here on the right is for the way the author uses the expression in this module. Remember that these words, like all words, can have different meanings in other contexts.

longest running (155) = being performed for more years than other acts

puzzled over (155) = tried to determine

relatively straightforward (156) = easy to understand

hard evidence (156) = scientific research evidence

(something) holds that (157) = claims that

black market (162) = buying and selling of things, like drugs, that are not legal

kingpins (165) = leaders

flashbacks (166) = a sudden recall of a past experience

one bout of (168) = an experience with

(his) world caved in (174) = (he) faced many serious life problems

saved from himself (174) = rescued from his problems

it is not uncommon (175) = a common occurrence

(after) going though (175) = completing

VOCABULARY BUILDING: Word Analysis

Instructions: Study the following table of common prefixes, suffixes, and roots and then guess the meanings of the terms in the table that follows. The number in parentheses ( ) refers to the page in the current module where you can find the word. You can find the definition for any word marked with a **G** in the textbook Glossary. Words that are not marked are used by the textbook author in other modules. Remember that these words, like all words, can have different meanings in other contexts.

Exercise 1. Disappear

Prefix/Root/Suffix	Meaning
dis/di-	away from/apart/not/without
proportion	part of a whole
-ate	having/resembling// having or holding an office
-gress	go/move/come
equ/equi-	equal
-vert	turn

Caution: "ate" is a suffix with many other meanings that depend on the context.

Word	Meaning
digress	
disadvantage	
disappear (164)	
disappear (164)	
disbelief	
discomfort	
discouraged	
disequilibrium	
disorganize	
displacement	
disproportionate	
dissociation	
distortions (172)	
distract	
distrust	
divert	
regress	
regression	

Exercise 2. Posthypnotic

Prefix/Root/Suffix	Meaning
pre-	before
post-	after
pro/proto-	forward/ahead/before/first/original
hibit	interfere/stop
cogn/cogni/cogno	to think/to be aware/to know

Word	Meaning
posthypnotic (158)	
predetermined (158)	
prohibition (168)	
professional (163)	
progress	
postsynaptic	
prehistoric	
premature	
precognition	
postgraduate	
cognition	
cognitive	
recognize	

Exercise 3. Amnesia

Prefix/Root/Suffix	Meaning
a/an-	not/without/lacking/from
mne	to recall
path	disease/feeling/suffering
alg	pain/suffering
esthe	pain/feeling
-ic	characteristic/ having to do with/having the power to/ belonging to
-ia	quality/condition/act/state/ result of/result of/process
orex	to desire
therap/therapy	treatment/cure

Word	Meaning
amnesia (158)	
apathy (169)	
analgesia (158)	
analgesic (165)	
anesthetic (163)	
therapeutic (166)	
anorexia	
anesthesia	
amoral	
chemotherapy (179)	

True-False

_____ 1. Stage hypnotism really isn't so remarkable, since everyone can be hypnotized.

_____ 2. According to the trance theory, during hypnosis a person enters a special, altered state of consciousness that is different from the normal waking state.

_____ 3. The debate in psychology about hypnosis concerns whether entertainers should be allowed to exploit hypnosis for profit.

_____ 4. One good use for hypnosis is to reduce pain during medical or dental procedures.

_____ 5. Hypnosis is more effective than any other technique in helping people quit smoking.

_____ 6. History shows that if our government would follow a consistent policy, one by one all illegal drugs could be eradicated.

_____ 7. Psychoactive drugs create effects on behavior by interfering with the normal activity of neurotransmitters.

_____ 8. The most harmful drugs are the illegal ones; the legal drugs may not be good for you, but they don't do any serious harm.

_____ 9. Research proves that in DARE (Drug Abuse Resistance Program) we finally have a program that works — if only we had the resolve to use it in every school in the nation.

_____ 10. Your risk for becoming an alcoholic rises significantly if members of your family were alcoholics.

Flashcards _for hip students..._

Special Quiz on Psychoactive Drugs: Sorry, but suspicious results may be sent home to your parents!

_____	1. alcohol	a.	America's number one cash crop
_____	2. caffeine	b.	creates a vicious circle of highs and intense craving for more
_____	3. cocaine	c.	most widely used drug in the world, relatively harmless
_____	4. ecstasy	d.	profound, long lasting sensory and perceptual distortions
_____	5. heroin	e.	responsible for most drug deaths
_____	6. LSD	f.	designer drug
_____	7. marijuana	g.	oldest drug made by humans, still society's biggest drug problem
_____	8. mescaline	h.	reemerging as crystal meth or ice
_____	9. nicotine	i.	opium poppy
_____	10. speed	j.	severe bad trips could lead to psychotic reactions

Scoring:

1 to 3 correct	_You've been in a monastery, right?_
4 to 6 correct	_I'm new on campus myself!_
7 to 9 correct	_This seems very suspicious._
all 10 correct	_Report to student health immediately — you know too much!_

Flashcards

Match each key term to the definition given in the textbook.

_____ 1. addiction

_____ 2. age regression

_____ 3. alcoholism

_____ 4. caffeine

_____ 5. cognitive-behavioral theory of hypnosis

_____ 6. designer drugs

_____ 7. hallucinogens

_____ 8. hypnotic analgesia

_____ 9. hypnotic induction

_____ 10. imagined perception

_____ 11. nicotine

_____ 12. opiates

_____ 13. posthypnotic amnesia

_____ 14. posthypnotic suggestion

_____ 15. psychoactive drugs

_____ 16. psychological dependency

_____ 17. stimulants

_____ 18. tolerance

_____ 19. trance theory of hypnosis

_____ 20. withdrawal symptoms

a. using hypnosis to take a person back in time to earlier period, such as early childhood

b. a reduction in pain reported by clients after undergoing hypnosis, instructions to relax

c. addictive drugs that come from the opium poppy, such as opium and morphine

d. dangerous drug that first produces arousal but then has calming effect [hint: it's legal!]

e. drugs that produce strange and unreal perceptual, sensory, and cognitive experiences

f. mild stimulant whose psychological effects include feelings of alertness, decreased fatigue

g. heavy drinking, usually over a long period, resulting in addiction and intense craving

h. says hypnosis is a special altered state of consciousness unlike normal waking state

i. chemicals that affect our nervous system and may alter consciousness, perception, mood

j. brain and body develop physical need for drug in order to function normally

k. manufactured or synthetic illegal drugs designed to produce psychoactive effects

l. says hypnosis is state of powerful social or personal pressure to conform to suggestions

m. experiencing sensations, perceiving stimuli, or performing behaviors from one's imagination

n. various methods to induce hypnosis, including asking subjects to close their eyes, go to sleep

o. drugs that increase activity of nervous system and result in heightened alertness and arousal

p. not remembering what happened during hypnosis if hypnotist told you that you wouldn't

q. strong psychological need, craving, or desire to use a drug to deal with a situation or problem

r. giving hypnotized subject a suggestion about performing certain behaviors upon waking up

s. brain and body react to a regular drug by building up resistance, requiring more for high

t. painful physical, psychological problems that occur after addicted person stops using drug

Multiple-Choice

_____ 1. Rod Plotnik tells the story about attending a stage hypnotist's act to illustrate the point that
  a. a trained psychologist cannot be hypnotized
  b. hypnotism produces remarkable effects, but we don't understand what it really is
  c. hypnotism is an art that many have attempted to learn, but only a rare few have mastered
  d. entertainment pays better than psychology

_____ 2. Which one of the following is _not_ a necessary part of inducing hypnosis?
  a. swing a watch slowly back and forth until the subject's eyes glaze over
  b. establish a sense of trust
  c. suggest what the subject will experience during hypnosis
  d. closely observe the subject and "suggest" what seems to be happening

_____ 3. The main issue in the psychological debate over hypnosis is
  a. not whether it exists, but how it is induced
  b. why subjects tend to play along with the hypnotist
  c. whether hidden observers really can spot stage hypnotist's tricks
  d. whether it is a special state of consciousness

_____ 4. Which one of the following is _not_ an effect claimed for hypnosis?
  a. age regression
  b. imagined perception
  c. hypnotic analgesia
  d. superhuman acts of strength

_____ 5. The hypnotist tells Janet, "When you wake up, you will not remember what you did on stage tonight." This is an example of
  a. posthypnotic amnesia
  b. hypnotic suggestion
  c. posthypnotic ordering
  d. hypnotic analgesia

_____ 6. Research into the use of hypnosis to change problem behaviors suggests that hypnosis
  a. is a miracle treatment in changing behavior
  b. does not help in attempts to change behavior
  c. can be useful in combination with other treatments
  d. is useful in helping people quit smoking, but not in weight loss

_____ 7. Many students are shocked to learn that the great psychologist Sigmund Freud had a serious drug problem
  a. cocaine
  b. nicotine
  c. alcohol
  d. marijuana

_____ 8. "Tolerance" for a drug means that the brain and the body
  a. adjust to the drug and use it with no ill effects
  b. no longer get any effect from using the drug
  c. shut out the drug, which passes harmlessly through the system
  d. develop a resistance to the drug and require larger doses to achieve the same effect

_____ 9. Basically, all illegal drugs work by interfering with the normal operation of
   a. neurotransmitters in the brain
   b. glucose in the blood
   c. DNA in the genes
   d. sensory receptors in the eyes, ears, nose, tongue, and skin

_____ 10. All of the following are stimulants _except_
   a. cocaine
   b. caffeine
   c. alcohol
   d. nicotine

_____ 11. One reason it is so tough to quit smoking is that the
   a. tolerance for nicotine develops so quickly
   b. physical addiction can continue for years after quitting
   c. withdrawal symptoms are so painful
   d. psychological dependency is deepened by the fact that smoking solves problems

_____ 12. Studies of national rates of alcoholism around the world suggest that alcoholism is
   a. strongly affected by cultural factors
   b. an individual problem, relatively unaffected by where the individual lives
   c. a genetic problem, independent of national origins
   d. a family problem, passed down through the generations

_____ 13. Despite all the drug abuse horror stories we hear, the truth is that the two most costly and deadly drugs in our society are
   a. heroin and cocaine
   b. marijuana and crack cocaine
   c. angel dust and mescaline
   d. alcohol and tobacco

_____ 14. The clear lesson of the history of attempts to suppress drugs is that
   a. when one drug becomes harder to get, people will switch to another
   b. we must abandon our on-again off-again enforcement strategies and declare an all-out war on drugs
   c. eventually people get tired of any drug
   d. legalization would reduce the problem to manageable dimensions

_____ 15. For years scientists have studied and debated the harmfulness of marijuana; the conclusion seems to be that marijuana
   a. eventually causes brain damage
   b. often leads to mental illness
   c. typically leads to the use of hard drugs
   d. long-term effects are unclear (beyond the obvious dangers of smoking)

Answers for Module 8

True-False
1. F
2. T
3. F
4. T
5. F
6. F
7. T
8. F
9. F
10. T

Flashcards
1. j
2. a
3. g
4. f
5. l
6. k
7. e
8. b
9. n
10. m
11. d
12. c
13. p
14. r
15. i
16. q
17. o
18. s
19. h
20. t

Multiple-Choice
1. b
2. a
3. d
4. d
5. a
6. c
7. b
8. d
9. a
10. c
11. c
12. a
13. d
14. a
15. d

Special Quiz On Psychoactive Drugs

1. g   2. c   3. b   4. f   5. i   6. j   7. a   8. d   9. e   10. h

Module 9

Classical Conditioning

The Paradox of Behaviorist Psychology

Most students begin reading about the psychology of learning with good intentions, but soon give up. It's just too darn complicated. They have run smack into The Paradox.

In truth, the basic principles of learning discovered by Pavlov, Skinner, and others (described in this module and the next) are elegantly simple, wonderfully powerful, and among the most useful products of psychology. Once you do understand them you'll say, "I sort of knew that already." The problem is the language they come wrapped in.

Ivan Pavlov was a pure scientist, a Nobel prize winner. Naturally, he used the precise, mathematical language of the laboratory. The psychologists who followed Pavlov, the ones we call behaviorists, also prided themselves on being laboratory scientists. One of the strongest points in favor of the behaviorist approach is its insistence that psychology stick to observable, measurable phenomena (no murky, mentalistic concepts like Freud's unconscious).

When students discover behaviorism, however, they do not enjoy the luxury of a long period in which to learn the technical language. We expect them to swallow it all down at one gulp. Most gag instead.

These poor psychology students have a point. Reform in our terminology is long overdue. The first term we could do without is "conditioning." We're really talking about *learning*. Classical conditioning and operant conditioning are also learning, each by a different route, but learning all the same. Even the terms "stimulus" and "response" say more about Pavlov's fame than about how human life really works.

We're Mad As Hell and We're Not Going to Take It Anymore!

Your instructor will tell you which terms to learn, but as you study you can make some mental translations. Keep in mind that we're always talking about *learning*. When you read "classical conditioning," remind yourself that you are reading about Pavlov's kind of learning, where a dog's natural reflex to drool at meat got connected to something else (a bell). When you bump into a technical term like Skinner's "positive reinforcement," make up an everyday-life story that illustrates the term: "If my little brother cleans up his room and my parents reward him with extra allowance money, he will be more likely to clean up his room again next week."

Don't let yourself be cheated out of what may be the most useful ideas in psychology, just because the language is difficult. Fight back!

Effective Student Tip 9

Adopt a Strategy of Effectiveness

You're probably getting more advice about how to be successful in college than you know what to do with. By itself, any specific piece of advice tends to get lost in the crowd. You need a way to pull the really good advice together and put it to regular use. You need a *strategy* of success.

An overall strategy is important because it gives you a way of evaluating any particular suggestion and of adjusting to whatever conditions arise. It is more than a single game plan, because it is both more comprehensive and more flexible. If your game plan for the next test is to work like the devil, what do you do if hard work doesn't seem to be enough?

Any plan is better than no plan, but I suggest a special kind of strategy, a strategy of effectiveness. The strategy of effectiveness is simply this: (1) You recognize that you have a basic need to be effective in everything you do, especially your college work, since that's your most important task right now. (2) You measure everything you do in college by asking, "Is this procedure getting the job done?" (In other words, is it effective?) (3) Whenever a method isn't working, instead of continuing to do the same ineffective things you make a specific procedural change.

Your response...

Do you have an overall strategy for getting through college? [Most students don't.]

Key Terms

Fight back! Translate the technical terms into everyday language about learning.

classical conditioning

cognitive learning

conditioned emotional response

conditioned nausea

conditioned response (CR)

conditioned stimulus (CS)

contiguity theory

discrimination

extinction

generalization

information theory

law of effect

learning

neutral stimulus

operant conditioning

phobia

preparedness

stimulus substitution

spontaneous recovery

systematic desensitization

taste-aversion learning

unconditioned response (UCR)

undonditioned stimulus (UCS)

Outline

- *INTRODUCTION*

  □ **Learning** *is one of those everyday terms about which we say, "I know what it means...," until we attempt a formal definition. How would you define learning? Seriously... give it a try.*

A. *Three Kinds Of Learning*

1. **Classical conditioning**

   a. Ivan Pavlov's famous experiment

   b. Conditioned reflex

   c. Learning through pairing stimuli

2. **Operant conditioning**

   a. **Law of effect** (E. L. Thorndike)

   b. Consequences and learning (B. F. Skinner)

   c. Learning through effects or consequences of actions

3. **Cognitive learning**

   a. Mental processes

   b. Observation and imitation

   c. Learning through observing and thinking

B. Procedure: Classical Conditioning

☐ *There is a beautiful logic to the way Pavlov worked out conditioning in his famous experiment with the drooling dog. Can you tell the story?*

1. How is salivation classically conditioned?

   a. Step 1: selecting stimulus and response

      (1) **Neutral stimulus**

      (2) **Unconditioned stimulus (UCS)**

      (3) **Unconditioned response (UCR)**

   b. Step 2: establishing classical conditioning

      (1) Neutral stimulus

      (2) Unconditioned stimulus (UCS)

      (3) Unconditioned response (UCR)

   c. Step 3: testing for conditioning

      (1) **Conditioned stimulus (CS)**

      (2) **Conditioned response (CR)**

2. Why does reading *Zoo World* make Carla anxious?

☐ *See if you can apply Pavlov's logic to the example of poor Carla. Use the three steps above.*

   a. Step 1: identifying the stimului and the response

   b. Step 2: establishing classical conditioning

   c. Step 3: testing for conditioning

C. Other Conditioning Concepts

1. **Generalization**

2. **Discrimination**

3. **Extinction**

4. **Spontaneous recovery**

D. Adaptive Value

1. What's the use of classical conditioning?

2. In each example, how does classical conditioning have survival value?

   a. **Taste aversion learning** in humans

   b. Taste aversion learning: explanation

      (1) **Preparedness**

      (2) Teaching coyotes not to kill sheep

3. Taste aversion learning in nature

   a. Survival value of classical conditioning

   b. Bluejays and monarch butterflies

4. Salivation and digestion

5. Emotions, fears, and phobias

   ☐ *Is there anything you are "phobic" about? What happens?*

   a. **Conditioned emotional response**

   b. **Phobia**

E. Two Explanations

1. What is learned?

2. **Stimulus substitution** theory (Pavlov)

   a. Criticisms

   b. **Contiguity theory**

3. **Information theory** (Robert Rescorla)

   a. Modern cognitive explanation (prediction)

   b. Backward conditioning

F. Research Focus: Little Albert

1. Research question: can emotional responses be classically conditioned?

2. Method

   a. John B. Watson and Rosalie Rayner

   b. Conditioning in humans

3. Results

4. Problems and conclusions

G. Cultural Diversity: Dental Fears

1. Role of classical conditioning

   a. Do cultural differences influence dental fears?

   b. What are the origins of dental fears?

   c. What are the effects of dental fears?

2. Role of culture in learning

H. Application: Conditioned Fear & Nausea

1. Classically conditioning physiological responses

2. Study: conditioned fear

3. Study: **conditioned nausea**

4. Study: **systematic desensitization**

5. Systematic desensitization procedure: three steps

   a. Step 1: Learning to relax

   b. Step 2: Developing an anxiety hierarchy

   c. Step 3: Imaging fearful stimulus and immediately relaxing

6. Effectiveness of systematic desensitization

Language Enhancement Guice

IDIOMATIC EXPRESSIONS AND CULTURAL TERMS

The following are idiomatic expressions and cultural terms found in the module. Some of them have more than one meaning; the definition given here on the right is for the way the author uses the expression in this module. Remember that these words, like all words, can have different meanings in other contexts.

The Nobel Prize (180) = A million dollar prize awarded each year by the Swedish Academy to people who have made major contributions to the world in such fields as medicine, biology, chemistry, economics, literature and world peace. The Nobel Prize is considered to be the highest academic honor a person can achieve.

widespread occurrence (183) = happens in many places

lesser magnitude (183) = not as strong

VOCABULARY BUILDING: Word Analysis

Instructions: Study the following table of common prefixes, suffixes, and roots and then guess the meanings of the terms in the table that follows. The number in parentheses ( ) refers to the page in the current module where you can find the word. You can find the definition for any word marked with a **G** in the textbook Glossary. Words that are not marked are used by the textbook author in other modules. Remember that these words, like all words, can have different meanings in other contexts.

Exercise 1. Consecutive

Prefix/Root/Suffix	Meaning
con	with/together
sequ/secut	follow
found	mix/pour together/confuse
duct	move/carry/lead/bring
anti-	against
-sepsis	decay/infection
phob	fear/terror/panic
agora-	market/ an open place

Caution: In other contexts "found" can mean begin or start.

Word	Meaning
consecutive	
successive	
confounding	
confession	
induction	bringing or placing a person into an office or position; a form of reasoning
conduct	
sequel	one development or stage follows another; an installment
execute	to carry out a plan or order; to punish by death
antiseptic (179)	
agoraphobia	fear of open places away from home

Exercise 2. Temper

Prefix/Root/Suffix	Meaning
a-	in/on
al	relating to/belonging to
ment	the act/means/result of
ive	tending to (be)/having to (be)
vert	turn
counter	against/opposite

Caution: See "Time" below.

Word	Meaning
aversion (184)	
aversive	
avert	
counterconditioning (191)	
counterphobic	

Exercise 3. Time

Prefix/Root/Suffix	Meaning
-re	back to a earlier condition/again/repeatedly
-tion/ion	the act/process/means/result of
flex	bend/curve
temper-	time
tempo	timing/rate of speed or motion as in music

Word	Meaning
temporal (G)	
contemporary	of the same or current time period, modern, people of the same age
temporary	for a short period of time, not permanent

GUESSING FROM CONTEXT

You won't find the following words and expressions from this module in the textbook Glossary, but they are useful in reading, writing, and talking about psychology and other academic subjects. See if you can guess their meanings by studying their contexts (their relationship to the words around them).

To do this, find the word or expression in your textbook and guess its meaning using the clues in the context. You may find clues in an explanation that immediately follows the word, in a synonym that appears nearby, or in the form of examples. After you have defined the terms, ask a native speaker what they mean or look them up in a dictionary to see if your guesses were correct.

exterminate (284)

preparedness (184)

necessitated (189)

appointments (191)

advocate (188)

True-False

_____ 1. Learning is a relatively permanent change in behavior as a result of experience.

_____ 2. Ivan Pavlov's famous explanation of learning was so persuasive that no other theory has challenged it since.

_____ 3. The key to Pavlov's experiment was finding a reward that would make the dog salivate.

_____ 4. At first, UCS → UCR, but after the conditioning procedure, CS → CR.

_____ 5. Once conditioning has taken place, _generalization_ may cause similar stimuli to elicit the response, but _discrimination_ should work to establish control by the specified stimuli.

_____ 6. The information processing theory says classical conditioning happens when a new stimulus replaces an old one through association.

_____ 7. Bluejays avoid eating monarch butterflies because of taste-aversion learning.

_____ 8. Automobile ads often include a gorgeous model in a low-cut evening gown because women typically make the decision about buying a car.

_____ 9. If you are like most people, the sound of the dentist's drill has become an unconditioned stimulus.

_____ 10. The goal of systematic desensitization is to _uncondition_ conditioned stimuli and make them neutral again.

For Psych Majors Only. . .

How Behaviorism Revolutionized Psychology: Living in an age of scientific psychology, it is hard for us to comprehend how profoundly behaviorism revolutionized psychology. William James, the 'father' of American psychology, was more a philosopher than psychologist. He and others in the new field relied on the method of introspection, rather than on laboratory research, to figure out how the mind worked.

Watson, extending Pavlov's scientific method to the study of human behavior, urged the following rule: Given the stimulus, predict the response; given the response, find the stimulus; given a change in response, find a change in the stimulus.

My mother took a psychology course when she attended the University of Wisconsin in the early 1920s. Psychology was only a small part of the philosophy department, but the air was charged with Watson's crusade. She still remembers her young professor's challenge to his students: _"Stimulus and response, stimulus and response — learn to think in terms of stimulus and response!"_

Flashcards

Match each key term to the definition given in the textbook.

_____ 1. classical conditioning

_____ 2. cognitive learning

_____ 3. conditioned emotional response

_____ 4. conditioned nausea

_____ 5. conditioned response (CR)

_____ 6. conditioned stimulus (CS)

_____ 7. contiguity theory

_____ 8. discrimination

_____ 9. extinction

_____ 10. generalization

_____ 11. law of effect

_____ 12. learning

_____ 13. neutral stimulus

_____ 14. preparedness

_____ 15. stimulus substitution

_____ 16. spontaneous recovery

_____ 17. systematic desensitization

_____ 18. taste-aversion learning

_____ 19. unconditioned response (UCR)

_____ 20. unconditioned stimulus (UCS)

a. stimulus that produces some result, but *not* the reflex being tested

b. feeling fear when experiencing a stimulus that initially accompanied a fearful event

c. feelings of nausea elicited by stimuli associated with receiving chemotherapy

d. says classical conditioning is a neural bonding of a neutral and an unconditioned stimulus

e. counterconditioning procedure in which person eliminates anxiety-evoking stimuli by relaxation

f. says classical conditioning occurs when two stimuli are paired close together in time

g. learning in which a neutral stimulus acquires the ability to produce a response (Ivan Pavlov)

h. stimulus which triggers or elicits some physiological reflex, such as salivation

i. learning to make a particular response to some stimuli but not to others

j. failure of a conditioned stimulus to elicit response when repeatedly presented alone

k. associating sensory cues (smells, tastes, sound, or sights) with an unpleasant response

l. biological readiness for some associations to be conditioned (learned) more easily than others

m. tendency for a stimulus that is similar to the conditioned stimulus to elicit same response

n. new response elicited by conditioned stimulus; similar to unconditioned response

o. learning that involves mental processes alone, may not require rewards or overt behavior

p. relatively permanent change in behavior resulting from experience

q. actions followed by pleasurable consequences tend to be repeated (E. L. Thorndike)

r. unlearned, innate, involuntary physiological reflex elicited by the unconditioned stimulus

s. formerly neutral stimulus that can elicit same response as unconditioned stimuli

t. tendency for conditioned response to reappear after being extinguished

Multiple-Choice

_____ 1. Rod Plotnik begins this module with the story of Carla, who canceled her subscription to *Zoo World*, to show how
  a. learning often occurs when we least expect it
  b. learning is more likely to occur in some environments than in others
  c. we can learn a response simply because it occurs along with some other response
  d. we can like something very much, then turn against it for no clear reason

_____ 2. All of the following are approaches to understanding how learning occurs *except*
  a. classical conditioning
  b. operant conditioning
  c. cognitive learning
  d. physical learning

_____ 3. Since S → R, then obviously UCS → UCR, so naturally CS →
  a. UCS
  b. UCR
  c. CR
  d. neutral stimulus

_____ 4. In Pavlov's experiment, the actual learning took place when the
  a. neutral stimulus was paired with the unconditioned stimulus
  b. conditioned reflex was presented again and again
  c. unconditioned stimulus was paired with the conditioned stimulus
  d. paired neutral and unconditioned stimuli were presented together in several trials

_____ 5. Psychologists like John B. Watson were excited by Pavlov's discovery because it
  a. provided the first look inside the thinking mind
  b. explained the operation of cognitive factors in learning
  c. explained learning in terms of behavior you could see and measure
  d. showed that canine and human brains work in much the same way

_____ 6. Conditioning seemed important to these early behaviorists because it held out the promise that psychology finally could become a/n
  a. practical, useful profession
  b. measurable, objective science
  c. proven theory
  d. established philosophy

_____ 7. After her bad experience in the dentist's office, Carla also became anxious when reading *Animals* magazine; this is an example of
  a. generalization
  b. extinction
  c. discrimination
  d. spontaneous recovery

_____ 8. But Carla did not feel anxious when reading *Time*; this is an example of
  a. generalization
  b. extinction
  c. discrimination
  d. spontaneous recovery

_____   9. When a conditioned stimulus (e.g., a tone) is repeatedly presented without the unconditioned stimulus (e.g., meat), _____ eventually will occur
   a. generalization
   b. discrimination
   c. extinction
   d. spontaneous recovery

_____   10. We seem to be biologically ready to associate some combinations of conditioned and unconditioned stimuli more easily than others, a phenomenon called
   a. conditioned nausea
   b. phobia
   c. taste-aversion learning
   d. preparedness

_____   11. From the point of view of a behavioral psychologist, a phobia is a/n
   a. expression of an unconscious conflict
   b. representation of a hidden wish
   c. conditioned emotional response
   d. unconditioned response

_____   12. According to Robert Rescorla's information theory explanation of Pavlov's experiment, the conditioned reflex gets established because
   a. the dog wants to do what Pavlov seems to want it to do
   b. the dog learns that the tone predicts the presentation of the food
   c. Pavlov unwittingly tips off the dog by looking at the food tray
   d. Pavlov simply waits until the dog makes the right response

_____   13. The reason for Little Albert's fame in psychology is the fact that
   a. Watson showed that conditioning occurred in humans, too
   b. Pavlov was unable to replicate his salivation procedure with Little Albert
   c. Rescorla used the Little Albert experiment to disprove Pavlov
   d. Carla learned not to fear the dentist through the example of this brave little boy

_____   14. A classically conditioned response often observed in patients receiving chemotherapy is
   a. conditioned nausea
   b. phobia
   c. taste-aversion learning
   d. preparedness

_____   15. Which one of the following is *not* necessary to the systematic desensitization procedure
   a. practice in relaxation techniques
   b. identification of unconscious conflicts
   c. a hierarchy of feared situations
   d. moving up and down through the hierarchy

Answers for Module 9

True-False	Flashcards	Multiple-Choice
1. T	1. g	1. c
2. F	2. o	2. d
3. F	3. b	3. c
4. T	4. c	4. d
5. T	5. n	5. c
6. F	6. s	6. b
7. T	7. f	7. a
8. F	8. i	8. c
9. F	9. j	9. c
10. T	10. m	10. d
	11. q	11. c
	12. p	12. b
	13. a	13. a
	14. l	14. a
	15. d	15. b
	16. t	
	17. e	
	18. k	
	19. r	
	20. h	

Operant & Cognitive Approaches

B. F. Skinner and the Behavioral Approach

Which psychologist has had the greatest impact on twentieth-century thought? The only obvious alternative to B. F. Skinner is Sigmund Freud himself. Even then, many would credit Freud for the most provocative ideas but give Skinner the award for actual laws of behavior and their practical applications. Skinner made psychology a science and discovered a series of principles that have become a permanent part of psychology.

As a scientist, Skinner spent his career pursuing principles of behavior that could be demonstrated in the laboratory. But he was equally concerned with what psychology is *not*. "I have feelings!" Skinner once protested, in his provocative manner. What he meant was that no matter how real and important feelings are, he refused to speculate about any psychological phenomena that could not be subjected to rigorous laboratory investigation. Rod Plotnik tells a fascinating story about how Skinner stuck to his scientific guns to the end of his life, even at the cost of offending those who had come to admire him.

Is "Cognitive Learning" a Contradiction in Terms?

For B. F. Skinner and the "radical" or "strict" behaviorists, as they came to be called, learning meant the principles of acquiring and modifying behavior as explained *without* reference to any nonobservable phenomena like cognition or mind. "Cognitive" learning, which Plotnik covers in this module, brings in what Skinner called nonobservable, and hence nonscientific, mental activity.

For most psychologists, even many of Skinner's young disciples like Albert Bandura, this uncompromising stand seemed to require a deliberate turning away from factors that were obvious and suggestive of further insights about learning. They were unwilling to leave so much out. So, without rejecting Skinner's classic discoveries, they entered the forbidden territory of the mind anyway. The result has been a very fruitful combining of behavioral principles and cognitive processes. Because the combined cognitive-behavioral approach has been willing to speculate about mental processes, it has developed many innovative and effective therapeutic applications. When the Skinnerians were at the peak of their influence, they assumed that since they understood the laws of behavior, it would be a simple matter to apply those laws to curing human psychological suffering. It didn't work out that way, since life is so much more complicated than the laboratory, and many of Skinner's frustrated followers drifted into the cognitive camp.

Effective Student Tip 10

Build Effective Routines

Anyone who loves computers also values orderly procedures. To get the most out of your computer, you must learn procedures and follow them.

Why not apply the same tactic to your college studies? When it comes to advice about how to do better in college, there are tons of useful techniques, hints, tips, tricks, and shortcuts out there. Become a consumer of useful procedures. Adapt them to your needs. Invent your own. Gather advice about how to be successful in school, but do it with a difference.

First, take a *procedural* point of view. Pay less attention to advice that is mainly sloganeering ("You *must* work harder!") and more to specific procedures (Try Tip 19, "Three Secrets of Effective Writing," for example.)

Second, gather all these useful procedures under the umbrella of *effectiveness*. Judge every procedure by whether it makes you a better student. If it works, keep it in your arsenal of useful procedures. If it doesn't, drop it. I once had a friend who decided to make himself lean and strong by eating *nothing but apples*. Excited about his new plan, for several days he was never without his bag of apples. It didn't work.

Your response...

What advice have you gotten that wasn't really very helpful? What was wrong with the advice?

Key Terms

Keep fighting back! Here is more technical laboratory language, but each key term is still about how we learn stuff. Try to make up a little story for each one.

behavior modification

biofeedback

biological factors

cognitive map

continuous reinforcement

critical [sensitive] period

cumulative record

discrimination

discriminative stimulus

ethologists

extinction

fixed-interval schedule

fixed-ratio schedule

generalization

imprinting

insight

law of effect

learning-performance distinction

negative punishment

negative reinforcement

noncompliance

observational learning

operant conditioning

operant response

partial reinforcement

pica

positive punishment

positive reinforcement

positive reinforcer

preparedness [prepared learning]

primary reinforcer

punishment

reinforcement

schedule of reinforcement

secondary reinforcer

self-injurious behavior

shaping

spontaneous recovery

superstitious behavior

time-out

variable-interval schedule

variable-ratio schedule

Outline

- **INTRODUCTION**

  I. **Operant conditioning**

  2. Observation and imitation

  A. *Operant Conditioning*

    1. Basic ideas: Thorndike and Skinner

      A. Thorndike's law of effect

        (1) **Law of effect**

        (2) Effects strengthen or weaken behavior

      B. Skinner's operant conditioning

        (1) **Operant response**

        (2) Voluntary behavior and consequences

2. Procedure: operant conditioning

   a. Skinner box

   b. **Shaping**

3. Shaping: reinforcing close approximations

☐ *You could almost say that the process of shaping is at the heart of operant conditioning. Why?*

4. Importance of immediate reinforcement

   a. Power of reinforcement (intended or not)

   b. **Superstitious behavior**

5. What is CACOB?

6. Principles of operant conditioning

   a. Toilet training and operant conditioning

   b. Food refusal and operant conditioning

7. Comparison: classical versus operant conditioning

☐ *How do classical conditioning and operant conditioning differ? What do they have in common?*

   a. Operant conditioning (Skinner)

   (1) *Voluntary* response

   (2) *Emitted* response

   (3) Consequence and reward

   (4) Immediate reinforcement

   (5) Behavior and consequences

   b. Classical conditioning (Pavlov)

   (1) *Involuntary* response

   (2) *Elicited* response

   (3) Conditioned response

   (4) Sequence

   (5) Expectancy

B. Reinforcers

1. CACOB

   a. **Reinforcement**

   b. **Punishment**

2. How can **pica** be treated?

3. Reinforcement: positive and negative

   a. **Positive reinforcement** and **positive reinforcer**

   b. **Negative reinforcement**

4. Punishment: positive versus negative

   a. **Positive punishment**

   b. **Negative punishment**

   c. Using punishment to treat a case of **self-injurious behavior**

5. Primary versus secondary reinforcers

   a. **Primary reinforcer**

   b. **Secondary reinforcement**

C. Schedules of Reinforcement

1. Skinner's genius

   a. **Schedule of reinforcement**

   b. **Cumulative record**

2. Two basic schedules of reinforcement

   a. **Continuous reinforcement**

   b. **Partial reinforcement**

3. Partial reinforcement: four different schedules

   ☐ *Can you think of an everyday life example of each schedule?*

   a. **Fixed-ratio schedule**

   b. **Fixed-interval schedule**

   c. **Variable-ratio schedule**

   d. **Variable-interval schedule**

D. Other Conditioning Concepts

1. **Generalization**

2. **Discrimination** and **discriminative stimulus**

3. **Extinction** and **spontaneous recovery**

E. Cognitive Learning

1. Three viewpoints on cognitive learning

   a. B. F. Skinner – against

   b. Edward Tolman – in favor (**cognitive map**)

   c. Albert Bandura – in favor (**observational learning**)

2. Observational learning

   ☐ *Some psychologists say Bandura's classic Bobo doll experiments disprove Skinner. How so?*

   a. Bobo doll experiments

   b. Modeling

3. Learning versus performance (**learning-performance distinction**)

4. Bandura's theory of observational learning

   a. Attention

   b. Memory

   c. Imitation

   d. Motivation

5. Using modeling to treat phobias

6. Insight learning

   a. **Insight** (Wolfgang Köhler)

   b. Insight in animals (how Sultan got the banana)

   c. Insight in humans (the "Ah ha" experience)

F. Biological Factors

1. Do animals learn to play?

   a. **Biological factors**

   b. Biological predispositions to behave

2. Imprinting

   a. **Ethologists**

   b. **Imprinting** (Konrad Lorenz)

      (1) **Critical [sensitive] period**

      (2) Irreversible

3. Prepared learning in animals and humans

   a. Incredible memory (birds) – **preparedness [prepared learning]**

   b. Incredible sounds (human infants)

   c. Conclusion

G. Research Focus: Noncompliance

1. Research question: how can parents deal with noncompliance?

   a. **Noncompliance**

   b. **Time-out**

2. Study: using time-out to reduce noncompliance

H. Cultural Diversity: East Meets West

1. Suzuki method (teaching violin) and Bandura's observational theory

2. Comparing learning principles: teacher Suzuki and researcher Bandura

   a. Attention

   b. Memory

   c. Imitation

   d. Motivation

I. Application: Behavior Modification

1. Problems of autistic children

2. **Behavior modification** for autistic children (Ivar Lovaas)

   a. Program

   b. Results

3. **Biofeedback**

4. How effective is spanking?

☐ *Do you believe in spanking? Were you spanked as a child? Do you spank your own children?*

   a. Spanking: positive punishment

   b. Time-out: negative punishment

Language Enhancement Guide

IDIOMATIC EXPRESSIONS AND CULTURAL TERMS

The following are idiomatic expressions and cultural terms found in the module. Some of them have more than one meaning; the definition given here on the right is for the way the author uses the expression in this module. Remember that these words, like all words, can have different meanings in other contexts.

swipe (195) = movement

ongoing (196) = directly observable

waltz (197) a type of dance

a task force (201) = a group of experts who work together to study and them make a report and recommendations about a scientific or social problem

profoundly mentally retarded (201) = a person with very low intelligence who cannot care for himself or herself

payoff (203) = reinforcement

layout (205) = a maplike arrangement

took no chances (204) = did not take any risks

VOCABULARY BUILDING: Word Analysis

Instructions: Study the following table of common prefixes, suffixes, and roots and then guess the meanings of the terms in the table that follows. The number in parentheses ( ) refers to the page in the current module where you can find the word. You can find the definition for any word marked with a **G** in the textbook Glossary. Words that are not marked are used by the textbook author in other modules. Remember that these words, like all words, can have different meanings in other contexts.

Exercise 1. Aversion

Prefix/Root/Suffix	Meaning
a/ab	away, from, away from
e/ex	out/out of/from
-mit	send
-licit	to pull
terminus	end/limit
vert/vers	to turn
-ion	the process/the act of
non-	not
comply	consent/yield/follow
-ance/ancy/ence/ ency	being
-ive	tending to (be)/having to (be)

Caution: The prefixes **a** and **e** can have many other meanings.

Word	Meaning
aversion (184)	
avert	
aversive	
exterminate (184)	
extinguish	
noncompliance (212)	
emit (201)	
elicit (199)	

True-False

_____ 1. Classical conditioning concerns involuntary (reflex) behavior while operant conditioning concerns voluntary behavior.

_____ 2. The secret of successful shaping is waiting until the animal emits the desired final target behavior, then immediately applying reinforcement.

_____ 3. The key to successful operant conditioning is making consequences contingent on behavior.

_____ 4. Positive reinforcement makes behavior more likely to occur again; negative reinforcement makes it less likely to occur again.

_____ 5. If you want effective learning, you must use primary reinforcers instead of secondary reinforcers.

_____ 6. Schedules of reinforcement are payoff rules that govern different patterns of work done and payment given.

_____ 7. Observational learning theory showed that there is a difference between learning a behavior and performing that behavior.

_____ 8. The difference between observational learning and operant conditioning is that the former does not depend on external reinforcement.

_____ 9. A good example of observational learning was when Sultan piled up several boxes so he could reach the banana.

_____ 10. The great power of reinforcement extends only so far — until it bumps into a biological restraint.

For Psych Majors Only. . .

How to Trade Bad Habits for Good: The central idea of behaviorism is that all human behavior is learned, the result of reinforcement through consequences. Your bad habits are not intrinsic parts of you, they are the result of learning. If that is true, then you can unlearn them, too, or crowd them out by learning new and better habits.

How can you accomplish this? By keeping the focus on behavior, understanding behavior as a transaction with the environment, and constructing better environments that support better habits. Of course this is easier said than done, because you have a long and largely forgotten learning history and also because social environments are complicated structures.

Have you noticed that nothing has been said about faults and weaknesses, blame or guilt? They have no place in behavior analysis. That's why the title of this box is not strictly accurate — habits are neither 'good' nor 'bad' in and of themselves. Behavior is simply behavior. How well any given behavior serves our purposes, however, leads to value judgments that can become guides to action.

Flashcards

Match each key term to the definition given in the textbook.

_____ 1. behavior modification

_____ 2. continuous reinforcement

_____ 3. fixed-interval schedule

_____ 4. fixed-ratio schedule

_____ 5. imprinting

_____ 6. insight

_____ 7. negative punishment

_____ 8. negative reinforcement

_____ 9. observational learning

_____ 10. partial reinforcement

_____ 11. positive punishment

_____ 12. positive reinforcement

_____ 13. preparedness or prepared learning

_____ 14. punishment

_____ 15. reinforcement

_____ 16. schedule of reinforcement

_____ 17. shaping

_____ 18. superstitious behavior

_____ 19. variable-interval schedule

_____ 20. variable-ratio schedule

a. presentation of a stimulus that increases probability of a behavior occurring again

b. rule that determines how and when occurrence of a response will be followed by a reinforcer

c. innate tendency of animals to be equipped to recognize and attend to certain cues

d. mental process marked by sudden occurrence of a solution; "ah ha" phenomenon

e. behavior that increases in frequency because of accidental pairing with a reinforcer

f. a consequence that occurs after behavior and increases likelihood of behavior occurring again

g. a reinforcer occurs following the first response that occurs after a fixed interval of time

h. result of watching; does not require learner to perform observable behavior or receive reward

i. simplest schedule; every occurrence of operant response results in delivery of reinforcer

j. a reinforcer occurs only after a fixed number of responses made by the subject

k. a situation in which responding is reinforced only some of the time

l. treatment or therapy that modifies problems by using principles of conditioning and learning

m. occurrence of an operant response that stops or removes an aversive stimulus

n. a consequence that occurs after behavior and decreases likelihood of behavior occurring again

o. inherited tendencies or responses displayed by newborn animals encountering certain stimuli

p. removal of reinforcing stimulus (taking away allowance) after response; decreases responding

q. a reinforcer occurs following the first response after a changing amount of time has gone by

r. presentation of an aversive stimulus (spanking) after a response; decreases responding

s. a reinforcer occurs after the subject makes a changing number of responses

t. successive reinforcement of behaviors that lead up to the desired behavior

Multiple-Choice

_____ 1. Rod Plotnik tells us about the starring performance of 1,800-pound Bart in _The Bear_ to make the point that
   a. although animals cannot begin to match human intelligence, they do have some capacity for learning
   b. the key to learning (and teaching) is perseverance: keep working
   c. you shouldn't believe that what you see in the movies reflects actual behavior in the wild
   d. operant conditioning procedures are powerful (no other technique could have produced Bart's learning)

_____ 2. Skinner gets the credit for operant conditioning instead of Thorndike because
   a. Thorndike stated a general principle; Skinner's research explained precisely how it works
   b. Thorndike's Law of Effect was essentially a restatement of Pavlov's conditioned reflex
   c. Skinner realized that there were biological limits on learning
   d. Skinner studied rats, pigeons, and other animals instead of limiting himself to cats

_____ 3. You could argue that Skinner's discoveries are more important than Pavlov's in that
   a. beginning a quarter of a century later, Skinner could build on Pavlov's discoveries
   b. Pavlov never worked with humans; Skinner did
   c. almost all important human behavior is voluntary (not reflex) behavior
   d. the conditioned reflex isn't fully explained until you bring in the concepts of both positive and negative reinforcement

_____ 4. The shaping procedure succeeds or fails depending on
   a. how long you are willing to wait for the target behavior to occur
   b. exactly which behaviors you reinforce
   c. how many times you reinforce the target behavior
   d. selecting the best one of several reinforcers

_____ 5. The basic principle of operant conditioning is that
   a. consequences are contingent on behavior
   b. conditioned stimuli produce conditioned responses
   c. the performance of undesired behaviors brings swift consequences
   d. consequences = CAROB (revenge is sweet)

_____ 6. The little child who gets a good hard spanking for running out into the street is experiencing an operant conditioning procedure called
   a. positive reinforcement
   b. negative reinforcement
   c. punishment
   d. extinction

_____ 7. The student on probation who finally buckles down and begins studying in earnest is under the control of an operant conditioning procedure called
   a. positive reinforcement
   b. negative reinforcement
   c. punishment
   d. extinction

_____ 8. When your date says, "I had a wonderful evening," you reply, "Gee, I was kind of hoping for a _____
    a. primary reinforcer
    b. secondary reinforcer
    c. token of your affection
    d. partial reinforcement

_____ 9. "Poor fool," you think to yourself when your friend tells you she lost on the lottery again, "another helpless victim of the _____ schedule of reinforcement"
    a. fixed-ratio
    b. variable-ratio
    c. fixed-interval
    d. variable-interval

_____ 10. Skinner opposed cognitive theories of learning to the end of his life because
    a. it is difficult to admit that the work of a lifetime was misguided
    b. they are based on philosophical speculation rather than on laboratory research
    c. they bring in the "mind," which he said couldn't be observed or measured directly
    d. you can't teach an old dog new tricks [just a joke!]

_____ 11. Although you haven't made a conscious effort to memorize the campus area, you probably get to any point on it relatively easily; Edward Tolman would say you
    a. exhibited attention, memory, imitation, and motivation
    b. learned through observation as you moved around campus
    c. can call on the power of insight when necessary
    d. automatically developed a cognitive map

_____ 12. Which one of the following was *not* an important outcome in Albert Bandura's famous Bobo doll experiment?
    a. more imitative behavior occurred when children were promised rewards before they watched the model pummeling Bobo
    b. the children learned even though they did not receive tangible rewards
    c. the children learned even though they were not engaging in any overt behavior
    d. some subjects did not imitate the model (proving learning had occurred) until they were reinforced for doing so

_____ 13. Which one of the following is *not* a factor in Bandura's theory of observational learning?
    a. attention
    b. memory
    c. rehearsal
    d. motivation

_____ 14. The important thing about the solution Sultan came up with for the out-of-reach banana problem was
    a. how an old conditioned reflex spontaneously recovered
    b. how he used trial and error
    c. how he built on previously reinforced behavior
    d. what was *missing* in his solution — namely, all the factors above

_____ 15. The Suzuki method of teaching violin to children closely resembles the processes of
    a. Pavlov's classical conditioning
    b. Bandura's observational learning
    c. Skinner's operant conditioning
    d. Kohler's insight learning

Answers for Module 10

True-False	Flashcards	Multiple-Choice
1. T	1. l	1. d
2. F	2. i	2. a
3. T	3. g	3. c
4. F	4. j	4. b
5. F	5. o	5. a
6. T	6. d	6. c
7. T	7. p	7. b
8. T	8. m	8. a
9. F	9. h	9. b
10. T	10. k	10. c
	11. r	11. d
	12. a	12. a
	13. c	13. c
	14. n	14. d
	15. f	15. b
	16. b	
	17. t	
	18. e	
	19. q	
	20. s	

Types of Memory

Nothing in This Module Is True

Psychobiology and cognitive psychology have made great strides in the last two decades. One of the results is a much clearer picture of how memory works. Even so, there is a sense in which none of it is true.

The answers we want are buried at least two layers down. First, how does the physical brain work? We are learning more about the brain every day, yet for all their discoveries neuroscientists have barely scratched the surface. The need to understand elusive electrical activity, not just gray matter, complicates the task. Second, how does the mind work? If the mind is an abstraction, a concept (unless you say mind and brain are the same thing), we cannot apprehend it directly, making it even more difficult to understand.

Today we are fond of comparing the mind to a computer, simply because the computer is the most powerful mechanical thinking device we know, and therefore makes a good comparison. Yet when we develop a *new* generation of thinking machines, perhaps based on liquid instead of silicone chips, we will stop comparing the mind to a computer and compare it to the new device instead, since the new device will seem much more like the human mind. The mind is not really a computer; the computer merely makes a good model for understanding the mind, at least today.

The Beauty of a Good Model

No wonder the dress looks so beautiful on the model sashaying down the runway in the fashion show — the model isn't an actual human being (obviously, no one is that tall, that thin, that perfect). Consequently, when draped around this abstraction of a human, we can see much more clearly how the clothing itself really looks.

A model helps us understand the real world because it is an ideal against which we can compare specific things. When we try to understand the mind, all we see are awkward elbows and knees. We need a model to help us visualize what it must really be like.

Many of the formulations presented in Module 11 are models of what the process of grasping the world and putting parts of it in our heads must be like. I think you can learn these theories better if you keep in mind the idea that they are models, not reality.

Effective Student Tip 11

High Grades Count Most

Here is a hard truth. Unfair, maybe, but true. Anyone who looks at your transcript, whether for admission to another school or for employment, is going to be looking for the *high* grades. It's difficult for them to tell exactly what 'C' means. In some schools, 'C' may mean little more than that you attended class. The grade 'B' begins to say more about your abilities and character, but it is an 'A' that is really convincing. No matter in what course or at what school, an 'A' says you did everything asked of you and did it well. That's a quality admissions people and personnel officers look for.

High grades have other rewards, too. You get on the school's honors list. You can join honors societies. You qualify for scholarships. With every 'A', your sense of effectiveness goes up a notch. You are more confident and enjoy greater self-esteem. (Keeps Mom and Dad happy, too!)

Tailor your work toward earning high grades. Take fewer courses, stay up later studying, write papers over, ruthlessly cut fun out of your life [just kidding].

Earning high grades in a few courses beats getting average grades in many courses. The fastest route toward your goal is a conservative selection of courses in which you do well, resulting in a good record and confidence in your effectiveness as a student.

Your response...

Can you remember a time when you thought you had an 'A', then didn't get it? What went wrong?

Key Terms

Many of these terms are based on a model of the mind. Get the model and it's easier to learn the terms.

automatic encoding

chunking

declarative [explicit] memory

echoic memory

effortful encoding

eidetic imagery

elaborative rehearsal

encoding

episodic memory

flashbulb memories

iconic memory

interference

levels of processing theory

long-term memory

maintenance rehearsal

memory

photographic memory

primacy effect

primacy-recency effect

procedural [implicit] memory

recency effect

repression

retrieval

semantic memory

sensory memory

short-term memory

storage

Outline

- *INTRODUCTION*

  1. **Memory**

  2. Three *processes* in memory

     a. **Encoding**

     b. **Storage**

     c. **Retrieval**

  A. *Three Types of Memory*

     ☐ *Can you see the logic of this model?*

     1. Why do we need three memory processes?

        a. **Sensory memory**

        b. **Short-term memory**

        c. **Long-term memory**

     2. Three process memory model

B. Sensory Memory: Recording

☐ *How do iconic and echoic memory work? What is their purpose?*

1. **Iconic memory**

2. **Echoic memory**

3. Functions of sensory memory

    a. Limits sensory input

    b. Decision time

    c. Stability, playback, and recognition

C. Short-Term Memory: Working

1. **Short-term** [working] **memory**

2. Two features of short-term memory

    a. Limited duration

        (1) From two to 30 seconds

        (2) **Maintenance rehearsal**

    b. Limited capacity

        (1) About seven items or bits (George Miller)

        (2) Memory span test

        (3) **Interference**

        (4) **Chunking**

3. Functions of short-term memory

    a. Attention

    b. Rehearsal

    c. Storage in long-term memory

D. Long-Term Memory: Storing

1. **Long-term memory**

2. Steps in the memory process

    a. Sensory memory

    b. Attention

    c. Short-term memory

    d. Encoding

    e. Long-term memory

    f. Retrieval

3. Facts about long-term memory

    a. Unlimited capacity

    b. Permanent storage

    c. Retrieval

4. Primacy versus recency

☐ *Take a moment to work out the logic of these concepts. They make sense if you understand the memory processes involved.*

    a. **Primacy effect**

    b. **Recency effect**

    c. **Primacy-recency effect**

5. Different kinds of long-term memories

    a. **Declarative [explicit] memory**

        (1) **Semantic memory**

        (2) **Episodic memory**

    b. **Procedural [implicit] memory**

E. Research Focus: Emotional Memories

1. Research question: why are emotional experiences better remembered?

2. Study: interfering with memories of emotional events

    a. Procedure

    b. Results

F. Encoding: Transferring

1. **Encoding**

   a. **Automatic encoding**

   b. **Effortful encoding**

2. Forms of encoding

3. Strategies of effortful encoding

   a. **Maintenance rehearsal**

   b. **Elaborative rehearsal**

4. **Levels of processing theory**

G. Repressed Memory

☐ *Do you remember seeing the story about a repressed memory of a gruesome murder in the news? Which side did you believe?*

1. What are repressed memories?

   a. Freud's theory of **repression**

   b. Problem for therapists

2. What is the therapist's role?

3. Can false memories be implanted?

4. Are repressed memories accurate?

5. Conclusions

H. Cultural Diversity: Oral Tradition

1. Encoding: comparing Africans and Americans

2. Remembering spoken information

I. Application: Unusual Memories

1. **Eidetic imagery**

2. **Photographic memory**

3. Flashbulb memory — revised

   a. **Flashbulb memories**

   b. Flashbulb memories and hormones

Language Enhancement Guide

IDIOMATIC EXPRESSIONS AND CULTURAL TERMS

The following are idiomatic expressions and cultural terms found in the module. Some of them have more than one meaning; the definition given here on the right is for the way the author uses the expression in this module. Remember that these words, like all words, can have different meanings in other contexts.

getting on with (their lives) (218) = continuing

blocked (218) = prevented

guard against (218) = prevent

a fair (220) = a market held at a specified time and place for the buying and selling of things

VOCABULARY BUILDING: Word Analysis

Instructions: Study the following table of common prefixes, suffixes, and roots and then guess the meanings of the terms in the table that follows. The number in parentheses ( ) refers to the page in the current module where you can find the word. You can find the definition for any word marked with a **G** in the textbook Glossary. Words that are not marked are used by the textbook author in other modules. Remember that these words, like all words, can have different meanings in other contexts.

Exercise 1. Encode

Prefix/Root/Suffix	Meaning
en /in-	in/into/within
code	a system of arbitrary symbols or signals used to represent words or ideas/a system of laws, rules, ethics
-cyclopedia	education/knowledge
re-	back/again and again
-ion	the act/means/results of
trans	to send/carry across/beyond
un-	not
-ence	act/condition/means
-trieve	to find

Word	Meaning
encode (228)	
enthusiasm	to be in excitement about something, inspired
encyclopedia	a summary of knowledge, books that summarize knowledge
reconstruction	
reconstruct	
repression	
transfer (220)	
transference (228)	

unreasonable (222)	
interference	
retain (220)	
retrieve (224)	
recollection	

STRUCTURAL CLUES: Leading Questions

On page 229 of this module Rod Plotnik explains that the deeper the level you process or encode information the more easily you can retrieve information. Plotnik presents several examples of the kinds of questions that promote deeper processing. Plotnik's text is very helpful in this way because he asks many well designed leading questions. His questions or problems are placed in the chapter to stimulate your curiosity and start you thinking about what is coming next. Many research studies have found that students who pay attention to questions and try to answer them before they continue to read are able to recall more information with greater accuracy than students who ignore them.

By reading these questions, you get a pretty good idea of the information on that page. But don't just read them; think about these questions before you start to read. Then, as you read, you can find out whether or not your answers were correct. It's tempting to skip them altogether, but they're there for a purpose — to make the reading task easier and give your reading a focus that makes reading more rewarding.

For example, turn to page 219 and the paragraph in the bottom box on the page and you will find the following question: "What is memory?" Before you read on, stop and think of an answer. After you have given this question some thought and generated your own answer, read on and compare your answer with the authors. You will find that the author has frequently incorporated provocative questions as the title of a section or as the first sentence in a new section.

Turn to page 220. You will find interesting questions framed in a box on the top and on the bottom of the page. The author has included questions like these in similar locations for each new section of each module for you to actively answer.

Practice using leading questions to preview module material by finding the following questions on the pages indicated. Guess the answers before you read the material on the page. Then read the material word-for-word and see if your guesses were correct. Here are several important questions selected from Module 11 along with their page numbers. Find each one in the chapter and examine how the author uses them to stimulate your interest in the text and start you thinking about the topic covered in the following paragraph or section. Whenever you find a leading question, stop and think about the possible answers to that question.

"What are repressed memories?" (230)

"What is the therapist's role?" (230)

"Can false memories be implanted?" (231)

"Are repressed memories accurate?" (231)

True-False

_____ 1. Memory involves three basic processes: encoding, storing, and retrieving.

_____ 2. There are four basic kinds of memory: flashbulb snapshots, temporary, impermanent, and permanent.

_____ 3. Without the stage called sensory memory, we would drown in a sea of visual and auditory sensations.

_____ 4. Short-term memory is capable of holding about a dozen bits of information for several minutes.

_____ 5. When you attempt to remember a list of animals, the recency effect takes precedence over the primacy effect.

_____ 6. If you are studying for the next psych exam, elaborative rehearsal will be a more effective strategy than maintenance rehearsal.

_____ 7. Encoding is transferring information from short-term to long-term memory.

_____ 8. The best way to get information into long-term memory is to repeat it over and over again.

_____ 9. A good strategy for remembering something is to associate it with some distinctive visual image.

_____ 10. When you find someone who has unusual powers of memory, you can be fairly certain that the person possesses a photographic memory.

For Psych Majors Only...

Gloomy Psychology: Here is a gloomy, possibly discouraging thought (considering how much you paid for your books): perhaps _nothing_ in psychology is really true. Perhaps everything you are slaving so hard to learn is simply the best understanding we have now, soon to be replaced by better ways of understanding how psychology works.

I suggested that the computer is merely a temporary model for understanding the mind. Let's go further and suggest that _all_ the wonderful theories you study in psychology are models, none ultimately "true." There is no "unconscious" region of the mind, no pure "schedule of reinforcement," and no ethereal "self." They are all fictions — fictions we need in order to make sense of the facts.

There is one happy possibility in this dismal thought. Think how eagerly psychology is waiting for the better model _you_ may construct one day. Keep working on your favorite theories.

Flashcards

Match each key term to the definition given in the textbook.

_____ 1. chunking

_____ 2. declarative [explicit] memory

_____ 3. echoic memory

_____ 4. effortful encoding

_____ 5. eidetic imagery

_____ 6. elaborative rehearsal

_____ 7. encoding

_____ 8. flashbulb memories

_____ 9. iconic memory

_____ 10. interference

_____ 11. long-term memory

_____ 12. maintenance rehearsal

_____ 13. photographic memory

_____ 14. primacy-recency effect

_____ 15. procedural [implicit] memory

_____ 16. repression

_____ 17. retrieval

_____ 18. sensory memory

_____ 19. short-term memory

_____ 20. storage

a. form of sensory memory that holds auditory information for one or two seconds

b. better recall of information presented at the beginning and at the end of a task

c. placing or storing information in memory by making mental representations

d. practice of intentionally repeating information so it remains longer in short-term memory

e. ability to examine material for 10-30 seconds then retain a detailed visual image for minutes

f. when new information overwrites previous information already in short-term memory

g. process of how encoded information is placed into relatively permanent mental holding

h. combining separate items of information into larger units, then remembering those units

i. making meaningful associations between new information and information already learned

j. transfer of information from short-term into long-term memory by working hard to do so

k. process of getting or retrieving information out of short-term or long-term storage

l. initial process that holds raw information for a brief period of time (instant to several seconds)

m. ability to form sharp, detailed visual images, then recall the entire image at a later date

n. process that can hold limited amount of information (7 items) for short period (2-30 sec)

o. vivid recollections, usually in great detail, of dramatic or emotionally charged incidents

p. memories for performing motor tasks, habits, conditioning; not conscious or retrievable

q. process of storing almost unlimited amounts of information over long periods of time

r. threat or trauma that pushes memory into the unconscious, from which it cannot be retrieved

s. form of sensory memory that holds visual information for about a quarter of a second

t. memories for facts or events (scenes, stories, faces, etc.); conscious and retrievable

Multiple-Choice

_____ 1. Rod Plotnik discusses Rajan Mahadevan, who memorized more than 30,000 digits of pi, because Rajan's rare abilities
   a. show that extreme concentration of mental ability in one area is usually accompanied by deficiencies in other areas
   b. are possessed only by people who are otherwise retarded or autistic
   c. could be duplicated by any of us... if we put our minds to it
   d. offer an extreme example of the memory processes we all use

_____ 2. Which one of the following is _not_ one of the three processes of memory?
   a. encoding
   b. storing
   c. deciphering
   d. retrieving

_____ 3. The function of sensory memory is to
   a. hold information in its raw form for a brief period of time
   b. make quick associations between new data and things you already know
   c. weed out what is irrelevant in incoming information
   d. burn sensations into long-term memory for later retrieval and inspection

_____ 4. _____ memory holds visual information for about a quarter of a second
   a. Chunking
   b. Iconic
   c. Pictorial
   d. Echoic

_____ 5. Thanks to _____ memory, incoming speech sounds linger just long enough so we can recognize the sounds as words
   a. chunking
   b. iconic
   c. verbal
   d. echoic

_____ 6. The statement below that describes short-term memory is:
   a. your perceptual processes react to it
   b. you freeze it briefly in order to pay attention to it
   c. you work with it to accomplish some immediate task
   d. you retrieve it later when you need it again

_____ 7. Out of change at the pay phone, you frantically repeat the 11-digit number you just got from Information over and over again; that's called
   a. chunking
   b. maintenance rehearsal
   c. memory span stretching
   d. duration enhancement

_____ 8. But wait a minute… You already know "1" and the area code, so you need only find something to associate with the prefix and the number; that's called
   a. chunking
   b. maintenance rehearsal
   c. memory span stretching
   d. duration enhancement

_____ 9. Why doesn't information in short-term memory simply become permanent? Probably because of
   a. limited storage space in the brain
   b. fascination with the new and different
   c. incompatibility with previously processed information
   d. interference caused by newly arriving information

_____ 10. If you attempt to remember a list of animal names, you will be more likely to remember the
   a. first few names
   b. last few names
   c. both the first and last few names
   d. neither the first or last few names, but the ones occurring in the middle of the list

_____ 11. Remembering how you did on your last psych test would be considered
   a. episodic information
   b. semantic information
   c. consequential information
   d. procedural information

_____ 12. The actual knowledge required for that test would be called
   a. episodic information
   b. semantic information
   c. consequential information
   d. procedural information

_____ 13. Your manual ability to write out the answers on the test would be called
   a. episodic information
   b. semantic information
   c. consequential information
   d. procedural information

_____ 14. The main problem with repressed memories of childhood abuse is that
   a. very few people can remember that far back
   b. we now know that the "unconscious" does not exist
   c. therapists may unwittingly help patients form memories which seem to explain their key problems
   d. so far, all the claimed cases of abuse in childhood have been proven to be lies

_____ 15. Rod Plotnik puts psychology to good use in his textbook by providing _____ to help you encode the material you must learn
   a. distinctive visual associations
   b. flashbulb memories
   c. maintenance rehearsal drills
   d. chunking strategies

Answers for Module 11

True-False
1. T
2. F
3. T
4. F
5. F
6. T
7. T
8. F
9. T
10. F

Flashcards
1. h
2. t
3. a
4. j
5. e
6. i
7. c
8. o
9. s
10. f
11. q
12. d
13. m
14. b
15. p
16. r
17. k
18. l
19. n
20. g

Multiple-Choice
1. d
2. c
3. a
4. b
5. d
6. c
7. b
8. a
9. d
10. c
11. a
12. b
13. d
14. c
15. a

Remembering & Forgetting

What If You Could Remember Nothing?

Imagine how terrifying amnesia must be? In one form of amnesia, you can't remember back before a certain point. In a less common form, you can't construct new memories. In either case, you are rootless, adrift in a world with no clear sense of past, present and future. You wouldn't really know who you are, why you exist, or what will happen to you.

What if you could *forget* nothing? Happily, there is no such psychiatric condition (although you could use such powers, with mid-term exams coming up). If you were incapable of ever forgetting anything you would be immobilized in a sea of indistinguishable bits and pieces of information, incapable of ever making a decision or taking action because the necessary review of past information and action would be never-ending.

The processes of remembering and forgetting are so immediate and so crucial that we take them for granted. But science, of course, takes nothing for granted. Rod Plotnik shows us what the science of psychology has learned about these vital memory processes.

Forget About It

When something is too painful to endure, a common reaction is to forget about it. Often victims of auto accidents experience temporary amnesia for the immediate events of the crash. All of us "forget" bad grades and other humiliating defeats.

As we have learned more about child abuse, we have come to realize how its victims often repress their trauma, in order to go on living. Uncovering these repressed memories has become an important part of psychotherapy. Many therapists are convinced that the suffering child cannot become well again unless the painful memories are dug out and worked through.

But memory is ever so much more complicated. Now we are also learning that it is quite possible to "remember" things that never happened. Rod Plotnik reveals the interesting and disturbing dangers of false memories, both those of eyewitness testimony. Is it really possible that a child could lie about having been sexually abused, or that an eyewitness to a crime could make the wrong identification? Forget about it!

Effective Student Tip 12

Manage Your Grade

True, we professors set the course standards and assign the final grades. Since most professors stick to the rules once they are established, however, *you* have almost total control over what that grade will be. But wishing doesn't make it so: you have to know how to make it happen. The trick is to take a management attitude toward your grades.

Taking charge and managing your grade involves six steps: (1) Understand your inner motivation concerning grades, to guard against self-sabotage. (2) Understand the details and logic of your professor's grading system. (3) Keep accurate records of your scores and grades (all of them, including any assignments or quizzes you missed). (4) Project your final grade from your current performance. (5) Determine what immediate steps you must take. (6) Make whatever adjustments seem necessary for effective pursuit of your goal.

Don't underestimate the importance of grades to your mental health. Rightly or wrongly, we interpret grades, like earnings, as powerful messages about our effectiveness.

You can passively allow your grades to happen to you, as many students do, or you can take charge and make them what you want.

Your response...

How important are grades to you? How much control do you seem to have over the grades you get?

Key Terms

These key terms touch on an area of psychology that researchers are just beginning to understand. But what could be more important than the way we orient ourselves to time and place?

amnesia	method of loci	recognition
cognitive interview	mnemonics	repression
forgetting curves	network hierarchy	retrieval cues
forgetting	network theory	retroactive interference
inadequate retrieval cues	nodes	source misattribution
interference theory	peg method	state-dependent learning
interference	proactive interference	tip-of-the tongue phenomenon
law of disuse	recall	

Outline

- *INTRODUCTION*

    ☐ *Were you surprised when you tried Rod Plotnik's quiz about the assault?*

    1. Recall versus recognition

        a. **Recall**

        b. **Recognition**

    2. Eyewitness testimony

    A. *Organization*

    1. Trash can versus **network theory**

    2. Network theory of memory organization

        a. Nodes

        b. Associations

        c. Network

    3. Network hierarchy

        a. **Nodes**

        b. **Network hierarchy**

    c. Searching the network hierarchy

    d. Memory organization: hierarchy or groups

        (1) Factual information

        (2) Personal information

        (3) New models

B. *Forgetting Curves*

  1. Unfamiliar and uninteresting information

    a. **Forgetting curves** (Hermann Ebbinghaus)

    b. Nonsense syllables

  2. Familiar and interesting information

  3. Two conclusions

C. *Reasons for Forgetting*

  1. **Forgetting**

  2. Five reasons for forgetting

    a. **Law of disuse** (old theory)

    b. **Repression** (Freud)

    c. **Interference**

    d. **Inadequate retrieval cues**

    e. **Amnesia**

  3. Interference

    a. **Interference theory**

        (1) **Proactive interference**

        (2) **Retroactive interference**

    b. Why did viewers forget the mugger's face?

  4. Inadequate retrieval cues

    a. **Retrieval cues**

    b. **Tip-of-the-tongue phenomenon**

  5. **State-dependent learning**

D. Biological Bases

1. Location of memories in the brain

    a. Cortex: short-term memory

    b. Cortex: recalling old memories

    c. Amygdala: adding emotional feelings

    d. Hippocampus: long-term memory

2. Mechanisms of memory

3. Chemical and structural changes

    a. Neurotransmitters

    b. Chemical changes

    c. Structural changes

E. Mnemonics: Memorization Methods

1. **Mnemonics**

2. **Method of loci**

3. **Peg method**

F. Cultural Diversity: Aborigines

1. Visual versus verbal retrieval cues

2. An experiment on Aborigines' memory

    a. Procedure

    b. Conclusions

G. Research Focus: False Memories

☐ *What are the implications of this research for psychologists and legal professionals?*

1. Research question: how suggestible are young children?

2. Study: creating false memories in young children

    a. Procedure

    b. Conclusions

H. Application: Eyewitness Testimony

1. Mistaken identities

2. Problems with eyewitness testimony

3. Can eyewitnesses be misled (Elizabeth Loftus)?

4. **Source misattribution**

5. **Cognitive interview** technique

Language Enhancement Guide

Mod 12 IDIOMATIC EXPRESSIONS AND CULTURAL TERMS

The following are idiomatic expressions and cultural terms found in the module. Some of them have more than one meaning; the definition given here on the right is for the way the author uses the expression in this module. Remember that these words, like all words, can have different meanings in other contexts.

(violent) jerk (239) = pull

jump haphazardly (240) = moved from place to place by chance

mugger (244) = a person who threatens, harms or robs others

nursery rhyme (245) = a poem or rhyme written for children

model (246) = a theory

Aborigine (250) = the original and often primitive native population of a region such as Australia

to testify in court (251) = to tell what you know about a crime in a court of law

VOCABULARY BUILDING: Word Analysis

Instructions: Study the following table of common prefixes, suffixes, and roots and then guess the meanings of the terms in the table that follows. The number in parentheses ( ) refers to the page in the current module where you can find the word. You can find the definition for any word marked with a **G** in the textbook Glossary. Words that are not marked are used by the textbook author in other modules. Remember that these words, like all words, can have different meanings in other contexts.

Exercise 1. Incongruous

Prefix/Root/Suffix	Meaning
contra/contro	against/opposite of/opposed to/contrary
congru	agreement/harmony/consistent/fitting
dict	to say/to speak
-ous	full of/characterized by
ent/ant-	being/doing/having/performing/showing
-ion	the act/means/results of
im/in-	not/without
plant	put/place
vert	change/turn/

Word	Meaning
controversy	
contradict	to express the opposite of (a statement or claim)
contradiction	
incongruous	
congruent	
dictation	
implant (321)	

True-False

_____ 1. Of the two ways to remember, recall is easier than recognition.

_____ 2. According to network theory, memory is organized like a gigantic map on which roads connect cities of related information.

_____ 3. Forgetting curves measure the length of time that pieces of information will remain in long-term memory.

_____ 4. Most psychologists explain forgetting by referring to the law of disuse.

_____ 5. Proactive interference occurs when you are trying too hard to remember new information.

_____ 6. Amnesia is the loss of memory that may occur following drug use, damage to the brain, or after severe psychological stress.

_____ 7. Although it is the brain that does the "thinking," the spinal cord stores the actual memories.

_____ 8. Both the method of loci and the peg method are mnemonic strategies.

_____ 9. It turns out that people _are_ different in mental ability — aborigines, for example, score lower than white Australians on intelligence tests.

_____ 10. Psychologists have discovered that introducing misleading information during questioning can distort eyewitness testimony.

Flashcards

Match each key term to the definition given in the textbook.

_____ 1. amnesia

_____ 2. cognitive interview

_____ 3. forgetting curves

_____ 4. forgetting

_____ 5. interference theory

_____ 6. interference

_____ 7. law of disuse

_____ 8. method of loci

_____ 9. network hierarchy

_____ 10. network theory

_____ 11. nodes

_____ 12. peg method

_____ 13. proactive interference

_____ 14. recall

_____ 15. recognition

_____ 16. repression

_____ 17. retrieval cues

_____ 18. retroactive interference

_____ 19. source misattribution

_____ 20. state-dependent learning

a. creating associations between number-word rhymes and items to be memorized

b. similar information learned later now blocks retrieval of information that was learned earlier

c. Freudian mental process that automatically hides emotionally threatening information

d. other related memories may block or prevent retrieval of some particular memory

e. arrangement of nodes so concrete ideas are at bottom of hierarchy, abstract ideas at top

f. says we forget information because newer information gets in the way and blocks retrieval

g. technique for questioning eyewitnesses by having them reconstruct details of event fully

h. creating visual associations between memorized places and items to be memorized

i. retrieving previously learned information without the aid of external cues

j. reminders created by forming vivid mental images of information or by association

k. related information learned earlier now blocks retrieval of information that was learned later

l. inability to retrieve, recall, or recognize information stored in long-term memory

m. loss of memory that may occur after brain damage, drug use, severe psychological stress

n. says we store related ideas in separate categories called nodes, all linked together

o. memory files that contain related information organized around a specific topic or category

p. easier to recall information when you are in the same physiological or emotional state or setting

q. memory error resulting from difficulty in deciding where a memory came from

r. identifying previously learned information with the help of external cues

s. measure amount of previously learned information subjects can recall across time

t. early theory of forgetting; said memories fade away and disappear across time if not used

Multiple-Choice

_____ 1. Your brow beading with perspiration, you struggle to answer these questions, desperately summoning your best powers of
   a. recall
   b. reflection
   c. recognition
   d. recollection

_____ 2. If you only glanced through the chapter, pray that the snap quiz will be
   a. essay
   b. multiple-choice
   c. short essay
   d. oral

_____ 3. According to _____ theory, memory is organized by nodes, associations, and hierarchies of information
   a. network
   b. trash can
   c. script
   d. abstraction

_____ 4. Which of the following groups of items would provide the best test in research on memory over time?
   a. names and faces of childhood friends
   b. commonly studied facts, such as state capitals
   c. foreign language vocabulary
   d. nonsense syllables

_____ 5. The data yielded by such research (above) would be
   a. rates of retention
   b. memory percentages
   c. forgetting curves
   d. cognitive charts

_____ 6. You know you said something terribly embarrassing, but you can't remember what it was — this is an example of
   a. the law of disuse
   b. repression
   c. interference
   d. inadequate retrieval cues

_____ 7. You were introduced to your friend's professor recently, but there was no time to chat and now you can't recall the professor's name — this is an example of
   a. the law of disuse
   b. repression
   c. interference
   d. inadequate retrieval cues

_____ 8. Of the main explanations of forgetting, the one with the least research support is
    a. the law of disuse
    b. repression
    c. interference
    d. inadequate retrieval cues

_____ 9. Proactive interference is when
    a. information learned later now disrupts retrieval of information learned earlier
    b. learning positive information interferes with the retrieval of negative information
    c. information learned earlier now disrupts retrieval of information learned later
    d. retrospective thinking interferes with potential learning

_____ 10. Retroactive interference is when
    a. information learned later now disrupts retrieval of information learned earlier
    b. learning positive information interferes with the retrieval of negative information
    c. information learned earlier now disrupts retrieval of information learned later
    d. retrospective thinking interferes with potential learning

_____ 11. We humans are very proud of our ability to "think," but, when we study creatures like the sea slug, "thought" begins to look more like
    a. molecular, chemical, and structural changes in the nervous system
    b. the thinking of a severely retarded person
    c. habits shaped through reward and punishment
    d. inherited tendencies somewhat modified by experience

_____ 12. Both the method of loci and the peg method work by
    a. causing learning to be strengthened through repeated practice
    b. creating strong associations that will serve as effective retrieval cues
    c. connecting material to be learned to the purpose it will be used for
    d. considering material to be memorized as easy and pleasant to learn

_____ 13. Aborigine children performed significantly better than white Australian children on memory tasks when
    a. only Aborigine objects were used
    b. the task involved auditory cues
    c. testing was done outdoors in a natural setting
    d. the task involved visual cues

_____ 14. Recent research on false memories of abuse in young children has shown that
    a. children can be coached to lie about trivial matters, but not about sexual abuse
    b. false memories can be created through repeated suggestions
    c. children make things up because they really can't remember very well at that age
    d. children tend to lie about most things if they can get something out of it

_____ 15. When evaluating eyewitness testimony, pay close attention to
    a. whether the eyewitness has anything to gain or lose by testifying
    b. how confident the eyewitness appears to be
    c. how the questions to the eyewitness are worded
    d. whether the eyewitness seems biased in favor of or against the defendant

Answers for Module 12

True-False
1. F
2. T
3. T
4. F
5. F
6. T
7. F
8. T
9. F
10. T

Flashcards
1. m
2. g
3. s
4. l
5. f
6. d
7. t
8. h
9. e
10. n
11. o
12. a
13. k
14. i
15. r
16. c
17. j
18. b
19. q
20. p

Multiple-Choice
1. c
2. b
3. a
4. d
5. c
6. b
7. d
8. a
9. c
10. a
11. a
12. b
13. d
14. b
15. c

Intelligence

The Social Psychology of Psychology

Perhaps no single topic reveals the interconnectedness of psychology and society more clearly than the complicated issue of intelligence. Delineating the nature and quality of human thought, captured in the concept of intelligence, has always been a primary goal of psychology. Yet few other subjects have entangled the science of psychology more controversially in the needs and passions of society.

Few would argue the importance of addressing the special needs of the super bright and the severely retarded. It seems obvious that something real is going on in both cases. But what about the rest of us, the great majority? How real are the differences among us that psychology measures with such precision, and, until recently, with such confidence? Questions like these evoke the central question of the social sciences.

The Nature-Nurture Debate in the Social Sciences

Heredity or environment? Personality or experience? Are we best explained by reference to our nature (what is built in) or to our nurture (how we are raised)? This is the essence of the nature-nurture debate, an old argument over basic assumptions that continues to rage in the social sciences. Two controversies illustrate the nature-nurture debate: (1) How important is what we inherit (genetics) compared to what we experience (learning)? (2) To what extent can we control our thoughts, feelings, and actions (free will) compared to control over us by outside forces (determinism).

You will find echoes of the nature-nurture debate in almost everything you read about psychological research and theory. Your basic orientation toward nature or nurture will influence what major theories in psychology you find most convincing, what giants of psychology you like and dislike, what research you believe or doubt, and even what "facts" you accept or reject. Whenever you come across an idea in psychology that arouses your strong interest, whether positive or negative, try examining the idea from the perspective of the nature-nurture debate. Odds are, the idea strongly supports or challenges your basic assumptions about life.

In the long run, thoughtful study of psychology will drive us more and more toward a middle position, an 'interactionist' point of view which sees humans as products of the interplay of heredity and environment, individual uniqueness and group pressure, rational choice and force of habit. Still, I am willing to bet that most of us will continue to feel the pull of our basic adherence either to the argument of nature or the argument of nurture.

Effective Student Tip 13

Risk a New Idea

You didn't come to college to stay the same. You intend to be a better and more fully developed person when you leave. You hope to grow in many ways, and one of the most important is mental. Intellectual growth requires a spirit of openness to change, of willingness to risk new ideas.

If you don't try out a new idea in college, you probably never will. As time goes on, work, family and responsibility all conspire to make most of us more cautious and more conservative. Never again will you encounter as many new and different ideas as in college. In one sense, the very mission of colleges and universities is to hit us with new ideas. If everything was dandy just the way it is now, we really wouldn't need colleges and universities.

When a professor or student throws out a challenging idea, seriously consider whether it might be true. If true, how would it change what you believe? If false, how do your own beliefs disprove it?

Accepting intellectual challenges will strengthen your ideas and your ability to defend them. You might even solve a problem you have been puzzling over. Most of the time, however, you will augment and improve your understanding of the world and yourself only slightly. This is a great victory. We call it growth.

Your response…

What startling new idea have you encountered recently? What was your reaction to that idea?

Key Terms

Understanding the controversies over intelligence will make these key terms easier to learn.

Binet-Simon Intelligence Scale

cultural bias

culture-free tests

ecological psychology

fraternal twins

Gardner's multiple-intelligence theory

gifted

identical twins

intelligence quotient

intervention program

mental age

mental retardation

nature-nurture question

normal distribution

organic retardation and cultural-familial retardation

psychometric approach

psychometrics

reaction range

reliability

Stanford-Binet

Sternberg's triarchic theory

two-factor theory

validity

Wechsler Adult Intelligence Scale-Revised (WAIS-R) [and Wechsler Intelligence Scale for Children-Revised (WISC-III)]

Outline

- *INTRODUCTION*

    1. Individual differences and intelligence

    2. **Psychometrics**

A. *Defining Intelligence*

    ☐ *Consider both the advantages and disadvantages of these definitions of intelligence. Which theory makes the most sense to you?*

    1. Two-factor theory (Charles Spearman)

        a. **Psychometric approach**

        b. **Two-factor theory**

    2. Multiple-intelligence theory

        a. **Gardner's multiple-intelligence theory**

        b. Highlights other areas, but how many areas are there?

    3. Information-processing approach

        a. **Sternberg's triarchic theory**

        b. Intelligence as cognitive processes of problem-solving, but how to test it?

    4. Which approach to use?

B. *Measuring Intelligence*

☐ *What is the essential difference between Binet's and Terman's approach to intelligence?*

1. Earlier attempts

   a. Head size (Francis Galton) and brain size (Paul Broca)

   b. Inherited factors

2. Binet's breakthrough (**Binet-Simon Intelligence Scale**)

3. **Mental age**: measure of intelligence

4. Terman's formula for IQ (**intelligence quotient**)

5. **Stanford-Binet** intelligence test

6. **Wechsler Adult Intelligence Scale-Revised (WAIS-R)** [and **Wechsler Intelligence Scale for Children-Revised (WISC-III)**]

   a. Verbal scale

   b. Performance scale

7. Two characteristics of a good test

☐ *These next two terms are absolutely essential to an understanding of science, and therefore to an appreciation of the basis of psychology. Can you define each term? Give an example of each?*

   a. **Reliability**

   b. **Validity**

C. *Distribution and Use of IQ Scores*

1. **Normal distribution**

2. **Mental retardation**: left end of normal distribution

   a. Severely mentally retarded

   b. Moderately mentally retarded

   c. Mildly mentally retarded

   d. **Organic retardation** and **cultural-familial retardation**

3. Middle of normal distribution

   a. Do IQ scores predict academic success?

   b. Do IQ scores predict job performance?

4. **Gifted**: right end of normal distribution

   a. What happens to gifted individuals?

   b. Terman's longitudinal study

D. Potential Problems of IQ Testing

1. Binet's warnings about intelligence tests

   a. Cognitive abilities, not innate intelligence

   b. Dangers of labeling

2. Racially discriminatory?

   a. Misapplications in educational decisions

   b. Special education

3. Culturally biased?

   a. **Cultural bias**

   b. Importance of accumulated knowledge

4. Culture-free?

   a. Culture-free tests

   b. **Ecological psychology**

5. Benefits of IQ tests

E. Nature-Nurture Question

1. **Nature-nurture question**

   a. **Fraternal twins**

   b. **Identical twins**

2. Twin studies

3. Adoption studies

4. **Reaction range**: interaction of nature and nurture

   a. Genes

   b. Environment

5. Racial controversy

    a. *The Bell Curve* (Richard Herrnstein and Charles Murray)

    b. Is there a 15-point difference between the IQ scores?

    c. Are African-Americans genetically inferior in intelligence?

F. Cultural Diversity: Immigration

1. Lewis Terman: IQ tests measure innate intelligence

2. Robert Yerkes: IQ scores classify races

3. United States Congress: IQ scores as the basis for laws

    a. Limiting immigration by quotas (Immigration Law of 1924)

    b. Mismeasurement examined (Stephen Jay Gould)

G. Research Focus: New Approaches

1. Research question: can intelligence be measured by brain scans?

2. Method and results

3. Conclusions

H. Application: Intervention Programs

1. **Intervention program**

2. Two kinds of intervention programs

    a. Abecedarian Project

    b. Head Start

3. IQ scores and intervention programs

4. Importance of intervention programs

Language Enhancement Guide

IDIOMATIC EXPRESSIONS AND CULTURAL TERMS

The following are idiomatic expressions and cultural terms found in the module. Some of them have more than one meaning; the definition given here on the right is for the way the author uses the expression in this module. Remember that these words, like all words, can have different meanings in other contexts.

small backward town (257) = a town that has not kept up with the changes of modern life

segregated (257) = to separate or isolate from others or from a main body or group

to work doubly hard (257)

is much to narrow (258) = limited, does not cover enough abilities

to be poorly related (260) = the two variables have a very low correlation

breakthrough (261) = a major scientific achievement

to do poorly (263) = get low grades

a class action suit (266) = an problem is brought to a court representing a large group of people

(he) had turned out so (268) = became

lower or upper class (269) = the social status of a person as determined by the income, educational level and occupation

VOCABULARY BUILDING: Word Analysis

Instructions: Study the following table of common prefixes, suffixes, and roots and then guess the meanings of the terms in the table that follows. The number in parentheses ( ) refers to the page in the current module where you can find the word. You can find the definition for any word marked with a **G** in the textbook Glossary. Words that are not marked are used by the textbook author in other modules. Remember that these words, like all words, can have different meanings in other contexts.

Exercise 1. Misconception

Prefix/Root/Suffix	Meaning
mis- (1)	bad/wrong
mis- (2)	to hate
concept	a thought/a mental image of a thing/ (see your textbook)
-ize	to make/to use/to become
-ion	the act/the process /means/result of
-ly (1)	having the characteristics of/ happening at a specific time or period
-ly (2)	in the manner of/to the degree/in the direction of
-al	relating to/characterized by/belonging to

Word	Meaning
misconception	
misconceive	
misunderstand	
mistake	
misogyny	to hate, fear or mistrust women
misandry	to hate, fear or mistrust men
misanthrope	to hate, fear or mistrust other human beings
conceptually	
conceptualize	
conceptualization	
conceptual	

STRUCTURAL CLUES : Skimming

In Module 11 of this study guide you learned to pay attention to leading questions. This is useful in approaching a text for the first time, and in preparation for your reading. Often, however, such as when you are preparing for a test, you need to identify specific information (or supporting ideas) quickly and easily. The technique for doing this is called skimming.

To skim a text, read it quickly and locate only the specific information you are looking for. You do this by hunting for the key words associated with the subject you are studying. You don't read anything else. Key words might be names, numbers, or whole phrases.

Practice this skill by following these steps:

1. Locate the paragraph on page 263 of the textbook on the right half side of the page entitled Validity.

2. Underline the following items in the paragraph: WAIS-R, IQ score, 0.30 to 0.70, IQ tests, Terman, very high IQs, 30%, 2%. Work as quickly as you can and read as few of the other words in the text as you can.

3. Now, skim the paragraph again and answer this question: *Does handwriting analysis have any validity as an intelligence or personality test?*

    The answer is "no." To find this, you should have skimmed the passage for the key phrase "studies have shown that handwriting...." You had to read only the sentence containing these words to get the answer.

Answer the following questions after you have skimmed the paragraphs indicated, and specify what key words you used to help you find the information:

1. Can the validity of a new test be determined by correlating a new test with one that has an established validity? (p. 263, par. 3)

2. If a person scores high on an IQ test is it possible for them to get low grades in college? (p. 263, par. 5)

3. In order for a person with outstanding cognitive abilities to do well in college what other abilities do they need? (p. 263, par. 5)

Answers: 1. Yes; key words: "correlated, validity, established." 2. Yes; key words: "Kay Jameson," "high IQ, low grades (do poorly)." 3. achievement (the amount of knowledge accumulated and motivation; key words: "abilities needed to do well in college."

True-False

_____ 1. The key issue in defining intelligence is whether it is essentially cognitive abilities or a combination of cognitive abilities and other skills.

_____ 2. It is generally true the larger the brain the more intelligent the person.

_____ 3. Alfred Binet gave us the concept of an intelligence quotient (IQ).

_____ 4. Lewis Terman's formula for determining IQ was mental age divided by chronological age times 100.

_____ 5. If you use a precise doctor's scale in an attempt to measure your intelligence, your results will be reliable, but not valid.

_____ 6. As a result of protest movements, all the major intelligence tests are now culture-free.

_____ 7. Measurements of intelligence have been used to support racial and ethnic discrimination.

_____ 8. Twin studies suggest that we inherit only a small percentage of our intelligence.

_____ 9. Adoption studies suggest that environment plays a significant role in determining intelligence.

_____ 10. Research shows that intervention programs like Head Start, while well meaning, have few long-term benefits.

Flashcards

Match each key term to the definition given in the textbook.

_____ 1. Binet-Simon Intelligence Scale

    a. common intelligence test; verbal, performance items arranged in order of increasing difficulty

_____ 2. cultural bias

    b. intelligence should be measured by observing how people solve problems in usual settings

_____ 3. culture-free tests

    c. computed by dividing child's mental age (MA) by child's chronological age (CA) times 100

_____ 4. ecological psychology

    d. defined by IQ scores above 130, as well as having some superior talent or skill

_____ 5. gifted

    e. degree to which a test measures what it is supposed to measure

_____ 6. intelligence quotient

    f. says intelligence is three skills — analytical thinking, problem solving, practical thinking

_____ 7. intervention program

    g. creates an environment that offers increased opportunities for intellectual, social growth

_____ 8. mental age

    h. says there can be seven kinds of intelligence: verbal, musical, logical, spatial, body, etc.

_____ 9. mental retardation

    i. area of psychology concerned with developing tests of abilities, skills, beliefs, and traits

_____ 10. multiple-intelligence theory (Gardner)

    j. first intelligence test; items measuring vocabulary, memory, common knowledge

_____ 11. nature-nurture question

    k. mental deficits resulting from genetic problems or brain damage

_____ 12. normal distribution

    l. question wording and background experiences more familiar to some social groups than others

_____ 13. organic retardation

    m. estimating intellectual progress by comparing child's score to average children of same age

_____ 14. psychometrics

    n. says intelligence is based on a general mental abilities factor (g) plus specific mental abilities

_____ 15. reaction range

    o. extent to which IQ scores increase or decrease as result of positive or negative environment

_____ 16. reliability

    p. how much genetic and environmental factors contribute to the development of intelligence

_____ 17. Stanford-Binet

    q. substantial limitations characterized by sub-average intellectual functioning

_____ 18. triarchic theory (Sternberg)

    r. vocabulary, experiences, social situations in test same as those of individual taking test

_____ 19. two-factor theory

    s. statistical arrangement of scores resembling the shape of a bell-shaped curve

_____ 20. validity

    t. consistency; a person's test score at one time should be similar to score on a similar test later

Multiple-Choice

_____ 1. Rod Plotnik is interested in Supreme Court Justice Clarence Thomas and his sister Emma Mae Martin because their stories
   a. show that some individuals seem destined for greatness
   b. illustrate the unpredictability of human abilities and behaviors
   c. show how unevenly intelligence is spread, even within one family
   d. illustrate the nature-nurture question in psychology

_____ 2. Charles Spearman's two-factor theory says that intelligence is a
   a. general factor (g) plus specific mental abilities
   b. group of separate and equally important mental abilities
   c. set of processes for solving problems
   d. combination of biological functions of the brain and nervous system

_____ 3. Both Howard Gardner's multiple-intelligence theory and Robert Sternberg's triarchic theory
   a. yield a single score that is useful for predicting academic performance
   b. measure each of the five known areas of intelligence
   c. take into account abilities not covered by standard IQ tests
   d. define intelligence in a way that is completely culture free

_____ 4. The information processing approach to intelligence emphasizes the
   a. machine-like efficiency with which our computer minds crunch numbers and sort data
   b. cognitive processes people use to solve problems
   c. biological changes in the brain and nervous system that result from information input
   d. single core ability on which all related intellectual skills are based

_____ 5. The first intelligence test was devised by
   a. Charles Spearman
   b. Louis Terman
   c. Alfred Binet
   d. Howard Gardner

_____ 6. The formula for IQ is
   a. level of schooling divided by actual age
   b. chronological age divided by mental age
   c. test score divided by grade in school plus 100
   d. mental age divided by chronological age times 100

_____ 7. Ten times your sister jumps on the scale and ten times it reads 115 pounds. "Wow," she exclaims, "I'm taller than the average American woman!" Her results are
   a. both reliable and valid
   b. neither reliable nor valid
   c. reliable, but not valid
   d. valid, but not reliable

_____ 8. If you measured the intelligence of everyone in the United States, a distribution of all the scores would look like a
    a. curve sloping gently upward to the right
    b. bell-shaped curve
    c. flat horizon line with a skyscraper in the middle
    d. curve that rises and falls at regular intervals

_____ 9. Terman's 35-year study of gifted persons revealed their lives to be
    a. no different from the average American's life
    b. plagued by the mental instability that goes with high intelligence
    c. lonelier, sadder, and more eccentric than average
    d. healthier, happier, and more successful than average

_____ 10. The problem with IQ tests is that they are
    a. completely culture-free
    b. seldom used to get children into the right classes in school
    c. sometimes used to label people and discriminate against them
    d. unable to predict how well a child will do in school

_____ 11. In the matter of intelligence, the nature-nurture question
    a. has been solved, for all practical purposes, by twin studies
    b. has been solved, for all practical purposes, by adoption studies
    c. remains unsolved, since the concepts of "nature" and "nurture" are too vague to be investigated by scientific research
    d. remains unsolved, since there is a complex interaction between nature and nurture in the formation of intelligence

_____ 12. Twin studies suggest that intelligence is
    a. about 90% inherited
    b. only slightly influenced by heredity
    c. about 50% determined by genetics
    d. a random phenomenon unaffected by heredity

_____ 13. Adoption studies suggest that intelligence
    a. can be positively affected by improved environmental conditions
    b. is essentially fixed at birth by heredity
    c. is lessened by the loss of one's biological parents
    d. does not change much, regardless of family environment

_____ 14. The story of IQ tests and immigration shows that
    a. good research can be used for bad purposes
    b. scientific research often reflects the prejudices of the times
    c. good research can be used to right injustice
    d. scientific research is politically neutral

_____ 15. Studies of the effectiveness of intervention programs like Head Start suggest that
    a. however well-intentioned, intervention programs don't work
    b. the main benefits of these programs go to the middle-class professionals they employ
    c. the short-term benefits fail to justify the high costs of these programs
    d. even if differences in IQ fade over time, there are other social benefits that justify continuing these programs

Answers for Module 13

True-False	Flashcards	Multiple-Choice
1. T	1. j	1. d
2. F	2. l	2. a
3. F	3. r	3. c
4. T	4. b	4. b
5. T	5. d	5. c
6. F	6. c	6. d
7. T	7. g	7. c
8. F	8. m	8. b
9. T	9. q	9. d
10. F	10. h	10. c
	11. p	11. d
	12. s	12. c
	13. k	13. a
	14. i	14. b
	15. o	15. d
	16. t	
	17. a	
	18. f	
	19. n	
	20. e	

Thought & Language

Can We Study Ourselves Scientifically?

Historians of science have pointed out that the accumulation of human knowledge seems backwards. We understood the far-away phenomena of astronomy centuries ago, gradually grasped the principles of physics and biology in modern times, but only now are beginning to penetrate the mysteries of the brain and the mind. The closer we are to something, the harder it is to study it objectively. Add to this difficulty an even greater one — we *are* the very thing we want to study. Natural scientists say this problem alone dooms social science to be inherently subjective and therefore not really scientific. Social scientists disagree, of course, but they admit that being objective about ourselves presents enormous challenges.

Processes That Make Us Human

As an animal lover, I welcome every discovery of animals engaging in behavior (like tool-using) previously thought to be the exclusive property of *Homo Sapiens.* Those of us who observe animals in the wild know that they communicate very effectively. Still, is it really language? (See Rod Plotnik's fascinating discussion of whether apes can acquire language.)

In our efforts to win greater respect for the rights and inherent value of other animals, some of us argue that we humans aren't so different and shouldn't consider ourselves morally superior. Nevertheless, we have to admit that humans have strikingly unique skills and abilities in three areas that perhaps define our species. We have unmatched intellectual potential, unrivaled flexibility in exploiting that potential, and a system of communication that preserves and extends those mental powers. In this module, Rod Plotnik continues the story of these quintessential human properties, helping us appreciate how interrelated they are.

Science is never easy, however. We all know what thought and language are, yet how do we describe and explain them? Our own subjective experience seems to get in the way of objective understanding. We have to fight for every piece of knowledge. Further complicating matters is the sad fact that science is not always neutral. In the previous module, Plotnik described times in our history when racial prejudice distorted the measurement of intelligence. After weighing all the evidence on whether other primates can acquire language, most psychologists have conclude that, however remarkable, the linguistic abilities of apes are not true language. So says science. Or is it our human prejudice?

Effective Student Tip 14

What Can You Do?

Some students freeze up when they get an assignment, fearing that, unless they instantly know what to do and how to do it, they're dead. The solution, if only they realized it, is right at hand. One of the best ways to tackle a new challenge is to draw on what you already do well. Step away from the course for a moment. What can you do competently right now?

Perhaps your work relates to the course (a business student at a bank, or a psychology student in a day-care center). Your experiences and observations would make great examples to use in class discussion or in written reports. Most professors delight in having students relate the subject matter of the course to the realities of the working world. If you learned how to operate a word processor at work, can you use it after hours to prepare papers so beautiful they will knock your professor's socks off? If you are an athlete, can you use your knowledge of effective training techniques to work out a schedule for gradually building up your academic skills?

You only start from square one once, and that was years ago. By now you have acquired many competencies, some quite special. Don't hesitate to use them.

Your response...

What are you really good at? Could that skill be used in your schoolwork? (Don't say "no" too quickly!)

Key Terms

Oh, oh... another tough set of key terms. This module covers two areas of psychology, thought and language, which are related but also separate and complete fields of study in their own right. Both are complicated and offer some highly technical facts and concepts [that's one of the terms]. Buckle down!

algorithms

analogy

availability heuristic

babbling

basic rules of grammar

Chomsky's theory of language

cognitive approach

communication

concept

convergent thinking

creative individual

creative thinking

critical language period

deductive reasoning

deep structure

definition theory

divergent thinking

dyslexia

environmental language factors

functional fixedness

grammar

heuristics

inductive reasoning

innate language factors

insight

language

morpheme

morphology

overgeneralization

parentese [motherese]

phonemes

phonology

problem solving

prototype theory

reasoning

semantics

sentences

single words

social learning approach

subgoals

surface structure

syntax [grammar]

telegraphic speech

theory of linguistic relativity

thinking

transformational rules

two-word combinations

word

Outline

- *INTRODUCTION*

    1. What is that thing?

    2. What is creativity?

    3. What is the **cognitive approach**?

        a. **Thinking**

        b. **Language**

A. Forming Concepts

☐ *Another of those deceptively common terms is* **concept**... *Can you define it formally?*

1. **Definition theory**

   a. Listing defining properties

   b. Problems with definition theory

2. **Prototype theory**

   a. Mental image

   b. Advantages of prototype theory

3. Prototype theory versus definition theory

   a. How definition theory explains forming concepts

   b. How prototype theory explains forming concepts

4. Functions of concepts

   a. Organize information

   b. Avoid relearning

B. Solving Problems

1. **Problem solving**

2. Two sets of rules for solving problems

   a. **Algorithms**

   b. **Heuristics**

3. Heuristics in everyday life: **availability heuristic**

4. Developing strategies for solving problems

   a. Changing one's mental set

      (1) **Functional fixedness**

      (2) **Insight**

   b. Using **analogies**

   c. Forming **subgoals**

C. Thinking Creatively

☐ *Do you consider yourself a creative person? How do you express your creativity?*

1. How is creativity defined and measured?

   a. **Creative thinking**

   b. **Creative individual**

   c. Psychometric approach

      (1) **Convergent thinking**

      (2) **Divergent thinking**

   d. Case study approach

   e. Cognitive approach

2. Are creativity and IQ related?

3. How do creative people think and behave?

   a. Focus

   b. Cognition

   c. Personality

   d. Motivation

4. Is creativity related to psychological problems?

D. Language: Basic Rules

1. Two principles of **language**

   a. **Word**

   b. **Grammar**

2. Four language rules

   a. **Phonology** and **phonemes**

   b. **Morphology** and **morphemes**

   c. **Syntax** [grammar]

   d. **Semantics**

3. Understanding language

    a. Mental grammar

    b. Innate program

4. Different structure, same meaning

    a. **Surface structure**

    b. **Deep structure**

    c. **Transformational rules**

    d. **Chomsky's theory of language**

E. *Acquiring Language*

1. Four stages in acquiring language

    a. **Babbling**

    b. **Single words** and **parentese [motherese]**

    c. **Two-word combinations**

    d. **Sentences**

        (1) **Telegraphic speech**

        (2) **Basic rules of grammar**

        (3) **Overgeneralization**

2. Acquiring a particular language

    a. Innate factors (Noam Chomsky)

        (1) **Innate language factors**

        (2) **Critical language period**

    b. Environmental factors

        (1) **Environmental language factors** (B. F. Skinner)

        (2) **Social learning approach** (Albert Bandura)

F. Reason, Thought, & Language

1. **Reasoning**: deductive or inductive

    a. **Deductive reasoning**

    b. **Inductive reasoning**

2. Why reasoning fails

3. Words and thoughts (Benjamin Whorf's **theory of linguistic relativity**)

4. How many words for snow?

5. Thinking in two languages

G. Research Focus: Dyslexia

1. Research question: what causes **dyslexia**?

2. Procedures and results

3. Conclusions

H. Cultural Diversity: Power of Words

1. Function of words

2. Cultural differences

3. Female-male differences

    a. Using words

    b. Using brains

I. Application: Do Animals Have Language?

☐ *What is the difference between* **communication** *and language?*

1. Four criteria for language

    a. Abstract symbols

    b. Express thoughts

    c. Complex rules of grammar

    d. Generate meaningful sentences

2. Dolphins: basic language (Louis Herman)

3. Gorillas and chimpanzees: signing

   a. Koko (Francine Patterson)

   b. Washoe (Beatrice and Allan Gardner)

   c. Criticisms (Herbert Terrace)

4. Bonobo: star pupil

   a. Kanzi (Sue Savage-Rumbaugh)

   b. Rules of grammar or only tools to get things?

Language Enhancement Guide

IDIOMATIC EXPRESSIONS AND CULTURAL TERMS

The following are idiomatic expressions and cultural terms found in the module. Some of them have more than one meaning; the definition given here on the right is for the way the author uses the expression in this module. Remember that these words, like all words, can have different meanings in other contexts.

formal schooling (279) = going to college or a school to learn a skill

would amount to much (279) = would become successful or famous

out on the street (279) = living on the street and not in a home

drifted from city to city (279) = going from city to city without any goal in life

flophouse (279) = an old hotel with very low rents

for instance (283) = for example

arbitrary (286) = determined by chance or impulse and not by logical reason or principle

VOCABULARY BUILDING: Word Analysis

Instructions: Study the following table of common prefixes, suffixes, and roots and then guess the meanings of the terms in the table that follows. The number in parentheses ( ) refers to the page in the current module where you can find the word. You can find the definition for any word marked with a **G** in the textbook Glossary. Words that are not marked are used by the textbook author in other modules. Remember that these words, like all words, can have different meanings in other contexts.

Exercise 1.

Prefix/Root/Suffix	Meaning
con-	with/together
di-	away from/apart/without/reverse of (**Caution**: di can also mean two or twice)
-metric	measure

un-	not
in-	in/into/within
-ate/natus	born
discrim	separate things/divide/show differences
-ate	having/resembling/holding office
flex	bend
ibility/ability	able to/able to make
verge	turn/incline
clude	to shut/ to close/to constrain/to end

Word	Meaning
converge (284)	
diverge (284)	
psychometric (284)	
unconventional (285)	
innate (287)	
discriminate (288)	
flexibility (291)	
conclusion (294)	

True-False

_____ 1. According to prototype theory, we form a concept by constructing a complete list of all the properties that define an object, event, or characteristic.

_____ 2. Today computer programs can beat all but the very best human chess players because they employ such powerful heuristics.

_____ 3. Good thinking: insight, analogy, subgoals. Bad thinking: functional fixedness.

_____ 4. Divergent thinking is a popular psychometric measure of creativity.

_____ 5. There is no scientific data to back up the common belief that creativity is related to an increased risk of mental instability.

_____ 6. Noam Chomsky bases his theory of language on the premise that humans have inborn language capabilities.

_____ 7. It is easier to learn a foreign language in grade school than in college.

_____ 8. Children complete the essential tasks of learning language during the three-word stage.

_____ 9. Eskimos probably think differently about snow because they have so many more words for it than other people do.

_____ 10. Despite fascinating research of dolphins, chimpanzees, and gorillas, so far it appears that only humans clearly meet the four criteria for true language.

Flashcards

Match each key term to the definition given in the textbook.

_____ 1. concept

_____ 2. convergent thinking

_____ 3. creative thinking

_____ 4. critical language period

_____ 5. deductive reasoning

_____ 6. definition theory

_____ 7. divergent thinking

_____ 8. dyslexia

_____ 9. functional fixedness

_____ 10. heuristics

_____ 11. inductive reasoning

_____ 12. morpheme

_____ 13. overgeneralization

_____ 14. parentese (motherese)

_____ 15. phonemes

_____ 16. prototype theory

_____ 17. semantics

_____ 18. telegraphic speech

_____ 19. theory of linguistic relativity

_____ 20. transformational rules

a. differences among languages result in similar differences in how people think and perceive

b. flexibility in thinking plus reorganization in understanding to produce innovative ideas

c. rules of thumb in problem solving that reduce the number of operations or allow shortcuts

d. a length of time from infancy to adolescence when language is easier to learn

e. beginning with a problem and coming up with many different solutions

f. using past experience to decide how probable a certain conclusion is; general to particular

g. mental set characterized by inability to see an object as having a function different from usual

h. beginning with a problem and coming up with a single correct solution

i. reading, spelling, and writing difficulties that may include reversing or skipping letters

j. way adults speak to young children; slower, higher than normal voice, simple sentences

k. we form a concept of an object by making a list of the actual properties that define it

l. the smallest meaningful combination of sounds in a language

m. applying a grammatical rule to cases where it should not be used ("I goed to store")

n. converting our ideas from surface structures into deep structures and back again

o. the basic sounds of consonants and vowels; any word can be broken down into phonemes

p. specifies the meaning of words or phrases when they appear in various sentences or contexts

q. we form a concept by first forming a mental image based on object's average characteristics

r. first considering a given number of statements then drawing conclusion; particular to general

s. distinctive pattern of speaking in which child omits articles, prepositions, parts of verbs

t. grouping objects, events, or characteristics on basis of some common property they all share

Multiple-Choice

_____ 1. Concepts are crucial to effective thinking because without them
   a. we would not know the rules for logical thought
   b. we would be overwhelmed by apparently unrelated pieces of information
   c. our cognitive processes would be just like those of a dog or cat
   d. our motivation to think would be greatly reduced

_____ 2. Most psychologists favor the _____ theory of concept formation because it _____
   a. definition ... is based on good, sound definitions
   b. definition ... accounts for the exceptions to the rule
   c. prototype ... is based on complete listings of essential properties
   d. prototype ... accounts for more objects using fewer features

_____ 3. Eventually, a computer program will beat the even best human chess player because
   a. increasingly more powerful algorithms will win
   b. good heuristics usually win
   c. computers can "think" faster than humans can
   d. there is an element of luck in any game

_____ 4. When your friend remarks pessimistically that crime is increasing ("Did you see that gruesome murder on the news last night?"), you recognize the operation of the
   a. accuracy algorithm
   b. availability heuristic
   c. prototype theory
   d. self-fulfilling prophecy

_____ 5. If you were not able to solve the nine-dot problem, it probably was because of
   a. functional fixedness
   b. lack of insight
   c. using poor analogies
   d. failure to establish subgoals

_____ 6. One of the best ways to finish your college assignments on time is to
   a. have the problem in the back of your mind, and wait for a sudden flash of insight
   b. use the analogy of other, similar assignments you have done before
   c. fix your thoughts on the function that is involved in the assignment
   d. break the assignment down into subtasks and subgoals

_____ 7. A serious problem with too many college courses is that they place all the emphasis on _____ thinking
   a. creative
   b. convergent
   c. divergent
   d. brainstorm

_____ 8. From most particular to most general in the rules of language, the correct order is
   a. morpheme, phoneme, syntax or grammar, semantics
   b. syntax or grammar, phoneme, semantics, morpheme
   c. phoneme, morpheme, syntax or grammar, semantics
   d. semantics, syntax or grammar, morpheme, phoneme

_____ 9. Which is the correct sequence of stages in children's acquisition of language?
   a. crying, begging, asking, reasoning
   b. senseless noises, listening, imitation, original productions
   c. babbling, one word, two word, three word, four word, etc.
   d. babbling, single word, two word combinations, sentences

_____ 10. According to Noam Chomsky, language operates at two levels:
   a. spoken words and censored words
   b. surface structure and deep structure
   c. obvious meaning and implied meaning
   d. sentences and telegraphic speech

_____ 11. The theoretical debate between Chomsky and B. F. Skinner concerns whether language abilities are _____ or _____
   a. innate ... learned through shaping by the environment
   b. universal ... different from one cultural group to another
   c. superficial ... deep-seated
   d. individual ... common to the group

_____ 12. "I goed to store" is an example of
   a. babbling
   b. parentese
   c. overgeneralization
   d. telegraphic speech

_____ 13. When you use past experience to reason from the general to the particular, you use
   a. deductive reasoning
   b. inductive reasoning
   c. convergent thinking
   d. divergent thinking

_____ 14. Benjamin Whorfs' theory of linguistic relativity theory might be proved by the observation that Eskimos have many more words for snow... except for the fact that
   a. they also have fewer words for rain
   b. snow is obviously such a crucial factor in their lives
   c. there is no relationship between language and thought
   d. the claim turned out to be untrue

_____ 15. The bottom line in the debate over whether other animals can acquire true language seems to be that
   a. dolphins may possess a system of communication far superior to human language
   b. only humans clearly meet the four criteria for true language
   c. the pygmy chimp is the only animal able to learn true language
   d. several of the higher primates can acquire the language skills of five-year-old children

Answers for Module 14

True-False
1. F
2. F
3. T
4. T
5. F
6. T
7. T
8. F
9. F
10. T

Flashcards
1. t
2. h
3. b
4. d
5. r
6. k
7. e
8. i
9. g
10. c
11. f
12. l
13. m
14. j
15. o
16. q
17. p
18. s
19. a
20. n

Multiple-Choice
1. b
2. d
3. a
4. b
5. a
6. d
7. b
8. c
9. d
10. b
11. a
12. c
13. b
14. d
15. b

Motivation

Does Learning Interest You?

Studying psychology offers a wonderful extra payoff: learning how to become a more effective student. Sometimes Rod Plotnik gives you an outright suggestion and sometimes you have to make the connection yourself, but each module contains a fact or an insight you can apply to becoming more effective in your college work. One of the most important ideas concerns motivation.

Module 15 introduces the idea of intrinsic motivation, the kind of motivation that goes beyond working for a specific, immediate, tangible payoff. Not that there's anything wrong with motivation through rewards. That's what gets us to work and makes us meet specific goals. In the long run, however, sustained pursuit of complex goals requires that extrinsic reinforcement be replaced by intrinsic motivation. That's why you get smiley faces on your papers in grade school, but not in college.

It is important to understand your motivation for attending college. If the real reason you enrolled was to please your parents or because all your friends went, you may have a difficult time mustering the energy and finding the time college work demands. If you find the activity of learning itself interesting, however, your college studies should be exciting and fun.

Our Motivation to be Effective

I think the most significant of all motivations may be the need to be effective. Oh sure, thirst, hunger, and sex are more immediate and can be insanely demanding, but what is it that we want all the time? We want to be effective in our dealings with the world, in our interactions with other people, and in managing our personal lives. Some call this a sense of mastery or control, but I like word effectiveness to convey our broad need to do things that work.

The idea comes from Robert W. White, who wrote persuasively about "competence motivation" a half-century ago. Unfortunately, his idea of competence has become so deeply woven into the fabric of modern psychology that we tend to overlook it. I think effectiveness is such a significant need that it deserves explicit recognition.

Perhaps you see why it is so important to do well in college. Success in college is the crucial measure of effectiveness at this point in your life. Examine your thoughts, feelings, and behavior. Doing something well (being effective) makes you pleased and happy, but when you are ineffective, you feel awful. Everything in your psychological makeup says you want to be effective in college.

Effective Student Tip 15

The One Day You Must Not Miss Class

The day the term paper is due? The day a surprise quiz is likely? The big exam? All these are important days to attend, but there is one day when you absolutely must not miss class. That's the day you don't have the assigned paper ready or aren't prepared for the test.

Of course this is exactly the day you are most tempted to cut. The embarrassment! The humiliation! Yet that's the day you can profit most from attending.

What you dread probably won't happen. Turns out you weren't the only one who goofed, and no one is led out and shot. Not planning to read the papers until the weekend anyway, the professor may take yours later. Some professors will reassign a tough paper, reschedule an exam, or even allow a retake.

One especially good thing can happen when you attend on that agonizing day: you learn more about yourself. Why did you procrastinate? Why did you trip yourself up by not leaving enough time? What are your true feelings about the teacher, and how did they come into play? If you go to class and discuss it, all of this becomes more clear, your relationship becomes more honest, and you take an important step toward becoming a more effective student. If you stay in bed, everything just gets worse.

Your response…

Have you ever avoided a class when there was a problem? What happened?

Key Terms

There are lots of key terms in this module because Rod Plotnik discusses several major areas of motivation, like hunger, sex, and aggression. But many of these terms are already part of your general knowledge.

achievement

AIDS

anorexia nervosa

biological hunger factors

biological needs

biological sexual factors

bulimia nervosa

central cues

cognitive factors in motivation

double standard for sexual behavior

drive-reduction theory

evolutionary theory of sexual differences

extrinsic motivation

fat cells

fear of failure

female circumcision

female hypothalamus

fixed action pattern

gender identity

gender roles

genetic hunger factors

genetic sexual factors

high need for achievement

HIV positive

homeostasis

incentives

inhibited female orgasm

instincts

interactive model of sexual orientation

intrinsic motivation

male hypothalamus

Maslow's hierarchy of needs

metabolic rate

motivation

need and drive

obesity

obesity gene

optimum [ideal] weight

organic causes

overweight

paraphilias

peripheral cues

premature [rapid] ejaculation

psychological causes

psychological hunger factors

psychological sexual factors

self-handicapping

set point

sex chromosome

sex hormones

sexual dysfunctions

sexual orientation [preference] (heterosexual, bisexual, homosexual)

social needs

Thematic Apperception Test (TAT)

transsexual

underachievers

Outline

- **INTRODUCTION**

  ☐ *What was the hardest thing you have ever done? The greatest victory you have ever achieved? How do you explain your behavior in these extreme situations?*

  1. **Motivation**

  2. Achievement

A. Theories of Motivation

☐ *It may help to think of four basically different explanations of motivation. Which theory makes the most sense to you?*

1. Instinct theory: innate factors

   a. **Instincts**

   b. **Fixed action pattern**

2. Drive reduction theory: biological factors

   a. **Need** and **drive**

   b. **Homeostasis**

   c. **Drive-reduction theory**

3. Incentive theory: environmental factors

   a. **Incentives**

   b. Pull rather than push theory

4. Cognitive theory: beliefs and expectations

   a. **Extrinsic motivation**

   b. **Intrinsic motivation**

5. Explaining human motivation

B. Biological & Social Needs

1. **Biological needs**

2. **Social needs**

3. Satisfying our needs (Abraham Maslow)

4. **Maslow's hierarchy of needs** [from lowest to highest]

   a. Physiological needs

   b. Safety needs

   c. Love and belongingness needs

   d. Esteem needs

   e. Self-actualization

C. Hunger

1. Animals: optimal weight

   a. **Optimum [ideal] weight**

   b. Natural regulation

2. Humans: optimal weight and overweight

   a. **Overweight**

   b. **Obesity**

3. Three types of factors that influence hunger

   a. **Biological hunger factors**

   b. **Psychological hunger factors**

   c. **Genetic hunger factors**

4. Biological hunger factors

   a. **Peripheral cues**

   b. **Central cues**

5. Genetic hunger factors

6. What we inherit

   a. **Fat cells**

   b. **Metabolic rates**

   c. **Set point**

   d. **Obesity gene**

7. Psychological hunger factors

   a. Learned associations

   b. Socio-cultural influences

   c. Personality variables

D. Sexual Behavior

☐ *Does sex, which Freud claimed was central to human psychology, cause any particular concerns or problems in your life? Good..., I thought not!*

1. Factors involved in sexual behavior

    a. **Genetic sexual factors**

    b. **Biological sexual factors**

    c. **Psychological sexual factors**

2. Genetic sex factors: female or male

    a. **Sex chromosome**

    b. Differentiation

3. Biological sex factors: estrogens or androgens

    a. **Sex hormones**

    b. **Male hypothalamus**

    c. **Female hypothalamus**

4. Psychological sex factors: gender identity, gender role, and sexual orientation

    a. 1st step: **gender identity**

        (1) **Transsexual**

        (2) Rare congenital problem

    b. 2nd step: **gender roles**

        (1) Stereotypic behaviors

        (2) Roles and behavior

    c. 3rd step: **Sexual orientation [preference]**

        (1) **Homosexual, bisexual**, and **heterosexual orientation**

        (2) **Interactive model of sexual orientation**

5. Sexual orientation: homosexual

   a. Genetic/biological factors

   b. Psychological factors

6. Male-female differences

☐ *Is the "double standard" still operating among the people you know?*

   a. **Double standard for sexual behavior**

   b. **Evolutionary theory of sexual differences**

      (1) Multiple partners

      (2) Preference for mates

      (3) Conclusion

7. Sexual problems and treatment

   a. **Paraphilias**

   b. **Sexual dysfunctions**

   c. **Organic causes**

   d. **Psychological causes**

   e. Four-stage model of human sexual response (William Masters and Virginia Johnson)

      (1) Excitement

      (2) Plateau

      (3) Orgasm

      (4) Resolution

   f. **Premature [rapid] ejaculation**

   g. **Inhibited female orgasm**

8. AIDS: Acquired Immune Deficiency Syndrome

   a. **HIV positive**

   b. **AIDS**

      (1) Risk for AIDS

      (2) Progression

      (3) Treatment

E. *Cultural Diversity: Female Circumcision*

☐ *If you believe in the ideal of cultural diversity, don't you also have to accept the practice of female circumcision among those who believe in it?*

1. Worthwhile tradition or cruel mutilation?

2. Issues involved in **female circumcision**

   a. What is its purpose?

   b. Are there complications?

   c. Is there a solution?

F. *Achievement*

☐ *Do you feel a strong need for achievement? How does achievement influence your life?*

1. **Social needs**

2. **Achievement**

3. How is the need for achievement measured?

   a. **Thematic Apperception Test (TAT)**

   b. David McClelland and John Atkinson

4. What is **high need for achievement**?

5. What is **fear of failure**?

   a. Motivation

   b. **Self-handicapping**

6. What is underachievement?

   a. **Underachievers**

   b. Paradox of underachievement

7. Cognitive factors in achievement

   a. **Cognitive factors in motivation**

      (1) **Extrinsic motivation**

      (2) **Intrinsic motivation**

   b. Should we pay people to donate blood?

G. *Research Focus: Immigrant Students*

1. Research question: how well do immigrant children do in school?

2. A study of academic performance

   a. Method and procedure

   b. Results and discussion

3. Conclusions

H. *Application: Eating Problems and Treatment*

☐ *Why are eating problems so common?*

1. Dieting: problems, concerns, and benefits

2. Eating disorders: bulimia nervosa and anorexia nervosa

   a. **Anorexia nervosa**

      (1) Personality and genes

      (2) Treatment

   b. **Bulimia nervosa**

      (1) Risk factors

      (2) Treatment

Language Enhancement Guide

IDIOMATIC EXPRESSIONS AND CULTURAL TERMS

The following are idiomatic expressions and cultural terms found in the module. Some of them have more than one meaning; the definition given here on the right is for the way the author uses the expression in this module.

some years ago (301) = many years ago

sheer granite wall (301) = a flat vertical granite wall

run marathons (303) = participate in a very long distance running contests

undertake (303) = to involve oneself in an activity, engage, carry on, to begin, participate

fulfilling (305) = to complete, to reach

Task Force (306) = a group of experts selected to study and make recommendations about a problem

triggers the development (311) = starts, initiates

risk factors (325) = symptoms or characteristics of a person that indicate the possibility of suffering an illness

VOCABULARY BUILDING: Word Analysis

Instructions: In each of the previous modules, the prefixes and suffixes used in each exercise were listed along with their meanings. Starting in this module you will be asked to analyze each term from memory using the following procedures:

1. Break each word in the table into its prefixes, roots and suffixes and guess the meaning of the word based on the meaning of its parts. If you do not remember the meaning of each part, look it up in the Prefix, Root, and Suffix Tables in the Appendix.

2. Find the word on the text page indicated in the brackets and redefine the word based on the context of the sentence, paragraph and chapter. Look up unmarked words in a college level dictionary. Remember that these words, like all words, can have different meanings in other contexts.

Word	Meaning
disability (301)	
underestimate (301)	
predispose (302)	
innately (302)	
intrinsic (322)	
extrinsic (322)	
deplete (307)	
distended (307)	
impregnated (310)	
circulate (311)	
controversial (313)	

GUESSING FROM CONTEXT

You won't find the following words and expressions from this module in the textbook Glossary, but they are useful in reading, writing, and talking about psychology and other academic subjects. See if you can guess their meanings by studying their contexts (their relationship to the words around them).

To do this, find the word or expression in your textbook and guess its meaning using the clues in the context. You may find clues in an explanation that immediately follows the word, in a synonym that appears nearby, or in the form of examples. After you have defined the terms, ask a native speaker what they mean or look them up in a dictionary to see if your guesses were correct.

optimum (306)

importance (310)

acquiring (312)

casual contact (317)

profound (318)

True-False

_____ 1. Animals have instincts; humans have fixed action patterns.

_____ 2. The concept of homeostasis supports the drive reduction theory.

_____ 3. The concept of intrinsic motivation rests on a recognition of the importance of external factors.

_____ 4. Maslow's hierarchy of needs nicely brings together both biological and social needs.

_____ 5. Humans are the only animal for whom learned cues to eating are more powerful than biological cues.

_____ 6. As one might expect, the male lion gets sex whenever he wants it.

_____ 7. The psychological factors in sexual development are (1) acquiring a gender identity, (2) learning a gender role, and (3) expressing a sexual orientation.

_____ 8. The percentage of people who are homosexual is rising rapidly.

_____ 9. Researchers believe they will find a cure for AIDS in the next year or two.

_____ 10. The dull truth is that the only realistic solution to weight problems is learning better eating behaviors.

Flashcards

Match each key term to the definition given in the textbook.

_____ 1. achievement

a. tendency of the body to return to and remain in a more balanced state

_____ 2. anorexia nervosa

b. traditional or stereotypic behaviors, attitudes, traits designated as masculine or feminine

_____ 3. bulimia nervosa

c. innate tendencies or biological forces that determine behavior

_____ 4. double standard for sexual behavior

d. practice in some traditional African cultures of cutting away the female's external genitalia

_____ 5. extrinsic motivation

e. problems of sexual arousal or orgasm which interfere with functioning adequately in sex

_____ 6. fear of failure

f. engaging in behaviors without external rewards because the behaviors are personally rewarding

_____ 7. female circumcision

g. a set of beliefs, values, expectations that subtly encourages sexual activity in males only

_____ 8. fixed action pattern

h. innate biological predisposition to a specific behavior in a specific environmental condition

_____ 9. gender identity

i. an ascending order with biological needs at the bottom and social needs at the top

_____ 10. gender roles

j. characterized by binge-eating and purging, excessive concern about weight

_____ 11. homeostasis

k. personality test in which subjects make up stories about characters in ambiguous pictures

_____ 12. instincts

l. a normal gene in which mutation causes a severe heredity obesity in mice (and humans?)

_____ 13. intrinsic motivation

m. engaging in behaviors that either reduce biological needs or help obtain incentives

_____ 14. Maslow's hierarchy of needs

n. process the body uses to maintain a certain stable amount of body fat throughout life

_____ 15. "obesity gene"

o. characterized by refusing to eat, intense fear of fat, distorted body image

_____ 16. paraphilias

p. desire to set challenging goals and to persist in pursuing those goals in the face of obstacles

_____ 17. self-handicapping

q. tendency to make up excuses for one's failures in performance, activities, or achieving goals

_____ 18. set point

r. sexual deviations characterized by repetitive or preferred sexual fantasies of nonhuman objects

_____ 19. sexual dysfunctions

s. one's subjective experience and feelings of being a male or female

_____ 20. Thematic Apperception Test (TAT)

t. avoiding experience of failure by choosing tasks that are either too easy or far too challenging

Multiple-Choice

_____ 1. Rod Plotnik tells the story of Mark Wellman's incredible climb to illustrate the fact that
   a. you can do anything you really put your mind to
   b. you should take risks in life, but also have strong ropes!
   c. the causes of human actions are complex, yet important to understand
   d. there must be a single source of motivation, as yet undiscovered

_____ 2. Early in this century, most psychologists believed that motivation was explained by
   a. drives and needs
   b. instincts
   c. environmental incentives
   d. beliefs and expectations

_____ 3. The newest theory of motivation places greatest emphasis on
   a. drives and needs
   b. instincts
   c. environmental incentives
   d. beliefs and expectations

_____ 4. The key idea of Maslow's hierarchy of needs is that
   a. unless social needs like esteem are satisfied, one cannot deal effectively with biological needs like safety
   b. basic biological needs must be satisfied before higher social needs can be dealt with
   c. unless you achieve level five, you are a defective person
   d. the higher needs are essential; the lower needs are incidental

_____ 5. Which one of the following is _not_ a biological cue for hunger?
   a. glucose in the blood
   b. the hypothalamus
   c. learned associations
   d. the walls of the stomach

_____ 6. Which one of the following is _not_ a genetic factor that influences body weight?
   a. fat cells
   b. metabolic rate
   c. set point
   d. responsiveness to food cues

_____ 7. Which one of the following is the best explanation of the common tendency of dieters to regain the weight they lose?
   a. fat cells
   b. metabolic rate
   c. set point
   d. obesity gene

_____ 8. Lions never go on talk shows; their sexual behavior is kept in line by the fact that
   a. females do most of the hunting
   b. hormones and pheromones prevail
   c. social roles and rules predominate
   d. a lioness's bite can be fatal

_____ 9. Which one of the following is the correct order of human sexual response?
   a. excitement – plateau – orgasm – resolution
   b. plateau – excitement – orgasm – resolution
   c. excitement – orgasm – plateau – resolution
   d. orgasm – excitement – resolution – plateau

_____ 10. The term "double standard" means the
   a. added burden modern women face of both working and caring for their families
   b. biological fact that women want one man but men want more than one woman
   c. social expectation that men will be more sexually active than women
   d. new idea that a woman can ask a man out and still expect him to pick up the check

_____ 11. What makes a person homosexual? Much of the new evidence points to
   a. social factors like having homosexual teachers
   b. biological factors like inherited tendencies
   c. family factors like overbearing mothers
   d. intellectual factors like fascination with art

_____ 12. The influence of culture in sexuality is clearly seen in the debate over
   a. celibacy
   b. paraphilias
   c. female circumcision
   d. sexual dysfunctions

_____ 13. The best motivation for superior academic performance is having a
   a. high need for achievement
   b. high fear of failure
   c. very efficient self-handicapping strategy
   d. reasonable excuse for occasional failure

_____ 14. Should we pay people to donate blood?
   a. yes — hospital supplies are always dangerously low
   b. yes — extrinsic rewards get results
   c. no — people should donate because it is the right thing to do
   d. no — payment might lessen the intrinsic motivation to give blood

_____ 15. Remember Oprah Winfrey's public battle with weight a few years ago? She eventually gained it all back because, as she later admitted, she
   a. had secretly been bulimic for years
   b. had always been terrified that she was potentially anorexic
   c. did not find a way to live in the world with food
   d. did not have the will power to say no to food

Answers for Module 15

True-False	Flashcards	Multiple-Choice
1. F	1. p	1. c
2. T	2. o	2. b
3. F	3. j	3. d
4. T	4. g	4. b
5. T	5. m	5. c
6. F	6. t	6. d
7. T	7. d	7. c
8. F	8. h	8. b
9. F	9. s	9. a
10. T	10. b	10. c
	11. a	11. b
	12. c	12. c
	13. f	13. a
	14. i	14. d
	15. l	15. c
	16. r	
	17. q	
	18. n	
	19. e	
	20. k	

Module 16

Emotion

A Gift of Nature

If space aliens dropped in for a visit, what would impress them most about us? Not our powers of logic and reason (theirs would be superior). It could be our emotions, which add the vitality to our life experience, that would impress them as truly marvelous. "What a wonderful gift nature has given you," they might tell us. We would be surprised, because feelings seem to create such problems for us.

In this module, Rod Plotnik carefully unravels the most important theories about what emotion is and how it works. All the theories keep coming back to two questions: (1) Does the body's reaction to a stimulus cause an emotion, or does an emotion trigger a physiological response? (2) Does a thought cause an emotion, or does an emotion trigger a thought? Plotnik shows us the competing answers psychology has offered.

Still, something seems to be missing. No one of these classic theories of emotion has yet triumphed, and none seems fully satisfying, no matter how intriguing the research findings are. What if all the answers are correct, but the questions are wrong? What if emotion is not separate from the perceptual process, but an integral part of it?

A Different View of Emotion

New discoveries in neuroscience are beginning to suggest that sensory data doesn't really become thought until it is charged by the force of emotion. Perception both transforms sensory experience to tell us what's out there and also uses emotion to tell us how important it is. Feelings and sensory data, both impermanent, are inseparable.

The new discoveries fit nicely with a different view of emotion, discovered by psychotherapist and writer Kenneth S. Isaacs. Dr. Isaacs says that feelings come and go in the perceptual process as instantly as sensory data, and that therefore emotion cannot build up in us. According to Isaacs, emotions are always benign and potentially useful parts of mental activity. Our problem is never with emotion itself, but with misunderstanding emotion. The mistaken idea that feelings are dangerous entities that must be gotten out, or at least controlled, robs many people of a rich emotional life and cripples others with extreme "affect phobia," expressed in a wide variety of symptoms.

Instead of fearing emotion, says Isaacs, we should welcome feelings as sources of information just as useful, yet just as fleeting, as any sight or sound that reaches us, then disappears. We couldn't get along without our emotions any more than we could do without other perceptual information. If Isaacs is correct, many ideas in psychology will have to be reconsidered.

Effective Student Tip 16

How to Beat Test Anxiety

In a famous experiment, dogs who received shocks in a closed box did not even try to escape when given shocks in an open box. The experimenter called it "learned helplessness." If we could ask them, the dogs might tell us that 'test anxiety' made them fail to jump over to the safe side.

Sometimes school can be like the shock box. Too many painful defeats, and you learn to accept failure as a normal part of life. You don't like it, but you have no experience of escaping it. So don't be too quick to say you are no good at tests. You may have learned to think so, but you can't really know until you take a test *for which you have prepared effectively.*

Scratch the surface of most test anxiety and you find ineffective techniques. The first thing to do is stop blaming yourself. Next, discard the idea that you simply have to try harder. Finally, dissect your weaknesses in note-taking, studying, and test-taking and replace them with better techniques.

You will begin to feel effective when you begin to be effective. As your sense of effectiveness increases, your ability to work out winning strategies will also increase. You may still experience some jitters (phobic effects linger), but who cares? Test anxiety will no longer rule your life.

Your response...

If you **were** brutally honest with yourself, what steps could you take to improve your test preparation?

Key Terms

Try to understand the battle of psychological theories that is reflected in many of these key terms.

---

adaptation level theory

affective-primacy theory

cognitive appraisal theories of emotions

cognitive appraisal theory

Control Question Technique

disgust

display rules

emotion

facial expressions

facial feedback theory

galvanic skin response

James-Lange theory

lie detector (polygraph) tests

peripheral theories of emotions

primacy question

psychoevolutionary theory of emotions

Schacter-Singer cognitive theory

universal emotions

Yerkes-Dodson law

Outline

- *INTRODUCTION*

  ☐ *Psychologists can't agree on how emotion works. What is your understanding of emotion?*

  1. From shark attacks to winning the lottery... highly emotional situations

  2. Four components of **emotion**

     a. Stimulus

     b. Subjective feeling

     c. Physiological responses

     d. Overt behaviors

  A. *Peripheral Theories*

  ☐ *In both of the two famous peripheral theories of emotion, the key is the sequence. Be sure to work it out for each theory.*

  ☐ *What do modern research findings say about each of the two theories?*

  1. Sequence for emotions

     a. **Peripheral theories of emotions**

     b. **Cognitive appraisal theories of emotions**

2. **James-Lange theory**: sequence for feeling an emotion

    a. Physiological changes

    b. Interpret changes

    c. Emotional feeling

    d. Sequence for emotions

    e. Criticisms

3. **Facial feedback theory**: sequence for feeling an emotion

    a. Physiological changes

    b. Interpret changes

    c. Emotional feeling

    d. Sequence for emotions

    e. Criticisms

B. Cognitive Appraisal Theory

1. **Cognitive appraisal theory**

2. **Schacter-Singer cognitive theory**

    a. Physiological arousal

    b. Interpret cues

    c. Emotional feeling

    d. Sequence for emotions

    e. Criticisms

3. Which comes first: feeling or thinking?

☐ *Why will your answer to the* **primacy question** *dictate which of the following two theories you tend to agree with more?*

    a. **Cognitive appraisal theory**: sequence for feeling an emotion

        (1) Stimulus

        (2) Interpret or appraise

        (3) Emotional feeling

        (4) Bodily response

        (5) Thinking before feeling

   b. **Affective-primacy theory**: sequence for feeling an emotion

      (1) Stimulus

      (2) Emotional feeling

      (3) Interpret or appraise

      (4) Bodily response

      (5) Feeling before thinking

C. Universal Facial Expressions

   ☐ *Why are some emotions universal? Why doesn't each culture have its own unique emotions?*

   ☐ *What does it mean when you tell someone, "I can read you like a book"?*

   1. **Universal emotions**

   2. Cross-cultural evidence

   3. Genetic evidence

D. Functions of Emotions

   ☐ *Considering all the pain and trouble they cause, wouldn't we be better off if we had no emotions?*

   1. Social signals

      a. **Facial expressions**

      b. More accurate than words

   2. Adaptation and survival

      a. **Psychoevolutionary theory of emotions**

      b. Signal intentions

   3. Arousal and motivation

      a. **Yerkes-Dodson law**

      b. Arousal and performance

E. Specific Emotions

1. Happiness

   a. **Adaptation level theory**

   b. Can money buy happiness?

2. Disgust

   a. **Disgust**

   b. Adaptive value

3. What examination of specific emotions reveals about emotional processes

F. Cultural Diversity: Display and Intensity

1. Display

   a. **Display rules**

   b. Belief systems

2. Intensity

   a. Display rules about intensity

   b. Which emotion is the most intense?

G. Research Focus: Emotions in the Brain

1. Research question: how does the brain process emotional information?

2. PET scans of brain processing emotion

   a. Method and procedure

   b. Results

      (1) Sadness

      (2) Happiness

   c. Discussion and conclusions

H. Application: Lie Detection

☐ *Have you ever taken a lie detector test? Would you do so willingly if asked?*

1. What is the theory behind lie detection?

   a. **Lie detector (polygraph) tests**

   b. **Galvanic skin response**

2. How is a lie detector test given?

   a. **Control Question Technique**

   b. Assessing galvanic skin responses

3. How accurate are lie detector tests?

   a. Error rates

   b. Employment and court restrictions

Language Enhancement Guide

IDIOMATIC EXPRESSIONS AND CULTURAL TERMS

The following are idiomatic expressions and cultural terms found in the module. Some of them have more than one meaning; the definition given here on the right is for the way the author uses the expression in this module. Remember that these words, like all words, can have different meanings in other contexts.

feel adrenaline pumping (329) = feel very emotionally excited and fearful

seemed like forever (329) = minutes felt like hours

lottery (329) = a contest in which tickets are sold, the winning tickets are selected in a random drawing and the winner gets a large sum of money

enormous windfall (329) = getting a large sum of money from a lottery

coming right at you (330) = moving directly toward you

going on in (331) = occurring, happening

universal (emotions) (334) = common to all people in the world

VOCABULARY BUILDING: Word Analysis

Instructions: Analyze each term from memory using the following procedures:

1. Break each word in the table into its prefixes, roots and suffixes and guess the meaning of the word based on the meaning of its parts. If you do not remember the meaning of each part, look it up in the Prefix, Root, and Suffix Tables in the Appendix.

2. Find the word on the text page indicated in the brackets and redefine the word based on the context of the sentence, paragraph and chapter. Look up unmarked words in a college level dictionary. Remember that these words, like all words, can have different meanings in other contexts.

Word	Meaning
sequence (330)	
conclude (331)	
intensify (331)	
reinterpret (332)	
appraisal (332)	
reaction (333)	
distress (335)	
diversity (337)	
nonharmful (339)	
hemisphere (339)	

STRUCTURAL CLUES: Cause and Effect

In Module 4 you saw some common transition expressions, words and phrases that show you the relationship between two ideas in a text. One of these was "as a result," which shows a cause and effect relationship. When you see "as a result," you know the next sentence or phrase contains the effect (or result) of the previous one. The following table lists several words and phrases that usually indicate a cause and effect claim, relationship or finding.

Words and Phrases that Imply Cause and Effect
X results from Y
X is due to Y
X is produced by Y
X is caused by Y
X is cured by Y
X is prevented by Y
X is a consequence of Y
X is changed by Y
X comes about as a result of Y
X makes Y occur

Practice identifying the causes and effects in the following sentences. First find and put a bracket around the word or phrase that indicates the cause. Then draw one line under the cause in each sentence and draw two lines under the results or effects. The first item provides an example.

1. We can conclude that <u>feelings of being hungry</u> or feeling full (result from a combination) of <u>peripheral and central cues, as well as from the influence of learned and social-cultural cues.</u>

2. According to the James-Lange theory, emotions result from specific changes in our bodies, and each emotion has a different physiological basis.

3. Today researchers argue that emotions may result not only from situational or environmental cues but also from our own cognitive processes, such as thoughts, interpretations, and appraisal.

4. In the next section we'll discuss how emotions may result in physical and psychological problems.

5. Researchers now have evidence to support the claim that homosexuality is due to a complex interaction between biological and social-learning factors.

6. According to cognitive appraisal theory, interpreting or appraising a situation as having a positive or negative impact on our lives produces a subjective feeling that we call an emotion.

As you read, look for these cause effect words and phrases as part of your effort to be an active reader who processes the material deeply. As you learned in Module 12 ("Remembering & Forgetting"), the deeper you process the more you will remember and the greater the accuracy of your recall.

True-False

_____ 1. Psychologists now agree that the James-Lange theory provides the best explanation of how emotions work.

_____ 2. Psychologists do not agree on whether feeling or thinking comes first in the process of experiencing emotions.

_____ 3. People all over the world recognize the expression of a few universal emotions.

_____ 4. Emotions are essential to our survival.

_____ 5. Human emotions, like the human appendix, are left over from our primitive past and are not really needed today.

_____ 6. There is a universal language of emotion expression that helps people understand each other.

_____ 7. The reason the joy of winning the lottery doesn't last is that human beings are seldom satisfied with what they have.

_____ 8. Display rules are cultural expectations that govern the presentation and control of emotional expression in specific situations.

_____ 9. People all over the world rate happiness as the most intense emotion.

_____ 10. Lie detector tests determine whether a statement is true or false.

For Psych Majors Only...

Emotion — Myths and Actualities: Which statements about emotion are true and which are false? Don't worry about your score, because these statements are more the foundation of a theory than a quiz. When you check the "answers," see if you can understand the theory (it was described in my module introduction).

_____ 1. Emotions can be dangerous.

_____ 2. Emotions have no constructive function.

_____ 3. Emotions, once evoked, remain in a kind of pressured storage until discharged.

_____ 4. Emotions, while in storage, become a source of damage to the person.

_____ 5. The necessary discharge of emotions must be accomplished very carefully so as to cause the least amount of damage.

_____ 6. Emotions are vital aspects of human functioning.

_____ 7. Emotions are automatic subjective responses to internal and external events.

_____ 8. Emotions serve the vital function of informing us of qualities of internal and external events.

_____ 9. Emotions are fleeting and in their initial reactive form are impossible to store or accrue.

_____ 10. Because emotions are fleeting, their discharge is not mandatory and their expression is optional.

Flashcards

Match each key term to the definition given in the textbook.

_____ 1. adaptation level theory

_____ 2. affective-primacy theory

_____ 3. cognitive appraisal theories of emotions

_____ 4. cognitive appraisal theory

_____ 5. Control Question Technique

_____ 6. disgust

_____ 7. display rules

_____ 8. emotion

_____ 9. facial expressions

_____ 10. facial feedback theory

_____ 11. galvanic skin response

_____ 12. James-Lange theory

_____ 13. lie detector [polygraph] tests

_____ 14. money

_____ 15. peripheral theory of emotions

_____ 16. primacy question

_____ 17. psychoevolutionary theory of emotions

_____ 18. Schacter-Singer cognitive theory

_____ 19. universal emotions

_____ 20. Yerkes-Dodson law

a. has four parts: (1) reacting (2) subjective feeling (3) physiological responses (4) overt behavior

b. brain interprets specific physiological changes as feelings or emotions; see bear, run, feel fear

c. must thinking come before we can experience a feeling, or can feeling come before thinking?

d. lie detection procedure utilizing both neutral questions and critical (emotional) questions

e. maybe it can't buy happiness, but it sure finances the illusion!

f. changes in sweating of fingers or palms that accompanies emotional experiences

g. inherited number of specific facial patterns or expressions that signal specific feelings

h. our interpretation of situation, object, or event can contribute to experiencing different feelings

i. communicate state of our personal feelings and provide social signals to others around us

j. we explain physiological arousal by interpreting environmental cues as causing the feeling

k. performance on a task is an interaction between level of arousal and difficulty of task

l. universal facial expression that involves closing eyes, narrowing nostrils, downward curling lips

m. specific cultural norms regulating when, where, and how much emotion we should express

n. emphasizes our body's physiological changes as giving rise to our subjective feelings

o. we evolved basic emotional patterns to adapt and solve problems important for our survival

p. brain interprets sensations from movement of facial muscles and skin as emotional feelings

q. we quickly become accustomed to receiving some good fortune [lottery], so initial joy fades

r. in some situations we feel an emotion before we have time to interpret or appraise the situation

s. measurement of changes in physiological responses caused by feelings such as guilt

t. emphasizes our interpretations or appraisals of the stimulus as giving rise to subjective feelings

Multiple-Choice

_____ 1. Rod Plotnik tells us about the surfer who was attacked by a shark [where does he *get* these stories?] to show that
   a. emotions play a major role in our lives
   b. sometimes you can feel all the emotions at once
   c. sometimes survival depends on having no emotions
   d. emotions (like the joy of surfing) can get in the way of common sense

_____ 2. Which one of the following is *not* a component of an emotion?
   a. appraising a stimulus
   b. physiological responses
   c. overt behaviors
   d. genetic variation

_____ 3. The _____ theory says emotions result from specific physiological changes in the body
   a. primacy
   b. James-Lange
   c. facial feedback
   d. cognitive appraisal

_____ 4. The _____ theory says emotions result from our brain's interpretation of muscle and skin movements that occur when we express an emotion
   a. primacy
   b. James-Lange
   c. facial feedback
   d. cognitive appraisal

_____ 5. The _____ theory says emotions result from our interpretation of a situation as having positive or negative impact on our lives
   a. primacy
   b. James-Lange
   c. facial feedback
   d. cognitive appraisal

_____ 6. The answer to the primacy question, as determined by research, is that
   a. thinking comes first
   b. feelings come first
   c. both occur at exactly the same time
   d. the debate is not yet resolved

_____ 7. Evidence for the universality of human emotions comes from the fact that people all over the world
   a. consider happiness to be the most intense emotion
   b. follow the same rules about how to show emotions
   c. recognize the universal emotions
   d. make up rules about how to show emotions

_____ 8. Which one of the following is *not* something emotions do for us?
   a. help us adapt and survive
   b. help us answer questions of fact
   c. motivate and arouse us
   d. help us express social signals

_____ 9. Which one of the following is *not* a basic emotion?
   a. indecision
   b. happiness
   c. surprise
   d. fear

_____ 10. Adaptation level theory explains why people who win big in the lottery
   a. don't come forward to claim their prizes right away
   b. often spend lavishly until they are right back where they started
   c. don't feel much happier than anyone else after a while
   d. often report that winning permanently changed them from discontented to happy persons

_____ 11. Cultural rules that govern emotional expression in specific situations are called
   a. display rules
   b. feelings guides
   c. primacy rules
   d. intensity rules

_____ 12. Cross-cultural research reveals that the most intense emotion is
   a. happiness
   b. disgust
   c. anger
   d. it differs from culture to culture

_____ 13. Lie detector tests measure
   a. whether a statement is true or false
   b. how much physiological arousal the subject feels
   c. whether the subject is basically honest or dishonest
   d. how much character a person has

_____ 14. In most courtrooms, lie detector test results are
   a. admissible, because they give scientifically derived evidence
   b. admissible, because the jury must hear any evidence available
   c. inadmissible, because of their potential for error
   d. inadmissible, because they would put lawyers out of work

_____ 15. [*For Trekkies only*] The subject matter of this module helps us understand why, in a perverse way, we find the character of _____ so fascinating
   a. Spock
   b. Uhuru
   c. Kirk
   d. Scotty

Answers for Module 16

True-False
1. F
2. T
3. T
4. T
5. F
6. T
7. F
8. T
9. F
10. F

Flashcards
1. q
2. r
3. t
4. h
5. d
6. l
7. m
8. a
9. i
10. p
11. f
12. b
13. s
14. e
15. n
16. c
17. o
18. j
19. g
20. k

Multiple-Choice
1. a
2. d
3. b
4. c
5. d
6. d
7. c
8. b
9. a
10. c
11. a
12. d
13. b
14. c
15. a

Emotion — Myths and Actualities Quiz

1. F 2. F 3. F 4. F 5. F 6. T 7. T 8. T 9. T 10. T

The first five items represent what Kenneth S. Isaacs calls *myths* about feelings, false beliefs that cause us to misunderstand emotion. The second five items represent what Isaacs sees as *actualities* of emotion, truths that could make us healthier and happier.

Infancy & Childhood

The Competent Child

One of the most striking changes in psychological thinking about child development in recent years has been the emerging view of the child as a competent person, right from the beginning. It had been thought that human infants were essentially helpless, completely dependent on the care of adults. Rod Plotnik shows how new research on newborns' abilities and better understanding of how children interact with adult caregivers has given us a new picture of childhood. We now see children as incredibly active, responsive persons who spend much of their day "working" at building relationships and creating environments most conducive to growth. If the little rug rats could talk, they would probably even claim that *they* are in charge, not us.

The Importance of Childhood in Psychology

One of psychology's most important contributions to modern knowledge is the idea of childhood as a separate, special phase of human life, with processes of development crucial for the rest of life. That idea seems obvious today, but not long ago most people thought of children simply as small adults, not really different in any special way, or as happy innocents enjoying a carefree period of freedom before the onset of adult concerns.

Once psychology recognized the importance of childhood, every comprehensive theory had to attempt to explain it. Not surprisingly, most of the 'big' theories in psychology are also theories of childhood. Sigmund Freud said children struggle through a series of conflicts in the first five years that essentially shape personality. Erik Erikson placed the most fundamental developmental tasks in the early years and showed how they affected all later growth. Jean Piaget claimed that mature thinking evolves just as obviously as the physical body, and illustrated the many ways in which children think differently than adults. Albert Bandura demonstrated that children learn even from the simple act of observing, and have a powerful tendency to imitate what they see around them. If you can master this module, with its heavy involvement of psychology's most famous names, you will have a good start on understanding the major theories of modern psychology.

Thinking about childhood inevitably leads to ideas about psychology in general. In order to explain what children are like, it is necessary to say what humans are like. In no time at all, we are back debating the nature-nurture question. If we find a strong urge in children to be competent, must that not mean we all have a need to be effective?

Effective Student Tip 17

Overstudy!

My favorite myth about tests is the often-heard lament, "I studied too hard!" The idea seems to be that what you learn has only a fragile and temporary residence in your head, and studying too much disorganizes it or knocks it right back out again. A sadder myth is the belief so many students have that they are "no good at tests," when the truth is that, for whatever reasons, they have not yet *done* well. No less misguided is the teeth-clenching determination to "do better next time," with no idea of what specific steps to take to bring that about.

A closer look would reveal that each of these misguided students is making the same mistake: not studying hard enough, or effectively enough. When I am able to persuade students to read the assigned chapters three or four times (they thought once was enough), the results amaze them. Almost invariably, their test grades go from 'D' or 'C' to 'B' or 'A.' Why? Because with more study, and better study, they are really mastering the material.

Determine how much studying you think will be enough for the next test. Then do more. Lots more. The single best way to improve your test scores is to overstudy the material.

Your response...

Have you ever studied much harder for a test than seemed necessary? What happened?

Key Terms

The inclusion of four major psychological theories in this module brings in many key terms. Group the terms by the famous psychologists who used them to build their theories.

accommodation

amniocentesis

anal stage

assimilation

attachment

cephalocaudal principle

child abuse and neglect

cognitive development

cognitive developmental theory

conception [fertilization]

concrete operations stage

conservation

developmental norms

developmental psychology

Down syndrome

egocentric thinking

embryonic period

emotional development

fetal alcohol syndrome (FAS)

fetal period

formal operations stage

gender identity

gender roles

gender schemas

genital stage

germinal period

inhibited children

insecure attachment

latency stage

maturation

motor development

nature-nurture question

object permanence

oral stage

ovulation

phallic stage

Piaget's cognitive stages

placenta

prenatal period

preoperational stage

principle of bidirectionality

prodigy

proximodistal principle

psychosexual stages

psychosocial stages

resiliency

secure attachment

sensorimotor stage

separation anxiety

social cognitive theory

social learning theory

social/personality development

temperament

teratogen

visual acuity

visual cliff

vulnerability

Outline

- ## INTRODUCTION

  ☐ *The nature-nurture question may be the most fundamental issue in the social sciences. It comes up again and again in psychology. Do you know the basic issues?*

  1. **Nature-nurture question**

  2. **Developmental psychology**

A. *Prenatal Influences*

1. Genetic factors: prodigies

   a. **Prodigy**

   b. Nature-nurture interaction

2. Genetic instructions

3. **Prenatal period**: three stages

   a. Germinal stage

      (1) **Germinal period**

      (2) **Ovulation**

      (3) **Conception [fertilization]**

   b. Embryonic stage

      (1) **Embryonic period**

      (2) Developing body organs

   c. Fetal period

      (1) **Fetal period**

      (2) Why some preemies do not survive

4. Birth defects

   a. **Amniocentesis**

   b. **Down syndrome**

5. Placenta and teratogens

   a. **Placenta**

   b. **Teratogen**

6. Drugs and prenatal development

   a. Multiple drug/cocaine usage

   b. Alcohol: **fetal alcohol syndrome (FAS)**

B. Newborn's Abilities

1. Sensing and perceiving

    a. Vision

        (1) **Visual acuity**

        (2) Patterns and faces

        (3) Depth perception (**visual cliff**)

    b. Hearing and touch

    c. Chemical senses: smell and taste

    d. Perceiving

2. Motor development

    a. **Proximodistal principle**

    b. **Cephalocaudal principle**

    c. **Maturation**

    d. **Developmental norms**

C. Emotional Development

1. Kinds of **temperament**

    a. Easy babies (40%)

    b. Slow-to-warm-up babies (15%)

    c. Difficult babies (10%)

    d. No-single-category babies (35%)

2. Role of temperament

3. **Emotional development**

4. **Attachment**

    a. When does attachment occur (**separation anxiety**)?

    b. Are there different kinds of attachment?

        (1) **Secure attachment**

        (2) **Insecure attachment**

    c. What are the long-term effects of attachment?

D. Research Focus: Temperament

1. Research question: are some infants born fearful?

2. Research methods for studying developmental changes

   a. Longitudinal method

   b. Cross-sectional method

3. A study of fear reactions (Jerome Kagan)

   a. Methods and procedure (**inhibited children**)

   b. Results and discussion

   c. Conclusions

E. Cognitive Development

☐ *When you are with young children, does their thinking seem like ours, except less developed, or does it seem quite different from adult thought?*

1. Piaget's theory of **cognitive development**

   a. **Assimilation**

   b. **Accommodation**

2. **Piaget's cognitive stages**

   a. **Sensorimotor stage**

      (1) Sensory experiences and motor actions

      (2) **Object permanence**

   b. **Preoperational stage**

      (1) Symbols

      (2) **Conservation**

      (3) **Egocentric thinking**

   c. **Concrete operations stage**

      (1) Mental operations

      (2) Conservation and classification

   d. **Formal operations stage**

      (1) Adult thinking and reasoning

      (2) Abstract ideas and hypothetical constructs

3. Evaluation of Piaget's theory

    a. Criticisms and support

        (1) Four stages

        (2) Active involvement

    b. Current directions

        (1) Genetic factors

        (2) Basic concepts

        (3) Primary and secondary cognitive abilities

F. Social Development

1. **Social/personality development**

    a. Freud's [five] **psychosexual stages**

    b. Erikson's [eight] **psychosocial stages**

    c. Bandura's [learning-based] **social cognitive theory**

2. Erikson and Freud: psychosocial and psychosexual stages

3. Erikson's first five (of eight) psychosocial stages

☐ *The heart of Erikson's theory is the potential problem at each stage. Do his ideas make sense?*

    a. Stage 1: trust versus mistrust

    b. Stage 2: autonomy versus shame and doubt

    c. Stage 3: initiative versus guilt

    d. Stage 4: industry versus inferiority

    e. Stage 5: identity versus role confusion

4. Freud's five psychosexual stages

☐ *The heart of Freud's theory is the conflict at each stage. Do you buy his descriptions?*

    a. **Oral stage**

    b. **Anal stage**

    c. **Phallic stage**

    d. **Latency stage**

    e. **Genital stage**

5. Importance of early years: resiliency

    a. **Vulnerability**

    b. **Resiliency**

6. Evaluation of Freud's and Erikson's theory

7. Gender identity and gender role

    a. **Gender identity**

    b. **Gender role**

    c. **Social learning theory**

    d. **Cognitive developmental theory** and **gender schemas**

8. Comparison of gender role theories

9. Gender differences (Carol Jacklin)

☐ *What position do you take in the debate over gender differences?*

    a. Are there gender differences in play and aggression?

    b. Are there gender differences in math abilities?

    c. Are there gender differences in verbal abilities?

    d. What can we conclude about gender differences?

10. Review: many developmental changes

G. *Cultural Diversity: Gender Roles*

1. Are gender roles different in different countries?

    a. Method

    b. Results and discussion

2. Conclusions

H. *Application: Child Abuse*

1. Kinds of abuse (**child abuse and neglect**)

2. Who abuses children (**principle of bidirectionality**)?

3. What problems do abused children have?

4. What are the treatments for child abuse?

Language Enhancement Guide

IDIOMATIC EXPRESSIONS AND CULTURAL TERMS

The following are idiomatic expressions and cultural terms found in the module. Some of them have more than one meaning; the definition given here on the right is for the way the author uses the expression in this module. Remember that these words, like all words, can have different meanings in other contexts.

tried hard (345) = made a great effort

had viewed (345) = had accepted

come down on the side of (345) = favored (the biological parents' rights)

universally hailed (346) = accepted by people all over the world

babyproof the house (351) = removing things on tables an shelves and locking doors so a crawling baby won't get hurt by pulling or playing with harmful items

major milestones (351) = important events and achievements

in this view (364) = this theory claims that

VOCABULARY BUILDING: Word Analysis

Instructions: Analyze each term from memory using the following procedures:

1. Break each word in the table into its prefixes, roots and suffixes and guess the meaning of the word based on the meaning of its parts. If you do not remember the meaning of each part, look it up in the Prefix, Root, and Suffix Tables in the Appendix.

2. Find the word on the text page indicated in the brackets and redefine the word based on the context of the sentence, paragraph and chapter. Look up unmarked words in a college level dictionary. Remember that these words, like all words, can have different meanings in other contexts.

Word	Meaning
ingesting (344)	
unpredictable (345)	
unusual (345)	
prenatal (346)	
premature (348)	
insecure (353)	
ambivalence (353)	
inhibited (354)	
uninhibited (355)	
temperament (355)	
egocentric (357)	
interaction (359)	

GUESSING FROM CONTEXT

You won't find the following words and expressions from this module in the textbook Glossary, but they are useful in reading, writing, and talking about psychology and other academic subjects. See if you can guess their meanings by studying their contexts (their relationship to the words around them).

To do this, find the word or expression in your textbook and guess its meaning using the clues in the context. You may find clues in an explanation that immediately follows the word, in a synonym that appears nearby, or in the form of examples. After you have defined the terms, ask a native speaker what they mean or look them up in a dictionary to see if your guesses were correct.

prodigies (346)

repertoire (352)

compensated (366)

diversity (367)

resiliency (362)

True-False

_____ 1. The nature-nurture question asks how much development owes to inheritance and how much to learning and experience.

_____ 2. The "visual cliff" is the distance after which visual acuity in newborns falls off quickly.

_____ 3. The cephalocaudal principle of motor development says that the parts closer to the head develop before the parts closer to the feet.

_____ 4. The concept of maturation is closer to "nature" than to "nurture."

_____ 5. Attachment is the close emotional bond that develops between infant and parent.

_____ 6. In Piaget's first stage of cognitive development, the child relates sensory experiences to motor actions.

_____ 7. When Piaget used the word "operations," he meant behaviors such as walking and talking that accomplish important tasks for the child.

_____ 8. In Erikson's scheme, each stage of life contains a "test" that, if failed, prevents you from entering the next stage.

_____ 9. Studies of "resilient" children tend to support Erikson's idea that later positive experiences can compensate for early traumas.

_____ 10. Ninety percent of abusive parents were themselves abused children.

Flashcards

Match each key term to the definition given in the textbook.

_____ 1. anal stage

_____ 2. attachment

_____ 3. cephalocaudal principle

_____ 4. concrete operations stage

_____ 5. formal operations stage

_____ 6. gender schemas

_____ 7. genital stage

_____ 8. latency stage

_____ 9. maturation

_____ 10. nature-nurture question

_____ 11. oral stage

_____ 12. phallic stage

_____ 13. preoperational stage

_____ 14. proximodistal principle

_____ 15. resiliency

_____ 16. sensorimotor stage

_____ 17. separation anxiety

_____ 18. temperament

_____ 19. teratogen

_____ 20. visual cliff

a. Freud's 3rd stage; infant's pleasure seeking is centered on the genitals

b. Freud's 2nd stage; infant's pleasure seeking centered on anus and functions of elimination

c. Piaget's 2nd stage; age 2-7; children learn to use symbols to think about things not present

d. Piaget's 3rd stage; age 7-11; children perform logical mental operations on present objects

e. parts closer to center of infant's body develop before parts farther away

f. developmental changes that are genetically programmed, not acquired through learning

g. close fundamental emotional bond that develops between infant and parent or caregiver

h. Freud's 5th stage; individual has renewed sexual desires fulfilled through relationships

i. how much genetic factors and environmental factors each contribute to development

j. personality, family, other factors compensating for increased life stresses to prevent problems

k. any disease, drug, or other environmental agent that can harm a developing fetus

l. Piaget's 1st stage; birth-age 2; infant interacts with environment with senses and motor action

m. Freud's 1st stage; infant's pleasure seeking focused on the mouth

n. infant's distress (loud protests, crying, and agitation) whenever parents temporarily leave

o. parts closer to the infant's head develop before parts closer to the feet

p. Freud's 4th stage; child represses sexual thoughts and engages in nonsexual activities

q. Piaget's 4th stage; from age 12; adolescents develop ability to solve abstract problems

r. stable behavioral and emotional reactions that appear early and are influenced by genetics

s. tabletop with checkerboard and clear glass surfaces to create illusion of a drop to the floor

t. sets of information and rules about how either a male or a female should think and behave

Multiple-Choice

_____ 1. Applying the nature-nurture question to Yehudi Menuhin, the child violin prodigy, we would ask whether his special abilities
    a. are a gift of God or an accident of nature
    b. are inborn or the product of learning and experience
    c. will stay with her or fade as she gets older
    d. will be as well received in other cultures as they have been in her native China

_____ 2. The briefest period of prenatal development is the
    a. germinal period
    b. embryonic period
    c. fetal period
    d. baby-making period [just kidding!]

_____ 3. If you believe what the textbook says about teratogens, you would tell all pregnant women to
    a. watch their weight gain very carefully
    b. get plenty of rest — even more as they approach delivery
    c. avoid alcohol entirely
    d. avoid becoming overly stressed

_____ 4. Infants first use their more developed arms, and then their fingers, whose control develops later — this is the
    a. cephalocaudal principle
    b. proximodistal principle
    c. principle of maturation
    d. principle of normal development

_____ 5. A longitudinal study of infant temperament found that
    a. infants develop a distinct temperament in the first two to three months
    b. infants' temperaments tend to mirror their parents' temperaments
    c. temperament is determined by the emotional state of the mother during pregnancy
    d. temperament fluctuates widely during infancy

_____ 6. The research on infant temperament tends to support the
    a. prenatal influences theory
    b. nature side of the nature-nurture question
    c. concept of gradual maturation
    d. nurture position in child development

_____ 7. The essence of Piaget's theory of cognitive development is that
    a. through thousands and thousands of mistakes, the child gradually builds a factual picture of the world
    b. a child's picture of the world is slowly, gradually shaped by a steady succession of learning experiences
    c. each stage is characterized by a distinctly different way of understanding the world
    d. the mind of a child is like the mind of an adult — there just isn't as much information in it

_____ 8. The concept of object permanence develops during the _____ stage
   a. sensorimotor
   b. preoperational
   c. concrete operations
   d. formal operations

_____ 9. Watching juice poured from a short, wide glass into a tall, narrow glass, the child cries, "I want [the tall] glass!" thus illustrating the problem of
   a. object permanence
   b. egocentric thinking
   c. classification
   d. conservation

_____ 10. If there is one idea Erikson's theory clearly modifies, it is
   a. Freud's emphasis on the critical importance of the first five years
   b. the idea that childhood development takes place in stages
   c. Piaget's emphasis on how children see the world
   d. Bandura's idea that children learn through social interaction

_____ 11. All of the following are positive outcomes in Erikson's first four stages, but which list is in the correct chronological order?
   a. trust – autonomy – industry – initiative
   b. trust – initiative – industry – autonomy
   c. trust – autonomy – initiative – industry
   d. autonomy – initiative – industry – trust

_____ 12. Perhaps the most attractive aspect of Erikson's theory is that he sees development as
   a. continuing throughout life, with many opportunities for reworking and rebuilding personality traits
   b. biologically predetermined in a positive direction, so that only extreme trauma results in negative personality traits
   c. arising from a foundation of essential human goodness and positiveness
   d. packed into the formative years, so that a happy child almost automatically becomes a happy adult

_____ 13. Which one of the following is _not_ an essential ingredient of resiliency?
   a. a positive temperament
   b. parents free from mental and financial problems
   c. a substitute caregiver
   d. social support from peers

_____ 14. The text asks, "When do you know whether you're a boy or a girl?" The answer is
   a. early in the first year
   b. between the ages of 2 and 3
   c. when you first observe other kids (as in bathing) and notice the obvious anatomical differences
   d. it's never really "learned" — it's something you always know

_____ 15. Treatment for child abuse involves at least two goals:
   a. arresting the abusing parent and removing the child from the home
   b. placing the child in a temporary foster home and enrolling the parent in counseling
   c. teaching the parent to substitute verbal for physical punishment and helping the child learn how to read the parent's moods
   d. overcoming the parent's personal problems and changing parent-child interactions

Answers for Module 17

True-False	Flashcards	Multiple-Choice
1. T	1. b	1. b
2. F	2. g	2. a
3. T	3. o	3. c
4. T	4. d	4. b
5. T	5. q	5. a
6. T	6. t	6. b
7. F	7. h	7. c
8. F	8. p	8. a
9. T	9. f	9. d
10. F	10. i	10. a
	11. m	11. c
	12. a	12. a
	13. c	13. b
	14. e	14. b
	15. j	15. d
	16. l	
	17. n	
	18. r	
	19. k	
	20. s	

Adolescence & Adulthood

All About You

If there is one module in the textbook that clearly is about *you*, this is it. If you are in college, you've just been an adolescent and now you're an adult. Therefore, it will be the hardest module to learn.

Say what?

When studying something like the brain or memory or language, even though it's all right on top our shoulders, it seems removed from our everyday knowledge. In a way, that makes it easier to objectify, and hence to learn.

The facts and theories of adolescence and adulthood, on the other hand, are so close to our everyday experience that it is difficult to obtain sufficient distance to allow getting a handle on them. As you read, you say "yes...," "yes...," yes...," but later it's hard to remember what ought to stand out as important to learn.

I suggest a three-step process in studying this material. First, give yourself credit for what you have learned from your own experience. Don't expect every idea in the module to be new to you. Second, recognize that many of the new ideas discussed in the module may be interesting, but have not yet been accepted as permanent contributions to knowledge. Find out from your professor what to master. Third, have one simple question in mind as you read and study: is this idea helpful? In other words, does what you are reading seem true about yourself, add to your knowledge, and deepen your understanding of adolescence and adulthood? Retain the facts and ideas that do.

The Elegance of Erik Erikson

In this module Rod Plotnik concludes his review of Erik Erikson's fascinating theory of development across the lifespan. (Erikson, considered a "neo-Freudian," does appear again in Plotnik's discussion of psychoanalytic personality theories in Module 19.)

To win a place in the educated public's understanding, a theory needs sharp edges and distinctive, even shocking, premises. We all remember Pavlov's confused dog, Freud's obsession with sex, Piaget's surprising ideas about how children think, and Skinner's untiring lever-pressing rats. Erik Erikson's elegant, almost poetic saga of human life lacks all that. Consequently, although psychologists respect Erikson highly, the educated public does not know his outlook very well. That's a shame, because it might be the most true-to-life theory of all.

Re-read Rod Plotnik's thoughtful discussion of Erikson in Modules 17 and 18. Put Erikson on your list of authors to read in the original.

Effective Student Tip 18

What the Professor Wants

I remember a student who would walk me to class and offer an admiring comment on my shirt, or some such, but then fail to turn in the assignment. Professors love compliments and admiring students. They're human, after all. That isn't what they really want, though.

Every professor wants to be an effective teacher. What your professor wants from you personally is that you really do *learn*. The best thing you can do for your professor is also the best thing you can do for yourself: learn, achieve your goals, and be successful.

Professors sometimes deceive themselves and each other by saying, "If I can help just one student, it's all worth while...," but they don't really believe it. Deep down, they wish *every one* of their students would learn and progress. Then they would know what they are doing is right, which would satisfy their own urge to be effective.

Like you, your professor wants to be effective, but because the measure of that effectiveness is your learning, only you can bring it about. Does it occur to you that you and the professor really need each other? Both of you want to be effective in life, and you can help each other achieve that effectiveness. Don't underestimate your power. The professor's fate is in your hands!

Your response...

Of all the teachers you have known, which one was closest and meant the most to you?

Key Terms

The key terms for this module are a mixed bag. Some are important terms from well-established theories, while others are interesting concepts from new research and thinking about adolescence and adulthood.

---

adolescence

adolescent egocentric thinking

aging by chance theory

aging by design theory

authoritarian parents

authoritative parents

BioPsychoSocial model

care orientation

cognitive development

commitment

companionate love

conventional level

estrogen

female secondary sexual characteristics

formal operations stage

gender roles

identity [self-identity]

intimacy

justice orientation

male secondary sexual characteristics

menarche

menopause

normal aging

passion

passionate love

pathological aging

perceptual speed

permissive parents

personality and social development

postconventional level

preconventional level

processing speed

puberty

reaction time

schema

self-esteem

testosterone

Outline

- *INTRODUCTION*

  ☐ *What was your own adolescence like? Do you remember it as the best of times or the worst of times?*

  1. **Adolescence**

  2. Major periods of change

  A. *Sexual Behavior*

  1. **Puberty**

  2. Girls during puberty

     a. Physical growth

     b. Female sexual maturity (**menarche** and **estrogen**)

     c. **Female secondary sexual characteristics**

     d. Early versus late maturing

3. Boys during puberty

    a. Physical growth

    b. Male sexual maturity (**testosterone**)

    c. **Male secondary sexual characteristics**

    d. Early versus late maturing

4. Sexually active or abstinent?

    a. Girls

    b. Boys

5. **BioPsychoSocial model**

6. Sexual behavior throughout adulthood

    a. Women's sexual behavior in late adulthood

    b. Men's sexual behavior in late adulthood

    c. Conclusions

B. Physical Changes

☐ *Did your body ever change in a way that was upsetting to you? What were your thoughts and feelings about it at the time?*

1. Kinds of aging

    a. **Normal aging**

    b. **Pathological aging**

2. Why do our bodies age?

    a. **Aging by chance theory**

    b. **Aging by design theory**

3. How do our bodies change with age?

C. Cognitive Changes

   1. **Cognitive development**

   2. Piaget's cognitive stages

      a. Stage 4: **formal operations**

         (1) Importance of formal operations

         (2) **Adolescent egocentric thinking**

         (3) Thinking abstractly and planning for the future

      b. Adolescent cognitive development

   3. Kohlberg's theory of moral reasoning

   ☐ *Each level has two stages. Do you agree with the logic of Kohlberg's progression?*

      a. Three levels of moral reasoning

         (1) **Preconventional level**

         (2) **Conventional level**

         (3) **Postconventional level**

      b. Evaluating Kohlberg's theory

         (1) Stages

         (2) Criticisms (Carol Gilligan)

            (a) **Care orientation** (females)

            (b) **Justice orientation** (males)

   4. Cognitive changes during adolescence

   ☐ *Which of Diana Baumrind's parenting styles describes your family?*

      a. Styles of parenting (Diana Baumrind)

         (1) **Authoritarian parents**

         (2) **Authoritative parents**

         (3) **Permissive parents**

      b. Conclusions

5. Cognitive changes throughout the life span

6. Stage 4: formal operations (Piaget)

7. Decline in cognitive processes

   a. **Reaction time**

   b. **Perceptual speed**

   c. **Processing speed**

8. Changes in specific cognitive skills

9. Cognitive changes with aging

10. Memory changes with aging

D. *Personality & Social Changes*

1. **Personality and social development**

   a. High self-esteem

   b. Low self-esteem

2. **Identity [self-identity]**

3. Patterns of **self-esteem**

   a. High self-esteem

   b. Low self-esteem

   c. Reversals

4. Adult stages

5. Erikson's psychosocial stages

   a. Stage 5: identity versus role confusion

   b. Stage 6: intimacy versus isolation

   c. Stage 7: generativity versus stagnation

   d. Stage 8: integrity versus despair

6. Development: consistency and change

E. Gender Roles, Love, & Relationships

1. **Gender roles**

   a. What are the traditional gender roles for adult makes and females?

   b. What are the functions of gender roles?

2. Falling in love

3. What is love?

   a. **Passionate love**

   b. **Companionate love**

4. Triangular theory of love (Robert Sternberg)

   a. **Passion**

   b. **Intimacy**

   c. **Commitment**

5. Long-term relationship (**schema**)

6. Success or failure in marriage

F. Cultural Diversity: Preferences for Mates

1. Measuring cultural differences

2. Desirable traits

3. Deciding to marry

G. Research Focus: Happy Marriages

1. Research question: how do couples maintain happy marriages?

   a. Methods and procedure

   b. Results and discussion

2. Conclusions

H. Application: Suicide

☐ *If you are like most of us, you know someone who committed suicide (or tried to). What happened?*

1. Teenage suicide

  a. What factors are related to teenage suicide?

    (1) Problems and symptoms

    (2) Precipitators

  b. What steps can be taken to prevent teenage suicide?

    (1) Identify risk factors

    (2) Crisis management

    (3) Hotline services

2. Suicide among the elderly

☐ *What is your own answer to the second question below?*

  a. Why is the rate of suicide among the elderly so high?

  b. Should euthanasia and assisted suicide be legal?

Language Enhancement Guide

IDIOMATIC EXPRESSIONS AND CULTURAL TERMS

The following are idiomatic expressions and cultural terms found in the module. Some of them have more than one meaning; the definition given here on the right is for the way the author uses the expression in this module. Remember that these words, like all words, can have different meanings in other contexts.

figured it out (373) = solved the problem

negotiate (373) = to accomplish a task

across all cultures (374) = for all cultures

telltale signs (388) = indicators

long-term (success) (399) = over many years or a life time

Center for Disease Control (393) = an agency of the Federal Government that studies the spread, causes, cure and prevention of disease

VOCABULARY BUILDING: Word Analysis

Instructions: Analyze each term from memory using the following procedures:

1. Break each word in the table into its prefixes, roots and suffixes and guess the meaning of the word based on the meaning of its parts. If you do not remember the meaning of each part, look it up in the Prefix, Root, and Suffix Tables in the Appendix.

2. Find the word on the text page indicated in the brackets and redefine the word based on the context of the sentence, paragraph and chapter. Look up unmarked words in a college level dictionary. Remember that these words, like all words, can have different meanings in other contexts.

Word	Meaning
abstinence (375)	voluntary holding back from an activity like eating or sex
conduction (377)	
immoral	
disuse (383)	
despair (385)	
integrity (385)	
unresolved (388)	
conflict (388)	
dissolve (390)	
insecurity (392)	

GUESSING FROM CONTEXT

You won't find the following words and expressions from this module in the textbook Glossary, but they are useful in reading, writing, and talking about psychology and other academic subjects. See if you can guess their meanings by studying their contexts (their relationship to the words around them).

To do this, find the word or expression in your textbook and guess its meaning using the clues in the context. You may find clues in an explanation that immediately follows the word, in a synonym that appears nearby, or in the form of examples. After you have defined the terms, ask a native speaker what they mean or look them up in a dictionary to see if your guesses were correct.

encountered (385)

precipitators (392)

True-False

_____ 1. New research shows that adolescence is a period of great psychological turmoil and severe emotional stress.

_____ 2. Girls normally experience the physical changes of puberty about two years earlier than boys.

_____ 3. For obvious reasons, early maturing girls are more confident and outgoing than late maturing girls.

_____ 4. Erik Erikson saw the key developmental issue of adolescence as the acquisition of a positive sense of identity.

_____ 5. The good news (too late for you) is that the happiest, best adjusted adolescents come from families using the permissive style of parenting.

_____ 6. Enjoy it while you can! The sad fact is that _all_ cognitive abilities eventually decline with age.

_____ 7. According to Erikson, the main task of young adulthood is to find intimacy by developing loving relationships.

_____ 8. Robert Sternberg's triangular theory of love explains why romantic love doesn't last — it has passion and intimacy, but it lacks commitment.

_____ 9. Regardless of culture, young adults all over the world ranked traits desirable in a potential mate in almost exactly the same way.

_____ 10. Most women report a kind of relief after menopause — at least they don't have to have sex anymore.

Flashcards _for the fun of it..._

A Special Rock 'n' Roll Quiz on Adolescence: Teenagers have always been aware of living in an emotional pressure cooker, and the music they listen to reflects their concerns. Can you match these worries of adolescence with the Golden Oldies that expressed them so memorably? After you try this quiz, how about making up one of your own? Perhaps you could base it on current hits.

_____	1. masculinity	a.	Love Potion Number Nine
_____	2. femininity	b.	Fifty Ways to Leave Your Lover
_____	3. self-esteem	c.	Walk Like a Man
_____	4. vulnerability	d.	Get a Job
_____	5. chastity	e.	Big Girls Don't Cry
_____	6. intimacy	f.	Little Sweet Sixteen
_____	7. romantic love	g.	Lonely Girl
_____	8. career	h.	Where Did My Baby Go?
_____	9. marriage	i.	Under the Boardwalk
_____	10. commitment _(not!)_	j.	Going to the Chapel

Flashcards

Match each key term to the definition given in the textbook.

_____ 1. adolescent egocentric thinking

_____ 2. aging by chance theory

_____ 3. aging by design theory

_____ 4. authoritarian parents

_____ 5. authoritative parents

_____ 6. care orientation

_____ 7. commitment

_____ 8. companionate love

_____ 9. estrogen

_____ 10. formal operations stage

_____ 11. gender roles

_____ 12. intimacy

_____ 13. justice orientation

_____ 14. menarche

_____ 15. menopause

_____ 16. passion

_____ 17. passionate love

_____ 18. permissive parents

_____ 19. puberty

_____ 20. testosterone

a. developmental period (9-17) of significant biological changes in sexual characteristics

b. gradual stoppage in secretion of estrogen, causing cessation of ovulation, menstrual cycle

c. making moral decisions based on issues of caring, avoiding hurt, and concerns for others

d. making a pledge to nourish the feelings of love and to actively maintain the relationship

e. less controlling; nonpunishing and accepting attitude; make few demands on their children

f. bodies age because of biological clocks that function like blueprints controlling cell death

g. continuously thinking about and having warm sexual feelings toward the loved one

h. the first menstrual period, a signal that ovulation may have occurred

i. attempt to control behavior of their children in accordance with absolute standard of conduct

j. bodies age because of naturally occurring problems or breakdowns in body's cells

k. traditional or stereotypic behaviors, attitudes, and personality traits of males and females

l. making moral decisions based more on issues of law and equality and individual rights

m. feeling physically aroused and attracted to someone through sharing and commitment

n. last Piaget cognitive stage (12-adulthood), when adolescents develop ability to think logically

o. having trusting and tender feelings for someone whose life is closely bound up with one's own

p. attempt to direct children rationally; loving, supportive; discuss rules with their children

q. difficulties in separating one's own thoughts and feelings from those of others

r. feeling close and connected to someone; it develops through sharing and communication

s. major male hormone; stimulates development of genital organs and sexual characteristics

t. one of the major female hormones; stimulates development of sexual characteristics

Multiple-Choice

_____ 1. Experts now believe that adolescence is *not* a period of
   a. great psychological turmoil
   b. considerable biological, cognitive, and social changes
   c. searching for personal identity
   d. dramatic positive or negative changes in self-esteem

_____ 2. When you compare the development of sexual maturity in girls and boys during puberty, you find that the changes are
   a. radically different in girls and boys
   b. parallel in girls and boys
   c. essentially the same, but occur about two years earlier in girls
   d. somewhat similar, except that the difference between a boy and a man is far greater than the difference between a girl and a woman

_____ 3. In terms of enjoying a psychological advantage in adjustment, the best thing to be is
   a. an early maturing girl
   b. a late maturing girl
   c. an early maturing boy
   d. a late maturing boy

_____ 4. In Erikson's psychosocial stage theory, an adolescent who does not develop a positive sense of identity is likely to suffer from
   a. isolation
   b. stagnation
   c. a sense of inferiority
   d. role confusion

_____ 5. Adolescent egocentric thinking is the belief that
   a. the demands of parents and society are less important than what the adolescent wants
   b. everyone else is as totally preoccupied with the adolescent's appearance, thoughts, and feelings as the adolescent is
   c. "I am smarter and more attractive than everyone else"
   d. "If I want it and need it, why shouldn't I have it?"

_____ 6. Lawrence Kohlberg based his theory of moral development on research into
   a. the behaviors that children of different ages listed as "good" or "bad"
   b. stories children made up when asked to illustrate good and bad behavior
   c. the correlation between how children rated their own behavior and how their teachers rated it
   d. the reasoning children used to solve problems that posed moral dilemmas

_____ 7. Your new friend seems to be competent, independent, and achievement oriented; you guess that she had _____ parents
   a. authoritarian
   b. authoritative
   c. permissive
   d. protective

_____ 8. According to the _____ theory, our bodies age because of naturally occurring problems or breakdowns in the body's cells
   a. aging by chance
   b. aging by design
   c. biological limit
   d. chronological aging

_____ 9. Which one of the following cognitive abilities does *not* decrease with aging?
   a. reaction time
   b. perceptual speed
   c. memorization
   d. interpretation

_____ 10. What we need in late adulthood [Stage 8], says Erikson, is
   a. recognition, respect, and honor from our family and colleagues
   b. a sense of pride in our acquisitions and our standing in the community
   c. a sense of contentment about how we lived and what we accomplished
   d. mainly good health — without it there is despair

_____ 11. What is this thing called love? Sternberg's triangular theory says love is a mix of
   a. romantic love, respect, and companionship
   b. romance, sharing, and loyalty
   c. infatuated love plus companionate love
   d. passion, intimacy, and commitment

_____ 12. Research suggests that the most important key to the success or failure of marriage is
   a. how couples decide on major purchases
   b. how couples handle conflicts
   c. whether both partners maintain good physical appearance
   d. whether both partners remain faithful

_____ 13. When 9,000 young adults all over the world listed traits they considered most desirable in a potential mate, the results showed that
   a. love is blind — there was little similarity in the traits chosen
   b. love is universal — all young people want the same things in a marriage partner
   c. cultures do exert strong influences on the mate preferences of their members
   d. cultural differences are breaking down so rapidly that few distinctions remain

_____ 14. When a young person commits suicide, our typical reaction is an anguished "Why? Why?"... but the truth is that
   a. nothing can stop a person who has decided to commit suicide
   b. there probably were signs of psychological problems and behavioral symptoms long before
   c. psychology has no answer to the riddle of why adolescents, with their whole lives before them, sometimes take their own lives
   d. adolescents who are contemplating suicide go to great lengths to disguise their intentions

_____ 15. Perhaps the main reason why the debate over assisted suicide is intensifying is that
   a. a doctor has invented a machine that makes it relatively easy
   b. psychologists, as scientists, are unwilling to become involved in a moral question
   c. morals in our country are breaking down
   d. so many Americans are living so much longer

Answers for Module 18

True-False	Flashcards	Multiple-Choice
1. F	1. q	1. a
2. T	2. j	2. c
3. F	3. f	3. c
4. T	4. i	4. d
5. F	5. p	5. b
6. F	6. c	6. d
7. T	7. d	7. b
8. T	8. o	8. a
9. F	9. t	9. d
10. F	10. n	10. c
	11. k	11. d
	12. r	12. b
	13. l	13. c
	14. h	14. b
	15. b	15. d
	16. m	
	17. g	
	18. e	
	19. a	
	20. s	

A Special Rock 'n' Roll Quiz on Adolescence

1. c   2. e   3. g   4. h   5. f   6. i   7. a   8. d   9. j   10. b

Freudian & Humanistic Theories

Big Theories to Answer Big Questions

In Modules 19 and 20, Rod Plotnik discusses personality theory, one of the most absorbing areas in all of psychology. Personality theories tackle the big questions, the questions we think about when we try to understand who we are and what meaning and purpose our lives have. We feel that we are unique individuals, but aren't we essentially like everyone else? We know we are growing and developing, but aren't we also somehow very much the same from year to year? We would like to change some things about ourselves, but why does that seem so difficult to do?

A theory of personality is necessarily comprehensive. The better it is, the more of our questions about ourselves it answers. As you study these two modules, pay attention to each theory's basic assumptions about human nature. Do you agree with them? To what extent can you see yourself in each theory? Does it describe you and explain your life?

But Do They Explain You?

I've said it before, but it's especially true for the two modules on personality: *challenge every new idea you meet*. Ask yourself, is that idea really true? Does that concept explain my own experience accurately? Does this theory capture how I feel about myself and life in general?

When Sigmund Freud says you have inborn sexual and aggressive tendencies, do you find them in yourself? When Abraham Maslow and Carl Rogers portray humans as fundamentally good, does that square with people as you know them? When Albert Bandura (next module) suggests that we are what we have learned to expect ourselves and the world to be, ask yourself if you are something more than a collection of past experiences. When Gordon Allport (also next module) paints your personality as a complex mosaic of tendencies to behave in certain ways, ask yourself if that captures all you are.

Finally, you might think about your own theory of personality. You do have one, even though you probably haven't tried to work it out in any detail. Anyone who studies psychology inevitably comes to have some sort of theory of personality — a global view of how all the facts and ideas in psychology fit together, and how they apply to everyday life. Reflecting on your own ideas about human nature will help you understand psychology's famous theories of personality.

Effective Student Tip 19

Three Secrets of Effective Writing

Too many students think the ability to write well is something you have to be born with. The truth is just the opposite. Any student can become a good writer. The *art* of writing requires curiosity and creativity, but we all have those qualities. The *craft* of writing is as learnable as cooking or carpentry. Three secrets of effective writing reveal how any serious student can get started on becoming a better writer.

Secret #1: Tell a *story* that is important to you. We organize our memory around stories. A well-told story is the most effective way to convey information.

Secret #2: Paint *word pictures*. We understand best what we can visualize. A beautifully worded description is the most effective way to create understanding in writing.

Secret #3: Think of writing as a *craft* (the artistry will come naturally, flowering as you work). One by one, learn the skills of good writing. Start by learning how to type a beautiful paper, the easiest procedure to learn and the one that has the most immediate effect on your reader.

When you think of writing as a craft, you realize that the goal is progress, not perfection. It doesn't really matter how good your next paper is, as long as it is better than the last one.

Your response...

What was the best paper you ever wrote? What made it so good?

Key Terms

Many of the key terms for this module have crossed over into the vocabulary of the educated person. All the more reason to make sure you learn them!

ability tests

anal stage

anxiety

cognitive unconscious

collective unconscious

conditional positive regard

conscious thoughts

defense mechanisms

deficiency needs

denial

displacement

dream interpretation

ego

fixation

free association

Freud's psychodynamic theory of personality

Freudian slips

genital stage

growth needs

holistic view

humanistic theories

id

latency stage

Maslow's hierarchy of needs

Oedipus complex

oral stage

personality

personality tests

phallic stage

phenomenological perspective

pleasure principle

positive regard

projection

projective tests

psychological assessment

psychosexual stages

rationalization

reaction formation

reality principle

reliability

repression

Rogers' self-actualizing tendency

Rogers' two kinds of selves

Rorschach inkblot test

self [self-concept]

self theory [self-actualization theory]

self-actualization

shyness

sublimation

superego

Thematic Apperception Test (TAT)

theory of personality

unconditional positive regard

unconscious forces

unconscious motivation

validity

Outline

- *INTRODUCTION*

    1. **Personality**

    2. **Theory of personality**

A. *Freud's Psychodynamic Theory*

    1. **Freud's psychodynamic theory of personality**

    2. Freud's key to unlocking the mind

3. Conscious versus unconscious forces

    a. **Conscious thoughts**

    b. **Unconscious forces**

    c. **Unconscious motivation**

4. Techniques to discover the unconscious

    a. **Free association**

    b. **Dream interpretation**

    c. **Freudian slips**

B. Divisions of the Mind

1. Iceberg analogy: conscious and unconscious levels

☐ *How do Freud's twin concepts of the pleasure principle and the reality principle make conflict inevitable in his personality theory?*

    a. **Id** and **pleasure principle**

    b. **Ego** and **reality principle**

    c. **Superego**

2. **Anxiety**

3. **Defense mechanisms**

☐ *Freud didn't mean that defense mechanisms are bad. Can you think of an everyday life example for each defense mechanism that shows how it promotes our adaptation and survival?*

    a. **Rationalization**

    b. **Denial**

    c. **Repression**

    d. **Projection**

    e. **Reaction formation**

    f. **Displacement**

    g. **Sublimation**

C. Developmental Stages

1. Development and fixation

   a. **Psychosexual stages**

   2. **Fixation**

2. Freud's five psychosexual stages

☐ *For this theory to make any sense, you must appreciate the conflict in each stage. Think about children you have known (including yourself!) and try to come up with examples for each stage.*

   a. **Oral stage**

   b. **Anal stage**

   c. **Phallic stage** and **Oedipus complex**

   d. **Latency stage**

   e. **Genital stage**

D. Freud's Followers & Critics

☐ *Why did Freud's most creative followers eventually become critics?*

1. Carl Jung and the **collective unconscious**

2. Alfred Adler

3. Karen Horney

4. Neo-Freudians (Erik Erikson)

5. Freudian theory today

   a. How valid is Freud's theory?

   b. Are the first five years the most important?

   c. Can Freud's concepts be tested?

   d. Is there evidence for unconscious forces?

      (1) A major Freudian assumption

      (2) A different explanation: **cognitive unconscious**

   e. What was the impact of Freud's theory?

E. *Humanistic Theories*

◻ The **humanistic theories** are a more varied collection than other major approaches to personality. What assumptions and characteristics do they have in common?

1. Three hallmarks of humanistic theory

    a. **Phenomenological perspective**

    b. **Holistic view**

    c. **Self-actualization**

2. Abraham Maslow and self-actualization

    a. **Maslow's hierarchy of needs**

        (1) **Deficiency needs**

        (2) **Growth needs**

    b. **Self-actualization**

    c. Characteristics of self-actualized individuals

3. Carl Rogers and self theory

◻ How and why does mental illness develop? Can you explain it using Carl Rogers' ideas?

    a. **Self theory [self-actualization theory]**

        (1) **Rogers' self-actualizing tendency**

        (2) **Self [self-concept]**

    b. Real self versus ideal self

        (1) **Rogers' two kinds of selves**

        (2) Contradictions and personality problems

    c. **Positive regard**

    d. Conditional and unconditional positive regard

        (1) **Conditional positive regard**

        (2) **Unconditional positive regard**

    e. Importance of self-actualization

f. Humanistic theory in practice

(1) Popularity and impact

(2) Evaluation

g. Popularity, impact, and evaluation of humanistic theories

F. Cultural Diversity: Achievement

1. What was different about the children of the boat people?

2. How did the Indochinese achieve such great success?

a. Primary values

b. Conclusions

G. Research Focus: Causes of Shyness

1. Research question: what causes **shyness**?

2. Answers from two very different theories of personality

a. Psychodynamic approach

(1) Unconscious fears and anxiety

(2) Unresolved conflicts

b. Social learning theory

(1) Observable, measurable components

(2) Relationship between genetic, emotional, and behavioral influences

3. Advantages and disadvantages of each theory

H. Application: Assessment — Projective Tests

1. **Psychological assessment**

a. **Ability tests**

b. **Personality tests**

2. **Projective tests**

3. Examples of projective tests

a. **Rorschach inkblot test**

b. **Thematic Apperception Test (TAT)**

4. Two characteristics of a good test: reliability and validity

   a. **Validity**

   b. **Reliability**

5. Usefulness of projective tests

   a. Advantages

   b. Disadvantages

Language Enhancement Guide

IDIOMATIC EXPRESSIONS AND CULTURAL TERMS

The following are idiomatic expressions and cultural terms found in the module. Some of them have more than one meaning; the definition given here on the right is for the way the author uses the expression in this module. Remember that these words, like all words, can have different meanings in other contexts.

turn away from (397) = ignore or reject

rocket to stardom (397) = become rich and famous very quickly

solitary confinement (397) = placed into a jail cell all alone for many weeks or months

to put life in order (397) = focus time and effort to achieve a goal

inner demons (397) = serious emotional conflicts and problems

in the light of (399) = based on

relatively large (400) = larger than other things when comparisons are made

living up to (409) = achieving the goals that other expect

VOCABULARY BUILDING: Word Analysis

Instructions: Analyze each term from memory using the procedures described earlier:

Word	Meaning
controversial (398)	
uncensored (399)	
repressed (399)	
mechanism (401)	
disregard (401)	
contradiction (402)	
retention (403)	
inadequate (413)	
projective (414)	
ambiguous (415)	

GUESSING FROM CONTEXT

You won't find the following words and expressions from this module in the textbook Glossary, but they are useful in reading, writing, and talking about psychology and other academic subjects. See if you can guess their meanings by studying their contexts (their relationship to the words around them).

To do this, find the word or expression in your textbook and guess its meaning using the clues in the context. You may find clues in an explanation that immediately follows the word, in a synonym that appears nearby, or in the form of examples. After you have defined the terms, ask a native speaker what they mean or look them up in a dictionary to see if your guesses were correct.

perplexing (397)

culminating (397)

sporadically (398)

turmoil (401)

gratification (403)

comprehensive (405)

optimal (412)

techniques (414)

assessment (414)

disadvantage (415)

True-False

_____ 1. Freud's famous personality theory is provocative, but hard to test scientifically.

_____ 2. Freud's key concept is the idea of conscious processes — how we understand reality.

_____ 3. Because almost all of Freud's main followers broke with him, today his ideas have little influence.

_____ 4. Free association is necessary because we cannot know the unconscious directly.

_____ 5. For Freud, most personality development takes place during the first five years of life.

_____ 6. Maslow and Rogers are pessimistic about the degree to which personality can change.

_____ 7. The hierarchy of needs helps explain why children who come to school hungry don't learn well.

_____ 8. Self-actualization means honestly recognizing your actual faults and weaknesses.

_____ 9. Rogers warns that a child who receives only unconditional positive regard will grow up spoiled and unrealistic about life.

_____ 10. For a personality test to be scientifically useful, it must possess the twin characteristics of reliability and validity.

Flashcards

Match each key term to the definition given in the textbook.

_____ 1. anxiety	a. making up acceptable excuses for behaviors that cause us to feel anxious
_____ 2. collective unconscious	b. others showing us warmth, acceptance, and love because we are valued human beings
_____ 3. conditional positive regard	c. unpleasant state that is associated with feelings of uneasiness, apprehension, arousal
_____ 4. dream interpretation	d. being locked into an earlier psychosexual stage because wishes were over- or undergratified
_____ 5. ego	e. positive regard dependent on our behaving in certain ways, meeting the standards of others
_____ 6. fixation	f. contains biological drives of sex and aggression that are source of all psychic or mental energy
_____ 7. free association	g. goal is to find safe, socially acceptable ways of satisfying id's desires, superego's prohibitions
_____ 8. Freudian slips	h. goal is applying moral values and standards of parents and society in satisfying one's wishes
_____ 9. id	i. child competing with same-sex parent for the affections and pleasures of opposite-sex parent
_____ 10. Oedipus complex	j. the inherent tendency to reach our true potentials
_____ 11. phenomenological perspective	k. how we see or describe ourselves; our self-perceptions, abilities, characteristics
_____ 12. pleasure principle	l. redirecting a threatening or forbidden sexual desire into a socially acceptable one
_____ 13. rationalization	m. mistakes we make in everyday speech which reflect unconscious thoughts or wishes
_____ 14. reality principle	n. influence of repressed thoughts, desires, or impulses on conscious thoughts and behaviors
_____ 15. self [self-concept]	o. Jung's theory of inherited ancient memory traces shared by all peoples in all cultures
_____ 16. self-actualization	p. talking about any thoughts, images that come to mind, providing clues to the unconscious
_____ 17. sublimation	q. satisfying a wish or desire only if there is a socially acceptable outlet available
_____ 18. superego	r. idea that our perception of the world, whether or not it is accurate, becomes our reality
_____ 19. unconditional positive regard	s. based on assumption that dreams contain underlying, hidden meanings and symbols
_____ 20. unconscious motivation	t. satisfaction of drives, avoidance of pain without concern for moral restrictions or social rules

Multiple-Choice

_____ 1. In psychology, the term "personality" means
   a. a fixed way of responding to other people that is based on our inherited emotional makeup
   b. a combination of long-lasting and distinctive behaviors, thoughts, motives, and emotions that typify how we react to other people and situations
   c. favorable and unfavorable personal characteristics
   d. how interesting and attractive we are to other people

_____ 2. In Sigmund Freud's psychodynamic theory of personality, the unconscious contains
   a. everything we are aware of at a given moment
   b. feelings and thoughts we remember from long ago
   c. material that can easily be brought to awareness
   d. repressed wishes, desires, or thoughts

_____ 3. Saying whatever comes to mind, even if it seems senseless, painful, or embarrassing, is part of the Freudian technique known as
   a. a defense mechanism
   b. a Freudian slip
   c. free association
   d. projection

_____ 4. The ability to create feelings of guilt gives the _____ its power
   a. superego
   b. ego
   c. id
   d. unconscious

_____ 5. A student who blames poor test performance on "tricky questions" — rather than admit to poor preparation — is using the defense mechanism of
   a. compensation
   b. denial
   c. projection
   d. rationalization

_____ 6. The defense mechanism in which unacceptable wishes are turned into their opposites is known as
   a. projection
   b. reaction-formation
   c. compensation
   d. rationalization

_____ 7. Which one of the following shows the correct order of Freud's psychosexual stages?
   a. oral – anal – phallic – latency – genital
   b. anal – latency – phallic – oral – genital
   c. genital – phallic – oral – anal – latency
   d. latency – anal – oral – phallic – genital

_____ 8. The concept of the collective unconscious was proposed by
   a. Carl Jung
   b. Alfred Adler
   c. Karen Horney
   d. B. F. Skinner

_____ 9. Unlike psychodynamic theories, humanistic theories of personality emphasize
   a. the continual operation of contradictory forces buried deep in our unconscious minds
   b. our capacity for personal growth, the development of our potential, and freedom to choose our destiny
   c. how difficult it is — even with therapy — to change personality significantly
   d. the importance of perceptions and beliefs

_____ 10. At the first level of Abraham Maslow's hierarchy, we find _____ needs
   a. self-actualization
   b. esteem
   c. love and belongingness
   d. physiological

_____ 11. By self-actualization, Maslow meant
   a. fulfillment of our unique potential
   b. having our deficiency needs satisfied
   c. being loved and loving someone in return
   d. gaining recognition and status in society

_____ 12. Why are so many people unhappy? Carl Rogers says it is because
   a. happiness is only possible when we become self-actualized
   b. happiness is only an illusion
   c. we have both a real self and an ideal self, and they are often in conflict
   d. we have a positive self and a negative self, and one always dominates

_____ 13. The story of the Indochinese "boat people" illustrates the basic assumption of _____ psychology that all humans possess _____
   a. humanistic ... a hierarchy of needs
   b. humanistic ... a tendency toward self-fulfillment
   c. psychodynamic ... a fierce determination to survive
   d. psychodynamic ... a tendency toward love as well as toward aggression

_____ 14. The old warning, "Of course Mommy loves you... when you're good!" is an example of Rogers' concept of
   a. self-actualization
   b. self-esteem needs
   c. conditional positive regard
   d. unconditional positive regard

_____ 15. Because they use _____ , projective tests often bring out unconscious material
   a. pictures of people
   b. simple materials
   c. ambiguous stimuli
   d. computer analysis

Answers for Module 19

True-False	Flashcards	Multiple-Choice
1. T	1. c	1. b
2. F	2. o	2. d
3. F	3. e	3. c
4. T	4. s	4. a
5. T	5. g	5. d
6. F	6. d	6. b
7. T	7. p	7. a
8. F	8. m	8. a
9. F	9. f	9. b
10. T	10. i	10. d
	11. r	11. a
	12. t	12. c
	13. a	13. b
	14. q	14. c
	15. k	15. c
	16. j	
	17. l	
	18. h	
	19. b	
	20. n	

Module 20

Social Learning & Traits

The Story of a Cold-Blooded Killer

Did you know that you are reading the work of a cold-blooded killer? One who could take out a long-bladed knife and charge at an enemy screaming "Kill!... Kill!..."? Of course the enemy in this case was a sack of straw and the killer was a draftee whose only real concern, in a time when our country was totally at peace, was how to get out of KP duty. An ironic twist: when it began raining half-way through the exercise, the officer in charge blew his whistle, loaded us into our trucks, and took us back to our dry barracks. The last thing he needed was a complaint from some concerned parents' congressman about how he was treating their boy!

The point of my "war story" is that I wasn't a killer at all (far from it!) and the officer who let us off easy was actually a good soldier. But what if there had been a real war? Maybe I would have acted on my army training. Then what would I have been?

The Genius and Fault of Modern Psychology

In Module 20 Rod Plotnik continues his survey of four dominant personality theories (psychoanalytic, humanistic, social learning, and traits) and raises one of the most fundamental questions in psychology: how stable is personality? (See Rod's discussion of person-situation interaction.) If the concept of personality is real, people must show a certain degree of consistency over a wide range of situations. But if people exhibit significantly different behavior in varying situations, how real is the idea of personality?

The genius of modern psychology is to help us see inside. You might say the psychoanalytic approach reveals the dark side of human nature and the humanistic approach the positive, but both place the truth inside. Trait theories also assume inner tendencies that guide our behavior, although through interplay with the environment. Social learning theory, based on the interaction of beliefs and past experience, introduces a dangerous question: could it be the other way around, with the situation determining the person?

The fault of modern psychology is its tendency to find the problem inside. We become so good at digging out the "real" reasons for psychological problems, as Freud taught us, that we can overlook obvious environmental causes like unemployment or discrimination or even pollution. We learn to manage stress, discover dysfunctions, and blame ourselves. Sometimes we miss the real problem.

By the way, I fudged at the bayonet drill years ago. I was too embarrassed to actually scream "Kill!... Kill!...," so I just pretended to yell. Does that added detail ruin my point?

Effective Student Tip 20

What Moves You?

When Monica scored her exam paper, she marked down how many questions she got right (32) and the corresponding letter grade ('D'). She handed me her answer sheet and fled. I began recording her score and grade, and then it hit me: by the grading standards I had written on the board, 32 was a 'C', not a 'D'.

A classmate chased her down the hall and when I showed Monica her mistake and asked her why, she said, "I guess because I always get a 'D'."

Like many students, Monica never did quite as well as I thought she would. Was her "slip of the pen" an indication of mixed motivation? Many students are not really sure why they are in school, why they have taken a certain class, or why they aren't doing as well as their abilities would suggest. All of these questions involve motivation, the basic forces that account for our actions.

Are you in college for your parents? Taking a course to "get it out of the way?" Cutting class without much idea why? These are common cases of mixed or poorly understood motivation. Don't let it happen to you. Try to discover your true motivation. Be alert for clues that alert you to possible confusion. You will be more successful, more easily, when you get your motivations and your goals in line. Honesty is the best policy.

Your response...

Try making a totally honest [and private] list of the reasons why you are in college.

Key Terms

These key terms from personality theory are somewhat less common that those in the previous module, but look how few of them there are to learn. Piece of cake!

Bandura's social-cognitive theory

Barnum principle

behavioral genetics

collectivistic culture

delay of gratification

factor analysis

five-factor model

heritability

individualistic culture

interpersonal conflict

locus of control

Minnesota Multiphasic Personality Interview (MMPI-2)

objective personality tests [self-report questionnaires]

person-situation interaction

quantum personality change

reliability

self-efficacy

social learning theory

structured interviews

trait theory

trait

validity

Outline

- *INTRODUCTION*

  ☐ *How do Rod Plotnik's two examples illuminate the concept and question of personality?*

  1. Nelson Mandela's strength and persistence

  2. Beverly Harvard's skills and determination

A. Social Learning Theory

  1. **Social learning theory** (Albert Bandura)

  2. Personality development: interaction of three factors

     a. Cognitive-personal factors

     b. Behavior

     c. Environmental influences

  3. Cognitive factors

     a. **Bandura's social-cognitive theory**

     b. Four cognitive factors that influence personality

        (1) Language ability

        (2) Observational learning

      (3) Purposeful behavior

      (4) Self-analysis

4. Three specific *beliefs* that influence *behavior*

   a. **Locus of control** (Julian Rotter)

      (1) Internal locus of control

      (2) External locus of control

      (3) Measuring locus of control

   b. **Delay of gratification** (Walter Mischel)

      (1) Preferred rewards and delay

      (2) Personality variables

   c. **Self-efficacy** (Albert Bandura)

      (1) Sources of information

      (2) Self-efficacy and performance

5. Evaluation of social-learning theory

   a. Strengths

      (1) Comprehensive approach

      (2) Experimentally based

      (3) Programs for change

   b. Criticisms and conclusions

B. Trait Theory

1. **Trait theory** and the **trait** (Gordon Allport)

2. Searching for traits

   a. How many traits can there be?

      (1) Allport's 18,000 terms

      (2) Reduced to 4,500 traits

   b. Aren't some traits related?

      (1) **Factor analysis** (Raymond Cattell)

      (2) Reduced list to 35 traits

3. Discovering the Big Five

    a. **Five-factor model** (OCEAN)

        (1) **O**penness

        (2) **C**onscientiousness

        (3) **E**xtraversion

        (4) **A**greeableness

        (5) **N**euroticism

    b. Big Five: supertraits

    c. Importance of the Big Five

4. Person versus situation (Walter Mischel)

    a. **Person-situation interaction**

    b. Resolving the contradiction

        (1) Traits

        (2) Observation

        (3) Predicting behaviors

5. Stability versus change

☐ *What is your age, relative to the Big Three-Oh? What does this suggest about your personality?*

    a. Stability

    b. Change

C. Genetic Influences on Traits

1. **Behavioral genetics**

2. How can two individuals be so alike?

3. Studying genetic influences

    a. Twin studies

    b. **Heritability**

4. Data from twin studies

5. Influences on personality

6. A big surprise

7. Conclusion

D. Evaluation of Trait Theory

1. How valid are the Big Five?

2. How consistent are individuals?

3. How strong are genetic factors?

E. Research Focus: Big Personality Changes

1. Research question: do people ever experience a sudden and major change in personality (**quantum personality change**)?

2. A study of personality change

   a. Method (**structured interviews**)

   b. Results

   c. Conclusions

F. Cultural Diversity: Resolving Conflicts

1. **Interpersonal conflict**

2. Cultural differences: the United States and Japan

   a. United States – **individualistic culture**

   b. Japan – **collectivistic culture**

3. Resolving interpersonal conflicts

   a. Strategies

   b. Overt or covert

G. Four Theories of Personality

☐ *Rod Plotnik gives you a beautiful summary of the important but complex material of Modules 19 and 20. Take advantage of his chart. Can you describe each theory and its key concepts?*

   a. Theory

      (1) Psychodynamic theory

      (2) Humanistic theories

      (3) Social learning theory

      (4) Trait theory

b. Key concepts

    (1) Psychodynamic theory

    (2) Humanistic theories

    (3) Social learning theory

    (4) Trait theory

H. Application: Assessment — Objective

1. **Objective personality tests [self-report questionnaires]**

2. Examples of objective tests

    a. Integrity tests

    b. **Minnesota Multiphasic Personality Inventory (MMPI-2)**

3. Two characteristics of a good test: reliability and validity

    a. **Barnum principle**

    b. **Validity**

    c. **Reliability**

4. Usefulness of objective tests

    a. Advantages

    b. Disadvantages

Language Enhancement Guide

IDIOMATIC EXPRESSIONS AND CULTURAL TERMS

The following are idiomatic expressions and cultural terms found in the module. Some of them have more than one meaning; the definition given here on the right is for the way the author uses the expression in this module. Remember that these words, like all words, can have different meanings in other contexts.

apartheid (419) = strict separation of races

mental toughness (419) = keeping one values and beliefs when others oppose them

went through the dictionary (424) = studied each page of the dictionary

giant leap forward (425) = a very important discovery

fast-food industry (436) = small restaurants like McDonald's and Burger King

horoscope (437) = a prediction about a person's future based on the position of planets and stars at the time of birth

VOCABULARY BUILDING: Word Analysis

Instructions: Analyze each term from memory using the following procedures:

1. Break each word in the table into its prefixes, roots and suffixes and guess the meaning of the word based on the meaning of its parts. If you do not remember the meaning of each part, look it up in the Prefix, Root, and Suffix Tables in the Appendix.

2. Find the word on the text page indicated in the brackets and redefine the word based on the context of the sentence, paragraph and chapter. Look up unmarked words in a college level dictionary. Remember that these words, like all words, can have different meanings in other contexts.

Word	Meaning
invest (418)	
adversity (419)	
oppression (423)	
unstable (424)	
extroversion (425)	
introversion	
stability (427)	
multiphasic (436)	

GUESSING FROM CONTEXT

You won't find the following words and expressions from this module in the textbook Glossary, but they are useful in reading, writing, and talking about psychology and other academic subjects. See if you can guess their meanings by studying their contexts (their relationship to the words around them).

To do this, find the word or expression in your textbook and guess its meaning using the clues in the context. You may find clues in an explanation that immediately follows the word, in a synonym that appears nearby, or in the form of examples. After you have defined the terms, ask a native speaker what they mean or look them up in a dictionary to see if your guesses were correct.

negotiate (418)

cherished (419)

perseverance (420)

profound (423)

spectrum (425)

enduring (432)

administered (437)

True-False

_____ 1. Social-learning theory combines reinforcement theory with ideas about how we think.

_____ 2. Gordon Allport and Raymond Cattell were early pioneers of social-learning theory.

_____ 3. One of the key ideas of social-learning theory is observational learning.

_____ 4. College students who think they "can't beat the system" ought to study the concept of locus of control.

_____ 5. The most important measure of self-efficacy is the ability to delay gratification.

_____ 6. A trait is a personal quirk — something that makes you different from everyone else in the world.

_____ 7. After a long search, researchers now believe that there are as many as 4,500 different personality traits.

_____ 8. One problem with the concept of traits is that they are not always consistent across situations.

_____ 9. Most changes in personality occur before the age of thirty.

_____ 10. Genetic influences can determine physical factors (like height), but not psychological factors like personality.

Flashcards _for psych majors only..._

Pioneers in Personality Theory: Modules 19 and 20 discuss many famous psychologists, whose names a psych major should know. Can you match these important pioneers to the phrase that fits their work or ideas?

_____ 1. Sigmund Freud   a. individual psychology

_____ 2. Carl Jung   b. "penis envy" is nonsense

_____ 3. Alfred Adler   c. hierarchy of needs

_____ 4. Karen Horney   d. personality traits

_____ 5. Abraham Maslow   e. delay of gratification

_____ 6. Carl Rogers   f. locus of control

_____ 7. Albert Bandura   g. collective unconscious

_____ 8. Walter Mischel   h. unconditional positive regard

_____ 9. Gordon Allport   i. observational learning

_____ 10. Julian Rotter   j. unconscious motivation

Flashcards

Match each key term to the definition given in the textbook.

_____ 1. Barnum principle

_____ 2. behavioral genetics

_____ 3. collectivistic culture

_____ 4. delay of gratification

_____ 5. factor analysis

_____ 6. five-factor model

_____ 7. heritability

_____ 8. individualistic culture

_____ 9. interpersonal conflict

_____ 10. locus of control

_____ 11. Minnesota Multiphasic Personality Interview (MMPI)

_____ 12. objective personality tests [self-report questionnaires]

_____ 13. quantum personality change

_____ 14. reliability

_____ 15. self-efficacy

_____ 16. social learning theory

_____ 17. structured interviews

_____ 18. trait

_____ 19. trait theory

_____ 20. validity

a. specific written statements requiring subjects to respond ("true" or "false") about applicability

b. experiencing a sudden and radical or dramatic shift in personality, beliefs, or values

c. personal beliefs of how capable we are of exercising control over events in our lives

d. a statistical measure estimating how much of a behavior is influenced by genetics

e. says personality is shaped by environmental conditions, cognitive factors, and behavior

f. approach for analyzing structure of personality by measuring, identifying, and classifying traits

g. places a high priority on attaining personal goals and striving for personal satisfaction (US)

h. beliefs concerning how much control (internal or external) we have over situations or rewards

i. degree to which a test measures what it is supposed to measure

j. places a high priority on group goals and norms over personal goals and values (Japan)

k. asking each individual same set of questions so same information is obtained from everyone

l. consistency; a person's test score at one time should be similar to score on a similar test later

m. postponing an immediate reward to persist in a task for the promise of a future reward

n. study of how inherited or genetic factors affect personality, intelligence, emotions, behavior

o. true-false self report questionnaire (567 items) describing normal and abnormal behaviors

p. complicated statistical method that finds relationships among many diverse items

q. listing a number of traits in such a general way (horoscope) that everyone sees self in it

r. a relatively stable and enduring tendency to behave in a particular way

s. categories are openness, conscientiousness, extraversion, agreeableness, and neuroticism

t. when one person interferes with a goal, wish, or expectation of another person

Multiple-Choice

_____ 1. One of the key concepts in Albert Bandura's social-learning theory is
   a. need for social approval
   b. observational learning
   c. self-actualization
   d. unconscious conflict

_____ 2. The only statement below that shows _internal_ locus of control is
   a. often exam questions are so unrelated to course work that studying is useless
   b. no matter how hard you try, some people just don't like you
   c. it is not always wise to plan too far ahead, because many things just turn out to be a matter of good or bad fortune
   d. when I make plans, I am almost certain I can make them work

_____ 3. Walter Mischel used children and marshmallows in his study of
   a. delay of gratification
   b. locus of control
   c. observational learning
   d. traits

_____ 4. Which one of the following is _not_ included by Bandura in the keys to determining our sense of self-efficacy?
   a. successes and failures we have experienced in the past
   b. comparing ourselves to others
   c. what others say about our capabilities
   d. the power of our conscience to make us feel guilty

_____ 5. One of the major contributions of social-learning theory to understanding personality is
   a. going beyond symptoms to the deeper emotional or unconscious causes of problems
   b. the development of successful programs for changing behavior and personality
   c. explaining the emotional and genetic causes of behavior
   d. offering a complete theory of personality and human nature

_____ 6. Do women make better cops? Evidence suggests that the answer is
   a. yes, at least for now, because women have a greater determination to succeed
   b. no, because women in our society tend to have a lower sense of self-efficacy
   c. yes, because personality traits shared by many women are useful in police work
   d. no, because the performance of male and female officers is about the same

_____ 7. A trait is a
   a. relatively stable and enduring tendency to behave in a particular way
   b. personal idiosyncrasy that distinguishes us from all others
   c. behavioral tendency that is genetically determined
   d. specific belief about the world which influences our personality

_____ 8. For years, research in personality has tried to identify the
   a. single trait that all humans share
   b. particular traits that make up a healthy personality
   c. most complete list of terms that deal with personality differences
   d. fewest number of traits that cover the largest range of human behaviors

_____ 9. The result of this effort (above) is the current belief that human personality is best described by
   a. five supertraits
   b. 35 basic traits
   c. 4,500 personality traits
   d. 18,000 descriptive terms

_____ 10. One of the sharpest attacks on the concept of traits was
   a. Mischel's argument that behavior changes in different situations
   b. Bandura's theory that we learn by observing others
   c. Maslow's discovery that needs are arranged in a hierarchy
   d. Allport's list of 18,000 terms that deal with personality differences

_____ 11. When are you most likely to make changes in your personality? Research says
   a. by age five
   b. before age 30
   c. after age 30
   d. when the end is near

_____ 12. The new area of psychology called behavioral genetics is providing evidence that
   a. twins are very different from single-birth children
   b. twins may appear outwardly similar, but in most respects they are quite different
   c. sharing a family environment is the major influence on personality
   d. inheritance sets a range of behaviors for many aspects of personality

_____ 13. How important are genetic factors in personality? Studies of more than 100 sets of twins suggest that
   a. about 40% of the development of personality traits is explained by genetics
   b. virtually all of the important personality traits are shaped by genetics
   c. while genetic influences are apparent, family environment is still the root of all the important features of personality
   d. the range of behaviors set by genetic influences is about 60-90%

_____ 14. Which one of the following is _not_ a criticism of trait theory?
   a. traits measured in one situation do not necessarily predict behavior in different situations
   b. data from questionnaires may paint too simplistic a picture of human personality
   c. there may be as few as five major traits that describe personality differences
   d. inherited factors should not be exaggerated, because most of the explanation for traits is due to environmental factors

_____ 15. A good example of a highly structured, objective personality test is the
   a. Minnesota Multiphasic Personality Inventory (MMPI-2)
   b. Rorschach Inkblot Test
   c. Thematic Apperception Test (TAT)
   d. traditional psychological interview

Answers for Module 20

True-False	Flashcards	Multiple-Choice
1. T	1. q	1. b
2. F	2. n	2. d
3. T	3. j	3. a
4. T	4. m	4. d
5. F	5. p	5. b
6. F	6. s	6. c
7. F	7. d	7. a
8. T	8. g	8. d
9. T	9. t	9. a
10. F	10. h	10. a
	11. o	11. b
	12. a	12. d
	13. b	13. a
	14. l	14. c
	15. c	15. a
	16. e	
	17. k	
	18. r	
	19. f	
	20. i	

Pioneers in Personality Theory Quiz

1. j   2. g   3. a   4. b   5. c   6. h   7. i   8. e   9. d   10. f

Health, Stress, & Coping

This Module Could Save Your Life!

O.K., maybe I'm exaggerating. Then again, maybe not. Remember Rod Plotnik's discussion of the relationship between illness and stress (in the section on psychosomatic symptoms)? Go back and check how much illness doctors estimate results from stress. The percentages are staggering.

It is becoming clear that stress is one of the greatest health hazards we face. We all feel it. Sometimes it seems that modern life not only is more stressful than 'the good old days' were, but that the number of our daily stressors continues to increase.

Does it have to be this way?

Ironically, considering its prevalence, stress is the one health hazard that is not inevitable, at least not in theory. Old age, eventually, is going to get each of us. Accidents will happen. We can't eliminate all disease. You won't solve the problem of environmental pollution all by yourself. Yet you are not doomed to be ravaged by stress.

What can you do about it? First, you can adopt a positive attitude and a healthy life style that will tend to protect you against stress. Second, you can learn how to manage the stress you can't escape. Module 21 explains how both of these safeguards work.

Never mind the grade on the test. Study this module to learn how to live a long and healthy life!

Should Stress Be Managed?

What about stress in *your* life? Do you enjoy a good balance between the demands of your environment and your mental and physical abilities to meet them? Or do you see signs in your behavior or your physical health that suggest too much stress in your life?

Often the suggestion of psychology seems to be that in order to avoid ulcers and heart attacks, we should learn how to "manage" the stress that is causing them. A different approach would be to think of stress as clues to aspects of life that aren't working effectively. While an ulcer certainly qualifies as a "clue," most stress clues are much more commonplace, and therefore are easy to overlook. Search for the small distortions in your everyday behavior (like swearing, irritation, speeding, and headaches) that could be evidence of stress. Look for feelings, thoughts, and actions that may betray problems in your life and suggest connections to pressures from your environment. Meditation and relaxation certainly are valuable, but changing your life and solving your problems, where possible, would be better.

Effective Student Tip 21

No One Is Lazy

All right, go ahead and call yourself "lazy," if it makes you feel better, but it's not good psychology. First, it may be what cognitive psychologists call a self-handicapping strategy, where you excuse yourself in advance for poor performance. ("I probably won't pass the test..., I'm too lazy to study!") Well, at least they can't say you're dumb, just lazy.

Second, I would argue that no one is lazy. Oh, sure, we humans like to lie around and we goof off a lot, but that probably has more to do with defending our freedom and autonomy against the regimentation of organized work. The natural tendency of all animals is activity. Watch children at play. Look at the time and energy we put into second jobs, hobbies, sports, and social activities. Normally, we prefer to be doing something, because only activity creates the opportunity to feed our constant hunger to be effective.

When we feel lazy we really are feeling ineffective. The task before us seems too difficult, too unrewarding, or too lacking in novelty and challenge. When you feel 'too lazy' to tackle your schoolwork, the real problem is that you haven't figured out how to handle it effectively, or how to make it deliver positive feedback attesting to your effectiveness.

Your response...

Many of my own students violently disagree with me on this Tip. What do you think?

Key Terms

Many of these key terms are as immediate as the morning newspaper, where, in fact, you may find them. Others are psychological terms that take the discussion of stress and coping a bit deeper. All are relevant to your daily life and important to your health and welfare.

alarm stage	fight-flight response	problem-focused coping
anxiety (Freud)	frustration	progressive relaxation
anxiety	general adaptation syndrome (GAS)	psychoneuroimmunology
approach-approach conflict		psychosomatic symptoms
approach-avoidance conflict	hardiness	relaxation response
avoidance-avoidance conflict	harm/loss appraisal	resistance stage
biofeedback	hassles	secondary appraisal
burnout	immune system	social support
case study	locus of control	stress management program
challenge appraisal	major life events	stress
conditioned emotional response	mind-body connection	threat appraisal
conflict	mind-body therapy	transcendental meditation (TM)
emotion-focused coping	negative affect	Type A Behavior
exhaustion stage	observational learning	uplifts
experiment	posttraumatic stress disorder	
	primary appraisal	

Outline

- *INTRODUCTION*

  1. **Stress**

  2. Coping

A. *Appraisal*

  1. **Primary appraisal**

  2. Three ways to appraise a stressful situation

     a. **Harm/loss appraisal**

     b. **Threat appraisal**

     c. **Challenge appraisal**

3. How quickly do we make appraisals?

4. How do primary appraisals affect levels of stress?

5. Why do people disagree on what is stressful?

6. Why are primary appraisals so important?

B. *Physiological Responses*

☐ *Can you explain why the fight-flight response was so valuable in our early evolution but has become such a problem in modern life? (See "For psych majors only..." box.)*

1. Primary appraisal and **fight-flight response**

2. Activation of the fight-flight response

   a. Appraisal

   b. Hypothalamus

   c. Sympathetic division

   d. Fight-flight response

3. Fight-flight: physiological responses

   a. Stress appraisal

   b. Respiration

   c. Heart rate

   d. Liver

   e. Pupils

   f. Hair

   g. Adrenal glands

   h. Muscle tension

4. Effects of stress

5. General adaptation syndrome (Hans Selye)

   a. **Psychosomatic symptoms**

   b. **General adaptation syndrome (GAS)**

      (1) **Alarm stage**

      (2) **Resistance stage**

      (3) **Exhaustion stage**

6. Mind-body connection

   a. **Mind-body connection**

   b. **Mind-body therapy**

7. Prevalence and kinds of psychosomatic symptoms

□ *Have you ever experienced psychosomatic symptoms?*

   a. Development of psychosomatic symptoms

      (1) Genetic predisposition and life-style

      (2) Prolonged stress

      (3) Psychosomatic symptoms

   b. Psychosomatic symptoms listed

8. **Immune system**

   a. **Psychoneuroimmunology**

   b. Evidence for psychoneuroimmunology

   c. Mind-body connection: the immune system

   d. Conditioning the immune system [to resist stress]

      (1) Psychological factors

      (2) Birth of psychoneuroimmunology

C. *Stressful Experiences*

1. Hassles and major life events

   a. **Hassles**

   b. **Major life events**

      (1) Importance of hassles (**uplifts**)

      (2) Importance of life events

      (3) Social Readjustment Rating Scale

2. Situational stressors

   a. **Frustration**

   b. **Burnout**

   c. Interpersonal violence (**posttraumatic stress disorder**)

3. Three common kinds of **conflict**

   a. **Approach-avoidance**

   b. **Approach-approach**

   c. **Avoidance-avoidance**

4. Five styles for dealing with conflict

   a. Avoidance

   b. Accommodation

   c. Domination

   d. Compromise

   e. Integration

5. **Anxiety**

   a. Developing anxiety

      (1) Classical conditioning – **conditioned emotional response**

      (2) **Observational learning**

      (3) Unconscious conflict – **anxiety (Freud)**

   b. Coping with anxiety

      (1) Extinction

      (2) Freudian defense mechanisms

D. Personality & Social Factors

☐ *Where would you locate yourself on each of the three dimensions below?*

1. **Hardiness**

   a. Definition

   b. Function

2. **Locus of control** and stress

   a. External locus of control

   b. Internal locus of control

3. **Negative affect** and stress

4. **Type A behavior**

    a. Can personality cause heart attacks?

    b. Revised definition of Type A behavior over three decades

5. **Social support**

    a. Functions of social support

    b. Social support as a buffer against stress

E. Coping: Problem versus Emotion

1. **Secondary appraisal**

2. Problem-focused or emotion-focused coping

    a. **Problem-focused coping**

    b. **Emotion-focused coping**

3. Choosing between coping strategies

F. Research Focus: Coping with Trauma

1. Research question: how do people cope with severe burns?

2. Research methods

    a. **Experiment**

    b. **Case study**

3. Questions

4. Coping with initial stressful affects

5. Coping with long-term stressful effects

6. Conclusions

G. Cultural Diversity: Tibetan Monks

☐ *Does Rod Plotnik's example of Tibetan Monks mean that modern science is flawed?*

1. Mind-body interaction

2. Control of temperature

3. Explanation and application

H. *Application: Stress Management Program*

☐ *Could you apply the basic principles of a* **stress management program** *to your own life?*

1. Changing thoughts

    a. Use challenge appraisals

    b. Substitute positive self-statements

2. Changing behaviors – take action

3. Changing physiological responses – learn to relax

    a. **Biofeedback**

    b. **Progressive relaxation**

    c. Meditation

        (1) **Transcendental meditation (TM)**

        (2) **Relaxation response**

Language Enhancement Guide

IDIOMATIC EXPRESSIONS AND CULTURAL TERMS

The following are idiomatic expressions and cultural terms found in the module. Some of them have more than one meaning; the definition given here on the right is for the way the author uses the expression in this module. Remember that these words, like all words, can have different meanings in other contexts.

the big deal (441) = a very important or serious event

scoops up (441) = picks up

put-down (444) = an insult

trigger (444) = start

getting more done (446) = completing all assignments

takes its toll on (446) = causes damage

breakdown (446) = disease and injury

(anxiety has) waned (453) = decreased

to deal with (459) = to think about, solve or prevent something

VOCABULARY BUILDING: Word Analysis

Instructions: Analyze each term from memory using the following procedures:

1. Break each word in the table into its prefixes, roots and suffixes and guess the meaning of the word based on the meaning of its parts. If you do not remember the meaning of each part, look it up in the Prefix, Root, and Suffix Tables in the Appendix.

2. Find the word on the text page indicated in the brackets and redefine the word based on the context of the sentence, paragraph and chapter. Look up unmarked words in a college level dictionary. Remember that these words, like all words, can have different meanings in other contexts.

Word	Meaning
transforms (443)	
impatient (444)	
psychosomatic (446)	
resistance (446)	
suppress (448)	
prematurely (449)	
postraumatic (451)	
comprise (454)	
encountered (456)	
demoralized (456)	
cohesive (457)	

GUESSING FROM CONTEXT

You won't find the following words and expressions from this module in the textbook Glossary, but they are useful in reading, writing, and talking about psychology and other academic subjects. See if you can guess their meanings by studying their contexts (their relationship to the words around them).

grimacing (441)

prestigious (441)

appraisal (442)

distinction (444)

symptoms (446),

prolonged (447)

susceptible (448)

commitment (454)

optimistic (455)

pessimistic (455)

True-False

_____ 1. Stress depends partly on how we evaluate a situation.

_____ 2. To "appraise" something means to feel very positive about it.

_____ 3. The fight or flight response goes back to the earliest days of the human species.

_____ 4. Some Tibetan monks have developed a type of yoga that allows them to levitate their bodies several inches off the ground.

_____ 5. One of the main ingredients of a stress management program is learning how to relax.

_____ 6. Research shows that small daily hassles are far more stressful than major life events.

_____ 7. The way we respond to frustration influences our levels of stress.

_____ 8. Conflict means the inevitable run-ins that occur when you have to work with someone else.

_____ 9. Your personality can influence how well you deal with stress.

_____ 10. One of the best prescriptions for successfully handling stress is to have many relationships that confer social support.

For Psych Majors Only...

It's a Jungle Out There: Imagine two of your prehuman ancestors venturing away from the trees looking for food. Suddenly they hear a low growling and see a huge cat with enormous fangs coming toward them. One (an early scientist) is delighted with the new creature and decides to go up and pet it. The other, feeling awful but also all charged up, makes an instant decision to run for the nearest tree and climb like never before. The survivor, whose makeup contained a little more of what became our fight-flight response, lived to contribute genes to the next generation. The other one made a contribution to the genes of the saber-toothed tiger.

Fast forward to today at the office. Suddenly the boss is standing over your desk saying something about a project that was supposed to be finished. Should you calmly explain that one of the reports you need hasn't arrived yet, or should you run for the nearest tree, like your ancestor did? Is it just another problem, or is it a real saber-toothed tiger? You get all charged up just trying to decide.

The situation in today's jungle of school, work, and relationships is much more complicated than it was for our ancestors. It's hard to tell the real emergencies, so we exhaust ourselves with constant false alerts. The fight-flight response was supposed to be for the rare enemy or tiger, not for the simple problems of daily life.

Flashcards

Match each key term to the definition given in the textbook.

_____ 1. anxiety

_____ 2. burnout

_____ 3. emotion-focused coping

_____ 4. exhaustion stage

_____ 5. fight-flight response

_____ 6. general adaptation syndrome (GAS)

_____ 7. hardiness

_____ 8. locus of control

_____ 9. major life events

_____ 10. mind-body connection

_____ 11. negative affect

_____ 12. posttraumatic stress disorder

_____ 13. primary appraisal

_____ 14. problem-focused coping

_____ 15. psychoneuroimmunology

_____ 16. psychosomatic symptoms

_____ 17. social support

_____ 18. stress

_____ 19. transcendental meditation (TM)

_____ 20. Type A Behavior

a. directs great sources of energy to muscles and brain creating preparation of body for action

b. protection from stress conferred by feelings of control, commitment, challenge

c. potentially disturbing or disruptive situations that we appraise as having significant impact

d. real physical symptoms but caused by psychological factors

e. relationship between central nervous system, endocrine system, and psychosocial factors

f. in a comfortable position, eyes closed, repeating a sound to clear one's head of all thoughts

g. feelings of doing poorly at one's job, physical and emotional exhaustion, demands too high

h. result of direct personal experience of an event involving actual or threatened injury or death

i. solving the problem by seeking information, changing our behavior, or taking some action

j. unpleasant state of feelings of uneasiness and apprehension with physiological arousal

k. continuum of beliefs about the extent to which one is in control of one's own future

l. anxious, threatening feeling of a situation being more than we can adequately handle

m. how thoughts, beliefs, emotions produce physiological changes

n. dealing with the problem by trying to reduce our emotional distress

o. three stages (alarm, resistance, exhaustion) of reactions body has to stressful situations

p. breakdown in internal organs or immune system due to long-term, continuous stress

q. moderation of stress by having groups, family, friends who provide attachment and resources

r. experiencing negative emotions, such as anger, hostility, rage, fear, or anxiety

s. theory that aggressive workaholism, anger, competition, hostility, can lead to a heart attack

t. our initial, subjective evaluation of situation in which we balance demands against our ability

Multiple-Choice

_____ 1. Which one of the following is *not* a type of primary appraisal?
   a. harm/loss
   b. threat
   c. challenge
   d. advantage/resource

_____ 2. Rod Plotnik lists people's reactions to a number of common stressors in order to illustrate the point that
   a. modern life has become almost unbearably stressful
   b. not everyone appraises these situations the same way
   c. there is a core of common experiences that everyone considers stressful
   d. the one thing everybody hates is waiting

_____ 3. The reason why the fight-flight response can harm our health is that
   a. every time it is triggered our bodies go though an automatic process of arousal
   b. overuse is a kind of "crying wolf" that eventually results in letting our guard down
   c. biologically, humans were designed for quiet, peaceful lives
   d. psychologically, humans do not tolerate challenge very well

_____ 4. Which one of the following is *not* a stage in the general adaptation syndrome?
   a. alarm
   b. attack
   c. resistance
   d. exhaustion

_____ 5. "Psychoneuroimmunology" means the study of
   a. the manner in which physical factors create psychological symptoms
   b. how disease can make a person psychotic or neurotic
   c. the interaction of physical and psychological factors in health
   d. this is a trick question — that is a made-up word

_____ 6. The total score on the Social Readjustment Rating Scale
   a. subtracts positive life events from negative life changes
   b. gives a precise cut-off point for becoming an ill or staying well
   c. reflects how well you cope with stress
   d. reflects how many major life events you have experienced in the past year

_____ 7. Having feelings of doing poorly, physically wearing out, or becoming emotionally exhausted because of stress at work is called
   a. frustration
   b. burnout
   c. conflict
   d. stress

_____ 8. According to Freud's explanation, we try to reduce anxiety by employing
   a. problem-focused coping at the ego level
   b. defense mechanisms at the unconscious level
   c. approach/avoidance choices at the ego level
   d. "snap out of it" coping messages at the superego level

_____ 9. Which one of the following is *not* an ingredient of hardiness?
   a. control
   b. commitment
   c. contentment
   d. challenge

_____ 10. The famous "Type A Behavior" research attempted to relate certain personality traits to
   a. hardy personality
   b. locus of control
   c. increased risk of cancer
   d. increased risk of heart attack

_____ 11. People in Roseto, Pennsylvania didn't follow healthy life styles, but they had lower rates of heart attacks, ulcers, and emotional problems, probably because
   a. the steep Pennsylvania hills forced them to exercise whether they wanted to or not
   b. being the home of the University of Pennsylvania, the town had superb medical facilities
   c. families in this small town were all related to each other, which had built up a good genetic background over many generations
   d. relationships with family and neighbors were extremely close and mutually supportive

_____ 12. Secondary appraisal means
   a. deciding what we can do to manage, cope, or deal with the situation
   b. our subjective evaluation of a situation to decide if we can deal with it
   c. the extent to which we appraise a situation as stressful after we have taken time to think about it objectively
   d. the extent to which we find a situation stressful the second time we encounter it

_____ 13. Sandra, the welfare mother in college whose struggles Rod Plotnik described, is using problem-focused coping when she
   a. divides her work into separate goals and sets time schedules
   b. tells herself it is more important to take care of her sick child than to study
   c. puts herself down for having to go on welfare
   d. feels uncomfortable around students from wealthy families

_____ 14. If Tibetan monks can raise their body temperature through meditation, then perhaps
   a. Western medicine — not Asian — represents the real medical fakery
   b. Western medicine should pay more attention to psychological factors
   c. every culture has a form of medicine that is best for its own members
   d. every culture develops some phenomena that can't be fully explained

_____ 15. The relaxation technique that involves learning to increase or decrease physiological signals from the body is called
   a. the relaxation response
   b. progressive relaxation
   c. biofeedback
   d. Transcendental Meditation (TM)

Answers for Module 21

True-False
1. T
2. F
3. T
4. F
5. T
6. F
7. T
8. F
9. T
10. T

Flashcards
1. j
2. g
3. n
4. p
5. a
6. o
7. b
8. k
9. c
10. m
11. r
12. h
13. t
14. i
15. e
16. d
17. q
18. l
19. f
20. s

Multiple-Choice
1. d
2. b
3. a
4. b
5. c
6. d
7. b
8. b
9. c
10. d
11. d
12. a
13. a
14. b
15. c

Disorders I: Definition & Anxiety Disorders

What Is Psychological Abnormality?

We can often recognize when a fellow human is psychologically 'abnormal,' but when we try to say exactly what makes the person abnormal, we find that it is not so easy.

Rod Plotnik begins this module with a hard problem for psychology and psychiatry: how to understand and treat mental disorders. In his examples of infamous criminals and everyday problems you will see that psychological science has not yet attained the agreement and precision of medical science. All doctors will agree on the diagnosis of a broken arm, but what about a broken mind? Since psychology has such a long way to go before it can claim a comprehensive and satisfactory definition of abnormality, perhaps I can be forgiven for trying my own definition.

One Try at a Definition of Psychological Abnormality

Psychological abnormality is a typically temporary condition of dysfunction and distress caused by deficits or breakdowns in the universal need to be effective. Lack of effectiveness can occur in any one or more of six areas of human psychological functioning (see Plotnik's six approaches to psychology).

The most damaging results of the loss of effectiveness are the corresponding breakdowns in those processes of regulation and self-regulation that are so crucial to the welfare of human beings, who lack guidance by instincts or reflexes. It is the loss of regulation and self-regulation that seems 'abnormal,' both to the troubled person and to others.

The basic remedy for psychological abnormality is to begin to take competent action. Restoration of competent action may require intervention in any one or more of six realms of psychological functioning. Treatment may include: (1) chemical intervention to restore regulation of a biologically based mental function; (2) understanding of basic psychological processes [especially emotion] and exploration of the past to discover origins of loss of effectiveness and patterns of ineffective behavior; (3) reversal of negative self-image and encouragement of more realistic thinking about the world; (4) modification of maladaptive habits and development of new skills and abilities; (5) projection of values and hopes into the future to identify desired and needed new capabilities, and (6) reconstruction and strengthening of social bonds that can help resurrect old competencies and encourage the acquisition of new ones.

Effective Student Tip 22

What 'Boring' Really Means

Students often complain that they aren't doing well because their classes and schoolwork are boring. I could suggest that *they* are interesting persons, and therefore have a duty to help make their classes interesting, but that wouldn't be fair. It would be more realistic to advise them to reconsider what boring really means.

Most students think certain people (not themselves) or certain activities are boring, but that is incorrect. Psychologically, boredom means being trapped, not being able to engage in an activity that is good for you. The next time you feel bored, ask yourself if there is anything taking place that allows you to grow and to express what is uniquely you. I'll bet you'll discover that 'boring' means not being able to exercise your urge to be effective.

Nothing is intrinsically boring. Every experienced teacher I've known had something worthwhile to say. Give me any example of activity or knowledge you might consider boring and I'll find someone, somewhere, whose great passion in life is pursuing exactly that activity or acquiring precisely that knowledge. Your schoolwork isn't boring, but perhaps you haven't yet found a way to connect it to the passions in *your* life.

Your response...

Think of something really boring. Now reconsider. Is there a way in which it might it *not* be boring?

Key Terms

The key terms in this module require you to be part lawyer, part historian, and part doctor. They will require more study than many other modules, but hard study will pay off. The next module is worse!

agoraphobia

animal models

clinical assessment

clinical diagnosis

clinical interview

cognitive-behavior therapy

cognitive-behavioral approach

conditioned emotional response

conversion disorder

Diagnostic and Statistical Manual of Mental Disorders-IV (DSM-IV)

exposure therapy

generalized anxiety disorder

insanity

labeling

maladaptive behavior approach

mass hysteria

medical model approach

mental disorder

obsessive-compulsive disorder

panic attack

panic disorder

personality tests

phobia

psychoanalytic approach

social norms approach

social phobias

somatization disorder

somatoform disorders

specific phobias

statistical frequency approach

taijin kyofusho (TKS)

Outline

- **INTRODUCTION**

    1. How did a serial killer go unnoticed?

        a. **Insanity**

        b. **Mental disorder**

    2. What's so scary about flying (**phobia**)?

    A. *Three Approaches*

    1. Why were witches burned in the middle ages?

    2. Three approaches to understanding and treating mental disorders

        a. **Medical model approach**

        b. **Cognitive-behavioral approach**

        c. **Psychoanalytic approach**

3. What is abnormal behavior?

    a. **Statistical frequency approach**

    b. **Social norms approach**

    c. **Maladaptive behavior approach**

B. Assessing Mental Disorders

☐ *Why is assessment of a mental problem more likely to be controversial than assessment of a problem of physical health?*

1. **Clinical assessment**

2. Clinical assessment: three methods

    a. Neurological exam

    b. **Clinical interview**

    c. **Personality tests**

3. Clinical assessment: Susan Smith

    a. Her past

    b. Her present

4. Clinical assessment: problems and importance

C. Diagnosing Mental Disorders

1. Diagnostic and Statistical Manual of Mental Disorders-IV

    a. **Clinical diagnosis**

    b. **Diagnostic and Statistical Manual of Mental Disorders-IV (DSM-IV)**

2. How is the DSM-IV used for clinical diagnosis?

    a. Axis I: Major clinical syndromes

        (1) Disorders usually first diagnosed in infancy, childhood, or adolescence

        (2) Organic mental disorders

        (3) Substance-related disorders

        (4) Schizophrenia and other psychotic disorders

        (5) Mood disorders

        (6) Anxiety disorders

        (7) Somatoform disorders

       (8) Dissociative disorders

       (9) Sexual and gender-identity disorders

   b. How are the five axes used in clinical diagnosis?

       (1) Axis I: Major clinical syndromes [see above]

       (2) Axis II: Personality Disorders

       (3) Axis III: General Medical Conditions

       (4) Axis IV: Psychosocial and Environmental Problems

       (5) Axis V: Global Assessment of Functioning (GAF) Scale

3. Advantages of DSM-IV

4. Potential problems with DSM-IV

   a. Problem of **labeling** of mental disorders

   b. Disorders with social or political implications

5. Frequency of mental disorders

D. Anxiety Disorders

☐ *Do you sometimes experience anxiety? How does it feel?*

1. **Generalized anxiety disorder**

   a. Symptoms

   b. Treatment

2. **Panic** disorder

   a. Symptoms (**panic attack**)

   b. Treatment

3. **Phobia**

   a. **Social phobias**

   b. **Specific phobias**

   c. **Agoraphobia**

4. **Obsessive-compulsive disorder**

☐ *No, you don't have the disorder, but what are some of your obsessive-compulsive behaviors?*

   a. Symptoms

   b. Treatment

      (1) **Exposure therapy**

      (2) Antidepressant drugs

E. Somatoform Disorders

☐ *Do you worry about your body or your health? Are your worries realistic or exaggerated?*

1. **Mass hysteria**

2. **Somatoform disorders**

   a. **Somatization disorder**

   b. **Conversion disorder**

F. Cultural Diversity: An Asian Disorder

☐ *What is* **taijin kyofusho (TKS)** *and what are its implications for psychiatry?*

1. Symptoms

2. Cultural influences

3. Social customs

4. Culture-bound disorders

G. Research Focus: Animal Model for Anxiety

1. Research question: which brain structures are involved with anxiety and fear?

   a. **Conditioned emotional response**

   b. **Animal models**

2. Fear in monkeys and the prefrontal cortex

3. Fear in rats and the amygdala

H. Application: Treating Phobias

☐ *Is there anything you are "phobic" about?*

1. Specific phobia: flying

    a. **Cognitive-behavioral therapy**

       (1) Thoughts

       (2) Behaviors

    b. **Exposure therapy**

2. Social phobia: public speaking

    a. Explain

    b. Learn and substitute

    c. Expose

    d. Practice

3. Drug treatment of phobias

Language Enhancement Guide

IDIOMATIC EXPRESSIONS AND CULTURAL TERMS

The following are idiomatic expressions and cultural terms found in the module. Some of them have more than one meaning; the definition given here on the right is for the way the author uses the expression in this module. Remember that these words, like all words, can have different meanings in other contexts.

hangover (446) = unpleasant physical effects due to drinking too much alcohol

con man (467) = a criminal who first gains your trust, then persuades you to hand over your money

[no male] would be caught dead (469) = would not under any conditions

drinking heavily (471) = drinking a lot of alcoholic beverages

time consuming (477) = activities that require much more time than required

vicious cycle (477) = repeating a "bad" self-defeating activity over and over again

VOCABULARY BUILDING: Word Analysis

Instructions: Analyze each term from memory using the following procedures:

1. Break each word in the table into its prefixes, roots and suffixes and guess the meaning of the word based on the meaning of its parts. If you do not remember the meaning of each part, look it up in the Prefix, Root, and Suffix Tables in the Appendix.

2. Find the word on the text page indicated in the brackets and redefine the word based on the context of the sentence, paragraph and chapter. Look up unmarked words in a college level dictionary. Remember that these words, like all words, can have different meanings in other contexts.

Word	Meaning
recurring (467)	
acrophobia (467)	
abnormal (468)	
evict (4369)	
maladaptive (469)	
adverse (469)	
disorder (470)	
antidepressant (471)	
interaction (477)	
somatoform (478)	
irresistible (479)	
insensitive (480)	
distorted (482)	
relapse (483)	

GUESSING FROM CONTEXT

You won't find the following words and expressions from this module in the textbook Glossary, but they are useful in reading, writing, and talking about psychology and other academic subjects. See if you can guess their meanings by studying their contexts (their relationship to the words around them).

sinister (467)

typical (467)

prosecution (467)

suspected (470)

diagnosis (472)

prevalence (474)

True-False

_____ 1. The psychiatrists who examined him all agreed that Jeffrey Dahmer was insane.

_____ 2. Although no one dreamed she would kill her own children, Susan Smith's neighbors had considered her a ticking bomb likely to explode at any minute.

_____ 3. When psychiatrists need to make diagnoses, they turn to DSM-IV.

_____ 4. Nearly 50% of all Americans report having had at least one mental disorder during their lifetimes.

_____ 5. Anxiety is a general problem that can result in many different disorders.

_____ 6. Panic disorder is more common among women than men.

_____ 7. Don't waste time worrying about your phobias — they usually disappear in a few months.

_____ 8. Experiences like going back inside to check that you turned off the oven show that obsessive-compulsive disorder is quite common.

_____ 9. Taijin kyofusho (TKS) is a social phobia characterized by a morbid fear of offending others.

_____ 10. Research has shown that drug treatment is superior to cognitive-behavior programs for getting rid of phobias.

For Psych Majors Only...

Psychology at its Most Real: Now, boys and girls, can you say "diathesis-stress theory?" You will by the time you are finished with this module and the next. These modules are tough, but getting a handle on the material now will help you in all your subsequent psychology courses, especially abnormal psychology.

These two modules are tough partly because the subject involves the technical terminology of medical science and the concept of the medical model of illness. You must learn to think and talk like a doctor. But the main reason is that the subject touches on the most difficult challenge faced by psychology: how to understand why things go wrong for troubled people and how to help them.

Have you noticed how frequently new discoveries about the causes and treatment of mental illnesses are in the news? The field of abnormal psychology is developing right before your eyes. Memorize what you must in these modules, but keep your eyes on the big picture, too.

Yes, these modules are tough, but they present psychology at its most real.

Flashcards

Match each key term to the definition given in the textbook.

_____ 1. agoraphobia

a. characterized by excessive and/or unrealistic worry or feelings of general apprehension

_____ 2. clinical interview

b. characterized by marked and persistent unreasonable fears about an object or situation

_____ 3. cognitive-behavioral approach

c. method of gathering information about relevant past and present behaviors, attitudes, emotions

_____ 4. Diagnostic and Statistical Manual... (DSM-IV)

d. characterized by anxiety of being in places or situations from which escape would be difficult

_____ 5. generalized anxiety disorder

e. points to causes of mental disorders as unconscious conflicts from psychosexual stages

_____ 6. insanity

f. problem that seriously interferes with ability to live a satisfying personal life, function in society

_____ 7. labeling

g. a behavior is abnormal if it occurs rarely or infrequently relative to the general population

_____ 8. maladaptive behavior approach

h. characterized by recurrent, unexpected panic attacks, continued worry about more attacks

_____ 9. mass hysteria

i. event that causes a group to all share the same fears, delusions, symptoms or behaviors

_____ 10. medical model approach

j. describes a uniform system for assessing specific symptoms, matching them to disorders

_____ 11. mental disorder

k. involve a pattern of recurring, multiple, significant bodily complaints over several years

_____ 12. obsessive-compulsive disorder

l. characterized by morbid fear of offending others through awkward social or physical behavior

_____ 13. panic disorder

m. a behavior is abnormal if it interferes with the ability to function as a person or in society

_____ 14. psychoanalytic approach

n. persistent, recurring irrational thoughts and irresistible impulses to perform act repeatedly

_____ 15. social norms approach

o. legal term meaning not knowing the difference between right and wrong

_____ 16. social phobias

p. a behavior is abnormal if it deviates greatly from accepted social standards or values

_____ 17. somatoform disorders

q. emphasizes that mental disorders result from deficits in cognitive processes, behavioral skills

_____ 18. specific phobias

r. process of identifying differences among individuals, placing them in specific categories

_____ 19. statistical frequency approach

s. views mental disorders as similar to physical diseases, with symptoms to diagnosis and treat

_____ 20. taijin kyofusho (TKS)

t. characterized by a marked and continuous irrational fear of performing in social situations

Multiple-Choice

_____ 1. The main issue in the Jeffrey Dahmer trial was whether Dahmer
    a. actually killed 15 young men, or only the one he was arrested for
    b. was under the influence of drugs when he killed
    c. knew the difference between right and wrong when he killed
    d. really intended to kill the five men who said they got away

_____ 2. The difference between the terms insanity and mental disorder is that
    a. insanity is more severe than a mental disorder
    b. insanity is a legal term while mental disorder is a medical term
    c. mental disorders are specific forms of insanity
    d. mental disorders do not qualify for insurance reimbursement

_____ 3. Which one of the following is _not_ a way of defining abnormal behavior?
    a. statistical frequency
    b. deviation from social norms
    c. maladaptive behavior
    d. slips of the tongue

_____ 4. Which one of the following is _not_ an approach to understanding and treating mental disorders?
    a. statistical frequency
    b. medical model
    c. cognitive-behavioral
    d. psychoanalytic

_____ 5. The most commonly used method for assessing abnormal behavior is the
    a. Rorschach inkblot test
    b. neurological examination
    c. personality test
    d. clinical interview

_____ 6. Rod Plotnik tells the story of Susan Smith in great detail to make the point that
    a. clinical diagnosis is a complicated yet vital process
    b. childhood sexual abuse almost always results in adult problems
    c. despite all we know about Susan Smith, we still can't understand why she did it
    d. her friends and neighbors should have seen the tragedy coming

_____ 7. The most widely used system of psychological classification is the
    a. Freudian Psychoanalytic System (FPS)
    b. Diagnostic and Statistical Manual of Mental Disorders-IV (DSM-IV)
    c. Disordered Mind Standards-III (DMS-III)
    d. Federal Uniform Code of Psychopathology (UCP)

_____ 8. A recent large-scale study showed that _____ of all Americans had at least one mental disorder during their lifetimes
    a. only 15%
    b. almost 50%
    c. fully 80%
    d. almost 100 %

_____ 9. The anxiety disorder that causes the greatest terror and suffering is
   a. panic disorder
   b. simple phobia
   c. generalized anxiety disorder
   d. social phobia

_____ 10. Rose is so afraid of being out in public that she stays at home all the time now; Rose suffers from
   a. a simple phobia
   b. a social phobia
   c. agoraphobia
   d. claustrophobia

_____ 11. Remember the case of Shirley, who had to do everything precisely 17 times? The theory is that she was trying to
   a. reduce or avoid anxiety associated with feeling or being dirty
   b. obey inner voices which told her God loves cleanliness
   c. cleanse her mind of confusing hallucinations
   d. please her mother, who used to punish her severely whenever she got her clothes dirty while playing

_____ 12. When 500 children gathered to perform in a concert suddenly became ill, the cause was determined to be
   a. mass hysteria
   b. mass delusion
   c. somatoform disorder
   d. somatization disorder

_____ 13. The key feature of somatoform disorders is
   a. pretending to be sick to avoid school or work
   b. real physical symptoms but no physical causes
   c. imagining physical symptoms that aren't really there
   d. psychological problems but no physical symptoms

_____ 14. Of all the mental disorders we know, it's a good bet you don't have to worry about getting TKS, mainly because you
   a. are in college, and therefore too old to get it
   b. are in college, and therefore too intelligent to get it
   c. got shots for it as a child
   d. don't live in Japan

_____ 15. Which one of the following is *not* a technique for treating a phobia?
   a. gradually exposing a client to the feared situation
   b. administering an antidepressant drug to the client
   c. hospitalizing the client until his or her fears begin to diminish
   d. teaching the client to become aware of thoughts about the feared situation

Answers for Module 22

True-False	Flashcards	Multiple-Choice
1. F	1. d	1. c
2. F	2. c	2. b
3. T	3. q	3. d
4. T	4. j	4. a
5. T	5. a	5. d
6. T	6. o	6. a
7. F	7. r	7. b
8. F	8. m	8. b
9. T	9. i	9. a
10. F	10. s	10. c
	11. f	11. a
	12. n	12. a
	13. h	13. b
	14. e	14. d
	15. p	15. c
	16. t	
	17. k	
	18. b	
	19. g	
	20. l	

Disorders II: Mood Disorder & Schizophrenia

The Story of a Troubled Person

One of the most perplexing and controversial problems of psychology is how to understand and treat human anguish and suffering. The great danger is that we may classify, label, and prescribe, without really understanding. Modern psychology has come a long way from the unthinking and often cruel 'treatment' in use not so long ago, but we are still far from having a reliable science of diagnosis and therapy.

I want to suggest an exercise that may help you think about the complexity of emotional disturbance, and show you that your own psychological sensitivity and insight into human suffering may be greater than you realize. The exercise is to write a brief paper about a troubled person you know. (You may simply write this paper in your mind, but if you do put it on paper it might fit an assignment in your psychology or English class.)

An Exercise in Understanding

Write about someone you know fairly well (a relative, friend, classmate, or coworker) who seems unable to enjoy the normal human satisfactions of love and work (Freud's definition of emotional disturbance). The reasons for the troubled person's distress could be anything from the psychological problems of severe depression or schizophrenia to the social problems of alcoholism or the trauma of child abuse. What you already know about the person is enough for this exercise.

How clear a picture of your troubled person can you draw? Include a description of personality, tell the life history briefly, and offer suggestions for treatment.

Your conclusion should reinforce two points: (1) your theory about why the person became troubled, and (2) what the story of this troubled person teaches us about human behavior — what lessons it has for our own lives.

You could use this exercise as an opportunity to think and write about your own life and problems. Even though you probably aren't a troubled person, you may have private doubts and worries or painful experiences you would benefit from exploring.

Effective Student Tip 23

Try, Try Again

I envied my brilliant classmates. I felt guilty when I read about the successes of others. "How did they do it?" I asked when I read about a new book or scientific breakthrough or business achievement. Now (taking nothing away from the few true geniuses among us) I realize that most successful people just kept trying.

Newly famous stars often ruefully acknowledge their "overnight success." They know they have been waiting tables and taking every part they could get for years before their big break. Perhaps they are uncomfortable with fame because they know it is illusory. The reality is the love for their craft that kept them working at it no matter how few the rewards.

Again and again, when you read about a new discovery or a great accomplishment, you find that a previously unheralded person, probably not much different from you or me, has been working at it for years. What these admirable people do have is persistence, a force psychology could do well to study in greater depth.

The moral is simply this: most great achievements result from a combination of an idea that won't let go of the person, sufficient time to work and rework the idea, and persistence in seeing it through. If at first you don't succeed...

Your response...

Looking back at your life, are there goals you wish you had pursued with greater determination?

Key Terms

You're in med school now. You've really got to work to learn all these key terms, but if you can do it you will gain a whole new world of understanding.

antidepressant drugs

antisocial personality disorder

atypical neuroleptic drugs

Beck's cognitive theory of depression

biological theory of depression

bipolar I disorder

case study

catatonic schizophrenia

dependent personality disorder

diathesis stress theory of schizophrenia

disorganized schizophrenia

dissociative amnesia

dissociative disorder

dissociative fugue

dissociative identity disorder

dopamine theory

dysthymic disorder

electroconvulsive therapy (ECT)

genetic marker

hallucinations

histrionic personality disorder

lithium

major depressive disorder

mood disorder

negative symptoms of schizophrenia

neuroleptic drugs

obsessive-compulsive disorder

paranoid personality disorder

paranoid schizophrenia

personality disorder

positive symptoms of schizophrenia

psychosocial factors

schizophrenia

schizotypical personality disorder

tardive dyskinesia

type I schizophrenia

type II schizophrenia

typical neuroleptics

Outline

- *INTRODUCTION*

  ☐ *How do Rod Plotnik's two examples differ qualitatively from those he used in the previous module?*

  1. Mood disorder

  2. Schizophrenia

A. *Mood Disorders*

  ☐ *Do you ever feel depressed? How does it affect you? How do you fight it?*

  1. **Mood disorder**

     a. Major depression (**major depressive disorder**)

     b. Bipolar disorder (**bipolar I disorder**)

     c. **Dysthymic disorder**

2. Causes of depression

    a. Biological factors

        (1) **Biological theory of depression**

        (2) Genetic factors

        (3) Neurological factors

    b. Psychological factors

        (1) **Psychosocial factors**

        (2) How much effect does stress have?

        (3) Stressful life events

3. Treatment of mood disorders

    a. Major depressive and dysthymic disorder

        (1) **Antidepressant drugs**

        (2) Prozac

        (3) Psychotherapy

    b. Bipolar I disorder

        (1) **Lithium**

        (2) Mania

B. *Electroconvulsive Therapy*

☐ *Why is ECT, which seems to work, such a controversial form of therapy?*

1. **Electroconvulsive therapy (ECT)**

2. Use of ECT

3. Effectiveness of ECT

    a. Results

    b. Modern ECT

    c. Potential risks

C. *Personality Disorders*

1. **Personality disorder**

2. Specific personality disorders

☐ *No, you're not sick, but which personality disorder is closest to your own personality?*

   a. **Paranoid personality disorder**

   b. **Schizotypical personality disorder**

   c. **Histrionic personality disorder**

   d. **Obsessive-compulsive personality disorder**

   e. **Dependent personality disorder**

   f. **Antisocial personality disorder**

3. Psychopath: antisocial personality disorder

4. Antisocial personality disorder: causes and treatment

   a. Causes

      (1) Psychological factors

      (2) Biological factors

   b. Treatment

D. *Schizophrenia*

1. Definition of **schizophrenia**

2. Schizophrenia symptoms

   a. Disorders of thought

   b. Disorders of attention

   c. Disorders of perception (**hallucinations**)

   d. Motor disorders

   e. Emotional (affective) disorders

3. Subcategories of schizophrenia

   a. **Paranoid schizophrenia**

   b. **Disorganized schizophrenia**

   c. **Catatonic schizophrenia**

4. Chances of recovery from schizophrenia

    d. **Type I schizophrenia**

    e. **Type II schizophrenia**

5. Causes of schizophrenia

    a. Biological factors: genetic predisposition

        (1) Genain quadruplets

        (2) **Genetic marker**

    b. Biological factors: brain changes

        (1) Ventricle size

        (2) Thalamus

        (3) Frontal lobe

    c. Environmental factors: diathesis theory

        (1) Environmental risk factors (50%)

        (2) **Diathesis stress theory of schizophrenia**

6. Treatment: typical neuroleptics

    a. **Positive symptoms of schizophrenia**

    b. **Negative symptoms of schizophrenia**

    c. **Neuroleptic drugs**

    d. **Typical neuroleptics**

    e. **Dopamine theory**

7. Treatment: atypical neuroleptics

    a. **Atypical neuroleptic drugs**

    b. Clozapine: second major advance

8. Problems with neuroleptics

    a. Side effects: typical neuroleptics (**tardive dyskinesia**)

    b. Side effects: atypical neuroleptics

    c. Relapse rate and long-term outcome

        (1) Typical neuroleptics

        (2) Atypical neuroleptics

E. Dissociative Disorders

☐ *What features do all the dissociative disorders have in common? (And don't say you forget.)*

1. **Dissociative disorder**

2. Three common dissociative disorders

    a. **Dissociative amnesia**

    b. **Dissociative fugue**

    c. **Dissociative identity disorder**

        (1) Occurrence and causes

        (2) Explanations and controversy

F. Cultural Diversity: Interpreting Symptoms

1. Spirit possession – cultural factors and symptoms

2. Therapists' expectations and gender roles – cultural factors and occurrence

    a. Dissociative identity disorder

    b. Major depression

G. Research Focus: Learning from Case Studies

1. Research question: what do we learn from case studies?

    a. **Case study**

    b. Three case studies

        (1) Chuck Elliot: bipolar I disorder

        (2) Michael McCabe: schizophrenia

        (3) Dick Cavett: major depressive disorder

2. Advantages and disadvantages of case studies

H. *Application: Dealing with Mild Depression*

   1. Mild depression

   2. **Beck's cognitive theory of depression**

   3. Maintaining or overcoming mild depression

      a. Problem: poor social skills; program: improve social skills

      b. Problem: lack of social support; program: increase social support

      c. Problem: negative thoughts; program: eliminate negative thoughts

Language Enhancement Guide

IDIOMATIC EXPRESSIONS AND CULTURAL TERMS

The following are idiomatic expressions and cultural terms found in the module. The definition given on the right is for the way the expression is used in this module.

was at her wits' end (487) = was confused and upset

hit bottom (488) = was at its lowest point

a ground breaking study (490) = a study with important new methods or findings

bewildering (496) = confusing

(out of my) funk (504) = depression

VOCABULARY BUILDING: Word Analysis

Instructions: Analyze each term from memory using the procedures described earlier:

Word	Meaning
unipolar (488)	
bipolar (488)	
relapse (490)	
reduce (491)	
pretreatment (491)	
impaired (492)	
antisocial (492)	
disobey (493)	
decreased (496)	
neurotransmitter (497)	
atypical (497)	
involuntary (498)	
dissociative (500)	
amnesia (500)	

GUESSING FROM CONTEXT

You won't find the following words and expressions from this module in the textbook Glossary, but they are useful in reading, writing, and talking about psychology and other academic subjects. See if you can guess their meanings by studying their contexts (their relationship to the words around them).

To do this, find the word or expression in your textbook and guess its meaning using the clues in the context. You may find clues in an explanation that immediately follows the word, in a synonym that appears nearby, or in the form of examples. After you have defined the terms, ask a native speaker what they mean or look them up in a dictionary to see if your guesses were correct.

episodes (487)

continuum (488)

considerable (489)

intriguing (489)

currently (489)

stigma (490)

dubious (491)

predispose (495)

complimentary (489)

True-False

_____   1. The most serious mood disorder is major depression.

_____   2. At the opposite pole from depression is mania.

_____   3. Rod Steiger knew what caused his depression, so he was able to cure it himself.

_____   4. The treatment of choice for bipolar I disorder and mania is lithium.

_____   5. The most common treatment for major depression is electroconvulsive therapy (ECT).

_____   6. People suffering from antisocial personality disorder are extremely shy and attempt to avoid other people.

_____   7. People suffering from Type I schizophrenia (more positive symptoms) have a better chance for recovery than those suffering from Type II schizophrenia (more negative symptoms).

_____   8. Antipsychotic drugs are effective, but they have serious side effects.

_____   9. Dissociative disorders and how they work: dissociative amnesia, forget; dissociative fugue, flee; dissociative identity disorder, split off.

_____   10. Although many people experience occasional mild depression, there is little they can do except tough it out.

Flashcards

Match each key term to the definition given in the textbook.

_____ 1. antidepressant drugs

_____ 2. antisocial personality disorder

_____ 3. bipolar I disorder

_____ 4. catatonic schizophrenia

_____ 5. diathesis stress theory of schizophrenia

_____ 6. disorganized schizophrenia

_____ 7. dissociative amnesia

_____ 8. dissociative fugue

_____ 9. dissociative identity disorder

_____ 10. dopamine theory

_____ 11. electroconvulsive therapy (ECT)

_____ 12. genetic marker

_____ 13. histrionic personality disorder

_____ 14. lithium

_____ 15. major depressive disorder

_____ 16. neuroleptic drugs

_____ 17. obsessive-compulsive disorder

_____ 18. paranoid personality disorder

_____ 19. paranoid schizophrenia

_____ 20. tardive dyskinesia

a. mineral salt, most effective treatment of bipolar I disorder because it reduces manic episodes

b. characterized by periods of wild excitement or periods of rigid, prolonged immobility

c. continually being in a bad mood, no interest in anything, getting no pleasure from activities

d. suddenly, unexpectedly travelling away from home and being unable to recall one's past

e. characterized by auditory hallucinations or delusions of being persecuted or of grandeur

f. used to treat serious mental disorders like schizophrenia by affecting neurotransmitters

g. an intense interest in being orderly, a perfectionist, and having control

h. marked by bizarre ideas, confused speech, childish behavior, great emotional swings

i. slow, involuntary, uncontrollable movements, twiching of mouth, lips from use of neuroleptics

j. administration of mild electrical current that passes through the brain and causes a seizure

k. act by increasing levels of a specific group of neurotransmitters believed to regulate mood

l. characterized by being unable to recall important personal information or events

m. characterized by fluctuating between episodes of depression and mania

n. a pattern of disregarding or violating rights of other without feeling guilt or remorse

o. a pattern of distrust and suspiciousness and perceiving others as having evil motives

p. says some people have a genetic predisposition interacting with life stressors to cause illness

q. says dopamine neurotransmitter system is somehow overactive and causes symptoms

r. characterized by excessive emotionality and attention seeking

s. presence of two or more distinct identities, each with its own pattern of perception and thought

t. identifiable gene, genes, or specific segment of chromosome directly linked to a trait or disease

Multiple-Choice

_____ 1. Rod Plotnik uses the example of Rod Steiger's illness to show that
   a. alcoholism is a huge psychiatric problem in America
   b. depression is a terrifying, crippling disorder
   c. anyone can become depressed at almost any time
   d. creative people are more likely to become mentally ill

_____ 2. Which one of the following is *not* a mood disorder?
   a. major depression
   b. bipolar I disorder
   c. antisocial personality disorder
   d. dysthymic disorder

_____ 3. Science now says the cause of depression is
   a. mainly biological
   b. mainly psychological
   c. mainly personal (optimistic versus pessimistic)
   d. both biological and psychological

_____ 4. When psychotherapy was compared to drug therapy in treating major depression, a surprising finding was that
   a. drug therapy was much more effective
   b. psychotherapy was much more effective
   c. neither had much positive effect
   d. both were effective, but neither prevented relapses

_____ 5. The most common treatment for bipolar I disorder and mania is
   a. ECT
   b. clozapine
   c. lithium
   d. dopamine

_____ 6. ECT is a controversial treatment for depression because it
   a. has serious side effects, such as memory loss
   b. is based on the use of antidepressant drugs
   c. has no effect at all on many patients
   d. is prescribed by psychiatrists but not by clinical psychologists

_____ 7. Jeffrey Dahmer represented an extreme case of _____ personality disorder
   a. histrionic
   b. paranoid
   c. antisocial
   d. schizotypical

_____ 8. The highest percentage of mental hospital inpatients are there because of
   a. major depression
   b. schizophrenia
   c. antisocial personality disorder
   d. dissociative amnesia

_____ 9. Which of the following are *not* symptoms of schizophrenia?
   a. disorders of thought
   b. disorders of attention
   c. disorders of perception
   d. disorders of moral character

_____ 10. Rod Plotnik tells us about the famous Genain quadruplets to illustrate the fact that
   a. science is filled with amazing coincidences
   b. there must be a genetic factor in schizophrenia
   c. children can "learn" to be schizophrenic from close contact with family members who are ill
   d. schizophrenia strikes in a random, unpredictable fashion

_____ 11. According to the _____ theory, schizophrenia is caused by abnormalities in neurotransmitters in the brain
   a. dopamine
   b. diathesis stress
   c. genetic marker
   d. tardive dyskinesia

_____ 12. The difference between dissociative amnesia and dissociative fugue is that
   a. in the former you stay in contact with reality; in the latter you become schizophrenic
   b. in the former you have memory gaps; in the latter you may wander away and assume a new identity
   c. in the former you forget more than in the latter
   d. these are really two different terms for the same experience

_____ 13. The case of "Burt Tate," who turned out to be a missing person named Gene Saunders, illustrates
   a. dissociative fugue
   b. dissociative amnesia
   c. dissociative identity disorder
   d. multiple personality disorder

_____ 14. An underlying cause often reported in dissociative identity disorder is
   a. physical trauma, such as a head injury
   b. unstable parents who give their children mixed messages about what they expect
   c. a flighty personality along with a tendency to overdramatize every situation
   d. severe physical or sexual abuse during early childhood

_____ 15. Which one of the following is *not* good advice if you are trying to break out of the vicious circle of mild depression?
   a. focus on positive events
   b. don't think about your problems
   c. give yourself credit
   d. take some action

Answers for Module 23

True-False	Flashcards	Multiple-Choice
1. T	1. k	1. b
2. T	2. n	2. c
3. F	3. m	3. d
4. T	4. b	4. d
5. F	5. p	5. c
6. F	6. h	6. a
7. T	7. l	7. c
8. T	8. d	8. b
9. T	9. s	9. d
10. F	10. q	10. b
	11. j	11. a
	12. t	12. b
	13. r	13. a
	14. a	14. d
	15. c	15. b
	16. f	
	17. g	
	18. o	
	19. e	
	20. i	

Therapies

The Contribution of Psychodynamic Psychology to Therapy

Psychotherapy is one of the great inventions of this century. Whether you consider it an art or a science, it is a young and constantly evolving process. Rod Plotnik discusses four current approaches to psychotherapy, each with numerous varieties and special techniques.

At the heart of most forms of psychotherapy lies a basic assumption and a fundamental process that come from psychodynamic psychology and the work of a great pioneer, good old You Know Who. Both the assumption and the technique are inherent in his theory of dreams, about which you read way back in Module 7.

A Model for Understanding Psychotherapy... and Life

The key idea is the distinction between manifest content and latent content. The manifest content of a dream is the story (however bizarre) we remember in the morning. The latent content is the disguised, unconscious wish hidden in the apparently meaningless story of the dream. The challenge to the dreamer, perhaps a patient in psychotherapy, is to gain insight into that latent content because it is a direct line [Our Hero called it the *via regia*, or royal road] to the unconscious. With the help of the therapist, the patient examines thoughts and feelings connected to the dream in the expectation that these associations will suggest an underlying meaning, a meaning that provides insight into the patient's 'dynamics,' or psychological life.

This key idea has broad implications. Freud saw dreams and other unconscious acts (slips of the tongue, losing things, forgetting, accidents) as miniature neuroses, reflecting the larger neuroses of which we all have more than a few. Therefore, we can interpret *any* behavior like a dream. Here's the formula. First, examine the behavior (a comment, an act, even a thought) very carefully. Exactly what happened? That's the manifest content. Next, search the manifest content for clues about what the *latent* content might be. Why did you forget the assignment? Lose your keys? Call your Honey the wrong name? Bingo! Insight into how your unconscious mind works.

This fundamental idea of psychodynamic psychology underlies most forms of therapy, and can be used as a model for understanding almost anything in life from the meaning of Shakespeare's plays to why your roommate is driving you crazy. Just answer two questions: What is the manifest content? What is the latent content?

Effective Student Tip 24

Take Teachers, Not Courses

Take at least a few courses far from your major area of study. Some advisors will urge you to take only courses that fit into your major, but that can be a mistake. One of the purposes of higher education is to broaden your horizons and show you worlds you scarcely know exist. When else will you have the opportunity to investigate ancient history, nutrition, figure drawing, astronomy, women's literature, and other fascinating subjects that aren't required for graduation?

Graduate students, who have been through it all and know all there is to know (just ask them), often say you should "take teachers, not courses." What they mean is that you should sign up for professors with reputations as especially stimulating teachers, without too much regard for how well the interesting courses fit into your official program.

You will come to know quite a bit about the faculty at your school. Some professors will begin to stand out as people you would like to study with and get to know. Try to give yourself at least a few of these experiences. You might learn more from an inspired, creative teacher in an unrequired course than from a dull teacher in the course that fits so neatly into your major.

Your response...

If neither time nor money mattered, what courses would you like to take just for your own interest?

Key Terms

Most of the key terms in this module are closely related to terms you have already learned in other modules.

behavior therapies

behavior therapy [behavior modification]

client-centered therapy

clinical psychologists

cognitive therapy

cognitive-behavior therapy

common factors

community mental health centers

counseling psychologists

deinstitutionalization

dream interpretation

eclectic approach

eye movement desensitization and reprocessing (EMDR)

free association

insight therapies

intrusive thoughts

medical therapy

meta-analysis

moral therapy

neuroses

phenothiazines

psychiatrists

psychoanalysis

psychodynamic psychotherapy

psychotherapy

resistance

short-term dynamic psychotherapy

systematic desensitization

transference

Outline

- *INTRODUCTION*

  □ *What parts did "Anna O" and "Little Albert" play in the history of psychotherapy?*

- A. *Historical Background*

  1. **Psychotherapy**

  2. Early treatment, reforms, and going backward

     a. Early treatments

     b. Reform movement (Dorothea Dix and **moral therapy**)

     c. Going backward

  3. **Phenothiazines** and deinstitutionalization

     a. Phenothiazines

     b. **Deinstitutionalization**

  4. Community mental health centers

     a. **Community mental health centers**

     b. New therapists and new approaches

B. Questions About Psychotherapy

1. Do I need professional help?

2. Are there different kinds of therapists?

   a. **Psychiatrists**

   b. **Clinical psychologists**

   c. **Counseling psychologists**

3. Are there different approaches?

   a. **Insight therapies**

   b. **Behavior therapy**

   c. **Medical therapy**

   d. **Eclectic approach**

4. How effective is psychotherapy?

   a. **Meta-analysis**

   b. Major findings

C. Insight Therapies

   ☐ *Rod Plotnik quotes from sessions illustrating the three insight therapies. Can you describe the different emphasis and style of each approach?*

1. **Psychoanalysis** (Sigmund Freud)

   a. Psychoanalysis: three major assumptions

      (1) Unconscious conflicts

      (2) Techniques of free association, dream interpretation, and analysis of slips of the tongue

      (3) Transfer strong emotions onto therapist

   b. Psychoanalytic therapy session

      (1) What happens in psychoanalysis?

      (2) What does the analyst do?

         (a) Free association

         (b) Interpretation

         (c) Unconscious conflicts

   c. Techniques to reveal the unconscious

     (1) **Neuroses**

     (2) Rat man: **free association**

     (3) Wolf-man: **dream interpretation**

   d. Case studies: Anna O., Rat Man and Wolf-Man

   e. Problems during psychoanalysis

     (1) Rat man: **transference**

     (2) Wolf-man: **resistance**

     (3) **Short-term dynamic psychotherapy**

   f. Psychoanalysis: evaluation

     (1) Evaluation

     (2) New directions (**psychodynamic psychotherapy**)

     (3) Popularity

     (4) Conclusion

2. **Client-centered therapy** (Carl Rogers)

   a. What happens in client-centered therapy?

   b. Origins of client-centered therapy

   c. Important factors in client-centered therapy

     (1) Empathy

     (2) Positive regard

     (3) Genuineness

   d. How effective is client-centered therapy?

3. **Cognitive therapy** (Aaron Beck)

   a. What happens in cognitive therapy?

   b. Origins of cognitive therapy

c. Important factors in cognitive therapy

    (1) Overgeneralization

    (2) Polarized thinking

    (3) Selective attention

d. How effective is client-centered therapy?

D. Behavior Therapy

☐ *In what ways is behavior therapy radically different from the insight therapies?*

1. **Behavior therapy [behavior modification]** (Joseph Wolpe)

    a. What happens in behavior therapy?

        (1) **Systematic desensitization**

        (2) Unconditioning process

            (a) Relaxation

            (b) Stimulus hierarchy

            (c) Exposure

            (d) Exposure: imagined or in vivo

    b. Origins of behavior therapy

    c. Important factors in behavior therapy

    d. How effective is behavior therapy?

2. **Cognitive-behavior therapy**

    a. Combining cognitive methods and behavioral methods

    b. Examples of therapies

E. Review: Evaluation of Approaches

☐ *Another great Plotnik summary! Can you master the basic elements of each approach?*

1. Four approaches to therapy

   a. Psychoanalysis

      (1) Background

      (2) Basic assumption

      (3) Techniques

   b. Client-centered therapy

      (1) Background

      (2) Basic assumption

      (3) Techniques

   c. Cognitive therapy

      (1) Background

      (2) Basic assumption

      (3) Techniques

   d. Behavior therapy

      (1) Background

      (2) Basic assumption

      (3) Techniques

2. Evaluation of different approaches

   a. How effective is therapy in general?

   b. Is one therapy approach more effective than another?

      (1) Small differences in specific disorders

      (2) **Common factors**

F. *Cultural Diversity: A Healer*

☐ *Hmmm... If the balian is generally successful, what does that suggest about the successes of Western psychotherapy?*

1. Case study: witchcraft

2. The balian, a local healer in Bali

   a. Healer's diagnosis: evil wind spirit

   b. Healer's treatment: exorcism and healing smoke

   c. Eastern healer versus Western therapist: effectiveness of treatment

      (1) Placebo effect

      (2) Common factors

G. *Research Focus: EMDR — Another New Therapy*

1. Research question: is EMDR an effective treatment for trauma?

   a. **Eye movement desensitization and reprocessing (EMDR)**

   b. Evidence from case studies

   c. Evidence from experiments

2. Results and conclusions

H. *Application: Cognitive-Behavior Techniques*

1. Thought stopping

   a. Self-monitoring of **intrusive thoughts**

   b. Thought stopping (thought-stopping procedure)

   c. Thought substitution (thought-substitution procedure)

2. Thought substitution

   a. Self-monitoring of irrational thoughts and rational thoughts

   b. Constructing matching list of rational thoughts

   c. Practicing thought substitution

3. Treatment for insomnia

   a. How can you stop worrying and go to sleep?

   b. A program for establishing an optimal sleep pattern

Language Enhancement Guide

IDIOMATIC EXPRESSIONS AND CULTURAL TERMS

The following are idiomatic expressions and cultural terms found in the module. Some of them have more than one meaning; the definition given here on the right is for the way the author uses the expression in this module. Remember that these words, like all words, can have different meanings in other contexts.

go away by itself (513) = stop

making blanket judgments (519) = making judgments without enough supporting evidence; overgeneralizing

kickstart (520) = a rapid start

VOCABULARY BUILDING: Word Analysis

Instructions: Analyze each term from memory using the procedures described earlier:

Word	Meaning
psychotherapy (512)	
insight (513)	
transference (516)	
repressed (515)	
projecting (516)	
resistance (516)	
disapproval (518)	
desensitize (521)	
noncompliance (522)	
intrusive (528)	

GUESSING FROM CONTEXT

You won't find the following words and expressions from this module in the textbook Glossary, but they are useful in reading, writing, and talking about psychology and other academic subjects. See if you can guess their meanings by studying their contexts (their relationship to the words around them).

persisted (509)

wretched (510)

reluctance (512)

assumption (514)

initially (520)

disillusioned 520)

progressive (521)

True-False

_____ 1. The history of therapeutic effort is a story of continual improvement in the treatment of the mentally ill.

_____ 2. Psychotherapists today are more likely to see themselves as eclectic than as adhering to one of the traditional approaches to psychotherapy.

_____ 3. The basic assumption of psychoanalysis is that since maladaptive behaviors are *learned*, they can be unlearned through training.

_____ 4. Transference is the process by which a patient carefully describes his or her problems so the therapist can analyze and solve them.

_____ 5. Although Freud is widely criticized, psychoanalytic ideas continue to be a force in psychotherapy today.

_____ 6. Rod Plotnik quotes from therapy sessions representing the major approaches; the point is that they all sound pretty much alike.

_____ 7. The systematic desensitization technique is essentially an unlearning experience.

_____ 8. Aaron Beck's cognitive therapy assumes that we have automatic negative thoughts that we say to ourselves without much notice.

_____ 9. Carl Rogers' client-centered therapy avoids giving directions, advice, or disapproval.

_____ 10. Research suggests that the new technique called Eye Movement Desensitization and Reprocessing (EMDR) will eventually replace all the traditional psychotherapies.

Flashcards *for psych majors only...*

The Story of Psychotherapy: You met many famous and intriguing characters from the history of psychology in this module, people like Anna O., Rat Man, and Little Albert (almost sounds like a circus, doesn't it?). If you were to arrange these names in historical order (as I have done below) and add what each contributed, you could construct a capsule history of the development of modern psychotherapy.

Try it. Match each name to the most appropriate phrase. As you do so, see if you can tell yourself the story of how the four strands of modern psychotherapy emerged, and how they differ from each other.

_____ 1. Dorothea Dix	a.	reduced hysterical symptoms by talking about them
_____ 2. Anna O.	b.	publicized the cruel treatment of "lunatics"
_____ 3. Sigmund Freud	c.	developed cognitive therapy for depressive thoughts
_____ 4. Rat Man	d.	developed a very positive client-centered therapy
_____ 5. Wolf-Man	e.	interpretation of his dreams revealed sexual fears
_____ 6. John B. Watson	f.	worked out a therapy called systematic desensitization
_____ 7. Little Albert	g.	believed emotional problems are conditioned (learned)
_____ 8. Carl Rogers	h.	conditioned to fear a rat in a famous experiment
_____ 9. Joseph Wolpe	i.	free association revealed his repressed memories
_____ 10. Aaron Beck	j.	developed psychoanalysis — the first psychotherapy

Flashcards

Match each key term to the definition given in the textbook.

_____ 1. behavior therapies

_____ 2. behavior therapy [behavior modification]

_____ 3. client-centered therapy

_____ 4. clinical psychologists

_____ 5. cognitive therapy

_____ 6. common factors

_____ 7. counseling psychologists

_____ 8. deinstitutionalization

_____ 9. dream interpretation

_____ 10. eclectic approach

_____ 11. free association

_____ 12. insight therapies

_____ 13. medical therapies

_____ 14. moral therapy

_____ 15. phenothiazines

_____ 16. psychiatrists

_____ 17. psychoanalysis

_____ 18. resistance

_____ 19. systematic desensitization

_____ 20. transference

a. involve use of psychoactive drugs to treat mental disorders by affecting neurotransmitters

b. reluctance to work through feelings, recognize unconscious conflicts and repressed thoughts

c. first group of drugs to reduce schizophrenic symptoms by blocking the effects of dopamine

d. involve the application of principles of learning to change client's specific problem behaviors

e. go to medical school, earn MD, take psychiatric residency and additional training

f. client is gradually exposed to the feared object while simultaneously practicing relaxation

g. technique that encourages clients to talk about any thoughts or images that enter their heads

h. release of patients from mental hospitals and their return to community to live fuller lives

i. belief that mental patients could be helped to function better by providing humane treatment

j. involves combining several or more techniques from many different approaches

k. assumes that our automatic negative thoughts distort perception, influence feelings, behavior

l. uses principles of conditioning to change disruptive behaviors and improve functioning

m. therapist shows compassion and positive regard in helping client reach full potential

n. search for hidden meanings, symbols providing clues to unconscious thoughts and desires

o. process by which patient expresses strong emotions toward therapist, a substitute figure

p. go to graduate school of psych or education and earn Ph.D., with work in a counseling setting

q. supportive and trusting relationship, accepting atmosphere, motivation to work on changing

r. involve therapist and client talking about the client's symptoms, problems, to identify cause

s. core idea is that repressed thoughts in the unconscious cause conflicts and symptoms

t. go to graduate school of psychology and earn Ph.D., including one year in clinical setting

Multiple-Choice

_____ 1. Rod Plotnik begins the module with the story of "Anna O." to make the point that
   a. Freud had some notable failures as well as famous successes
   b. talking about your problems seems to help
   c. the real credit for inventing psychoanalysis should go to Dr. Breuer
   d. talking won't help unless the client also does something positive

_____ 2. John B. Watson's famous experiment with Little Albert was designed to show that
   a. ethical standards of psychological research are much more stringent today
   b. psychological problems affect babies as well as children and adults
   c. fear of rats is almost natural and may be inborn
   d. emotional problems can be viewed as learned behavior

_____ 3. In the history of the treatment of mental illness, Dorothea Dix is famous for
   a. charging admission to watch the crazy antics of the "lunatics"
   b. inventing early treatment techniques like the strait jacket and bleeding
   c. publicizing the terrible living conditions and poor treatment of the mentally ill
   d. emptying the mental hospitals of almost half of their patients

_____ 4. The discovery of antipsychotic drugs led directly to
   a. deinstitutionalization
   b. the reform movement
   c. reinstitutionalization
   d. the community mental health center

_____ 5. In order to become a _____ you need a medical degree and a residency with further training in psychopathology and treatment
   a. clinical psychologist
   b. counseling psychologist
   c. social worker
   d. psychiatrist

_____ 6. When asked which approach they use in therapy, a majority of psychologists indicated a preference for the _____ approach
   a. psychodynamic
   b. behavioral
   c. eclectic
   d. cognitive

_____ 7. How effective is psychotherapy? Studies suggest that psychotherapy is
   a. an effective treatment for many mental disorders
   b. no more effective than just waiting
   c. no more effective than doing nothing
   d. an effective treatment, but only if continued for more than a year

_____ 8. The only one of the following who was a patient of Freud's was
   a. Anna O.
   b. Rat Man
   c. Dorothea Dix
   d. Joseph Breuer

_____ 9. Which one of the following is *not* a technique used in psychoanalysis?
   a. free association
   b. dream analysis
   c. analysis of performance
   d. analysis of transference

_____ 10. Rod Plotnik's fascinating example of the balian, a local healer in Bali, suggests that the success of Western psychotherapy
   a. demonstrates the superiority of modern medicine
   b. results from its assumption that the problem lies inside the sufferer
   c. depends on having intelligent and educated patients
   d. owes much to what are called common factors in psychotherapy

_____ 11. Which one of the following is *not* a step in the systematic desensitization procedure?
   a. relaxation
   b. stimulus hierarchy
   c. stimulus sensitizing
   d. exposure

_____ 12. Aaron Beck discovered that depressed people tend to interpret the world through
   a. carefully planned negative statements
   b. thoughtless repetitions of what other people believe
   c. secretly hostile beliefs
   d. automatic negative thoughts

_____ 13. In his cognitive therapy, Beck attempts to make clients aware of
   a. the importance of education in the contemporary world
   b. adaptive thought patterns like open-mindedness, acceptance, love, and will power
   c. maladaptive thought patterns like overgeneralization, polarized thinking, and selective attention
   d. how much better they could be if they would just "think about it"

_____ 14. The central assumption of Carl Rogers' client-centered therapy is that
   a. each person has the tendency and capacity to develop his or her full potential
   b. psychotherapy must be freely available in community mental health centers
   c. we must struggle to overcome our basic human selfishness and hostility
   d. therapy should focus on real behavior, not vague thoughts and feelings

_____ 15. Which one of the following is *not* a step in the thought substitution procedure?
   a. through self-monitoring, write a list of your irrational thoughts
   b. compose a matching list of rational thoughts
   c. practice substituting rational thoughts whenever you have irrational ones
   d. if you catch yourself thinking irrationally, administer a predetermined punishment, like no TV that night

Answers for Module 24

True-False
1. F
2. T
3. F
4. F
5. T
6. F
7. T
8. T
9. T
10. F

Flashcards
1. d
2. l
3. m
4. t
5. k
6. q
7. p
8. h
9. n
10. j
11. g
12. r
13. a
14. i
15. c
16. e
17. s
18. b
19. f
20. o

Multiple-Choice
1. b
2. d
3. c
4. a
5. d
6. c
7. a
8. b
9. c
10. d
11. c
12. d
13. c
14. a
15. d

The Story of Psychotherapy Quiz

1. b   2. a   3. j   4. i   5. e   6. g   7. h   8. d   9. f   10. c

Social Psychology

The Material That Was Difficult Because It Seemed Easy

Well, not really easy — you'll have to study this module as carefully as the others — but obvious, in a sense. One of the difficulties in studying social psychology is that so many of the facts and ideas it presents seem like things you already know. That makes it hard to get a handle on what to "learn." Here's an idea that may make it easier.

Because you are a human being, you have been a social psychologist all your life. If there is one essential human skill, it is how to live with each other. I don't mean this in a preachy way, but in the sense that our instincts, what few we have, tell us very little about interacting with others. Therefore, we must learn to observe, understand, and predict what other people will do (and what we will do) in any given situation. We soon become experts in human interaction. See? You've been studying this stuff all your life.

The beauty of social psychology is that it can take us outside ourselves and help us see our behavior more objectively, and hence more clearly. Such awareness, which social psychology owes to anthropology and sociology, helps correct the tendency of psychology to focus too much on individual, internal factors. There's a price you pay for this insight, however. Theories in social psychology typically involve fancy names and complicated explanations. Don't be afraid. The social psychologists you'll study are talking about what you do every day. Try to understand it that way. Give yourself credit for understanding what seems obvious. Translate what does not seem clear into the language of your own experience.

The Cross-Cultural Approach to Psychology

If you counted them, you would discover that there are more key terms in this module than almost any other. Another module with almost the same number of key terms is Rod Plotnik's presentation of "The Incredible Nervous System." And that's no accident. Just as Module 4 helped define the psychobiological approach to psychology, Module 25 defines the other end of the spectrum — the cross-cultural approach (some might call it the sociocultural approach). In the earlier module, we were almost off the chart into biology, hence the need for many new terms. Here, we are deep into sociology, and once again need a whole new vocabulary.

One problem sociologists have is that they are talking about things that are utterly familiar, like attitudes, helping, groups, and aggression. Sometimes it almost seems like they invent fancy names for their concepts because what they are describing is so familiar. But they wouldn't do that, would they?

Effective Student Tip 25

Honor Your Need to be Effective

Most of my tips have been quite specific, because I wanted them to be actions you could take immediately. If they worked, you won a victory here and there and perhaps did better in the course. I hope they also contribute to a body of strategies that will make you a stronger student in the courses still to come.

In truth, however, I have an even larger goal in mind. That goal is for you to begin to understand that the need to be effective is the essence of your human motivation. If I am right, you feel a need to be effective not only in your schoolwork but more importantly in everything you do.

My argument is simply this: We humans have almost no instincts to guide us. The only way we can tell whether what we are doing is right is the extent to which it works for us. We know our actions are working when they make the world give back what we want and need. In other words, the extent to which the actions we take are effective becomes the measure of our happiness and satisfaction in life.

Whatever situation you may be in, school or employment or relationship, honor your need to be effective by paying attention to how well your actions are working for you and how good you feel about what you are doing.

Your response...

I am convinced that we all have a constant need to be effective. Do you feel that need in yourself?

Key Terms

These terms are especially important because they help define the cross-cultural approach to psychology.

actor-observer effect

aggressive behavior

altruism

arousal-cost-reward model of helping

attitude

attributions

bystander effect

catharsis

central route for persuasion

cognitive dissonance

cognitive miser model

compliance

conformity

consensus

consistency

counterattitudinal behavior

covariation model

crowd

debriefing

decision stage model of helping

deindividuation

diffusion of responsibility theory

discrimination

distinctiveness

evaluative function

event schemas [scripts]

external attributions

foot-in-the-door technique

frustration-aggression hypothesis

fundamental attribution error

group cohesion

group norms

group polarization

groups

groupthink

informational influence theory

internal attributions

interpreting function

modified frustration-aggression hypothesis

obedience

peripheral route for persuasion

person perception

person schemas

predisposing function

prejudice

prosocial behavior [helping]

role schemas

schemas

self schemas

self-perception theory

self-serving bias

social cognition

social comparison theory

social facilitation

social inhibition

social learning theory

social psychology

socially oriented group

stereotypes

task oriented group

Outline

- ## INTRODUCTION

  ☐ *What basic areas of social psychology does Rod Plotnik illustrate with his examples of Lawrence Graham and David Koresh?*

  1. **Social psychology**

  2. **Social cognition**

A. Perceiving Others

1. **Person perception**

   a. Physical appearance

   b. Need to explain

   c. Influence on behavior

   d. Effects of race

2. Physical appearance

   a. What makes a face attractive

   b. Does an attractive face help?

   c. Psychological characteristics contributing to attractiveness

3. **Stereotypes**

   a. Development and kinds of stereotypes

      (1) **Prejudice**

      (2) **Discrimination**

   b. Functions of stereotypes

      (1) Source of information

      (2) Thought-saving device

4. **Schemas**

   a. Kinds of schemas

      (1) **Person schemas**

      (2) **Role schemas**

      (3) **Event schemas [scripts]**

      (4) **Self schemas**

   b. Advantages and disadvantages of schemas

      (1) Advantage

      (2) Disadvantage

B. *Attributions*

    1. **Attribution**

    2. Internal versus external attributions (Fritz Heider)

        a. **Internal attributions**

        b. **External attributions**

    3. Kelley's model of covariation

        a. **Covariation model** (Harold Kelley)

            (1) **Consensus**

            (2) **Consistency**

            (3) **Distinctiveness**

        b. Applying Kelley's covariation model

    4. Biases and errors in attribution

        a. **Cognitive miser model**

        b. Common biases in making attributions

            (1) **Fundamental attribution error**

            (2) **Actor-observer effect**

            (3) **Self-serving bias**

C. *Research Focus: Attributions & Grades*

    1. Research question: can changing student's attributions change their grades?

        a. Kinds of attributions

        b. Method: changing attributions

        c. Results and discussion

    2. Conclusions

D. Attitudes

1. Definition of attitudes

   a. **Attitude**

   b. Features of all attitudes

      (1) Evaluative

      (2) Targeted

      (3) Predisposes behavior

2. Components of attitudes

   a. Cognitive

   b. Affective

   c. Behavioral

3. Functions of attitudes

   ☐ *What was your attitude toward Shannon Faulkner and her goal?*

   a. **Predisposing function**

   b. **Interpreting function**

   c. **Evaluative function**

4. Attitude change

   ☐ *Read the famous 'boring task' experiment several times, until you really understand it.*

   a. **Cognitive dissonance** (Leon Festinger)

      (1) Adding or changing

      (2) **Counterattitudinal behavior**

   b. **Self-perception theory** (Daryl Bem)

5. **Persuasion**

   ☐ *Can you think of examples from current events for the two routes?*

   a. Two routes to persuasion

      (1) **Central route for persuasion**

      (2) **Peripheral route for persuasion**

   b. Elements of persuasion

    (1) Source

    (2) Message

    (3) Audience

E. *Social & Group Influences*

1. **Conformity** (Solomon Asch)

  a. Conformity in Waco

  b. Asch's experiment

    (1) Procedure

    (2) Results

2. **Compliance**

  a. Conformity and compliance

  b. **Foot-in-the-door technique**

3. **Obedience** (Stanley Milgram)

  a. Milgram's experiment

    (1) Would you punish a learner for making errors?

    (2) What would you do if the subject stopped answering?

  b. Milgram's results

    (1) Why people obey

    (2) Were Milgram's experiments ethical?

      (a) Debriefing

      (b) Experimentation today

4. Helping: prosocial behavior

  a. **Prosocial behavior [helping]**

  b. **Altruism**

  c. Why people help (empathy, personal distress, norms or values)

    (1) **Decision stage model of helping**

    (2) **Arousal-cost-reward model of helping**

5. Group dynamics and membership

   a. **Groups**

   b. Group influence

   c. Group cohesion and norms

      (1) **Group cohesion**

      (2) **Group norms**

   d. Why do we form groups?

      (1) **Social comparison theory**

      (2) **Task oriented group**

      (3) **Socially oriented group**

6. Being in a crowd

   a. Social facilitation and inhibition

      (1) **Social facilitation**

      (2) **Social inhibition**

   b. Deindividuation in crowds

      (1) **Crowd**

      (2) **Deindividuation**

   c. The bystander effect

      (1) **Bystander effect**

      (2) **Informational influence theory**

      (3) **Diffusion of responsibility theory**

7. Group decisions

   a. **Group polarization**

      (1) Risky shift

      (2) Polarization

   b. **Groupthink**

F. Aggression

☐ *Do you believe that human beings are naturally aggressive?*

1. **Aggressive behavior**

2. Model of aggressive behavior

   a. Biological factors

      (1) Violent humans

      (2) Mutant mice

   b. Social learning factors (**social learning theory**)

      (1) Cognitive patterns

      (2) Television

   c. Environmental factors

      (1) **Frustration-aggression hypothesis** (Dollard)

      (2) **Modified frustration-aggression hypothesis** (Leonard Berkowitz)

3. Sexual aggression

   a. Kinds of rapists

      (1) Power rapist

      (2) Sadistic rapist

      (3) Anger rapist

      (4) Acquaintance or date rapist

   b. Rape myths

G. Cultural Diversity: National Attitudes

☐ *What, in general, are your attitudes toward Russia and the Russian people?*

1. Attitudes and behavior

2. Persuasion

3. Attitude change

4. Prejudice and discrimination

H. Application: Controlling Aggression

 1. Controlling aggression in children

  a. Cognitive-behavioral deficits

  b. Program to control aggression

 2. Controlling aggression in adults

  a. **Catharsis**

  b. Cognitive-behavioral program

 3. Controlling sexual aggression

  a. Knowing the risk factors

  b. Strategy of increasingly forcefulness

Language Enhancement Guide

IDIOMATIC EXPRESSIONS AND CULTURAL TERMS

The following are idiomatic expressions and cultural terms found in the module. Some of them have more than one meaning; the definition given here on the right is for the way the author uses the expression in this module.

 wink of an eye (534) = very quickly

 harassment (541) = to continually annoy, upset or bother another person

 laid down rules (544) = made or listed rules

 ask for a favor (545) = to ask another person to perform a kindness or service

VOCABULARY BUILDING: Word Analysis

Instructions: Analyze each term from memory using the following procedures:

1. Break each word in the table into its prefixes, roots and suffixes and guess the meaning of the word based on the meaning of its parts. If you do not remember the meaning of each part, look it up in the Prefix, Root, and Suffix Tables in the Appendix.

2. Find the word on the text page indicated in the brackets and redefine the word based on the context of the sentence, paragraph and chapter. Look up unmarked words in a college level dictionary. Remember that these words, like all words, can have different meanings in other contexts.

Word	Meaning
subarea (533)	
polygamist (533)	
distorted (534)	
inaccurate (535)	
covariation (537)	
insubordination (540)	
renounce (542)	
inconsistent (542)	
counterattitude (542)	
peripheral (543)	
incredible	
conformity (544)	
compliance (545)	

GUESSING FROM CONTEXT

You won't find the following words and expressions from this module in the textbook Glossary, but they are useful in reading, writing, and talking about psychology and other academic subjects. See if you can guess their meanings by studying their contexts (their relationship to the words around them).

To do this, find the word or expression in your textbook and guess its meaning using the clues in the context. You may find clues in an explanation that immediately follows the word, in a synonym that appears nearby, or in the form of examples. After you have defined the terms, ask a native speaker what they mean or look them up in a dictionary to see if your guesses were correct.

affluent (533)

prestigious (533)

patronizing (535)

conserve (535)

tolerated (536)

intriguing (536)

perseverance (538)

corresponding (540)

preaching (542)

assaulted (544)

accomplice (545)

True-False

_____ 1. The words "prejudice" and "discrimination" mean the same thing.

_____ 2. A schema is an unfair stereotype we apply to a person who is different.

_____ 3. Attributions are our attempts to understand and explain people's behavior.

_____ 4. An attitude is a tendency to respond to others in a quirky, overly-sensitive manner.

_____ 5. Cognitive dissonance occurs when an audience hears so many contradictory arguments that they lose sight of the main issue.

_____ 6. Advice for all you budding politicians: if the facts are on your side, take the central route to persuasion; if they aren't, take the peripheral route.

_____ 7. The famous "electric shock" experiment showed that if you pay people enough they will follow just about any orders.

_____ 8. It is the social-psychological phenomenon of deindividuation that can make a crowd dangerous.

_____ 9. Because of the pooling of many talents and ideas, group decisions are usually superior to individual decisions.

_____ 10. Good advice on how to avoid date rape: know the risk factors and meet unwanted advances with increasing forcefulness.

For Psych Majors Only...

Classic Experiments: The classic experiments in social psychology are among the most elegant in psychology, if not in all of science, but they may seem complicated on first reading. Go through the explanations in the textbook more than once, and make sure you understand the logic of each experiment. The research Rod Plotnik writes about is well worth understanding and remembering. These experiments are important building blocks of modern psychology, and you will come across them repeatedly in your further studies.

There is a great irony surrounding these famous experiments: most of them could not be conducted today. Plotnik explains why in his discussion of the ethics of psychological research.

Flashcards

Match each key term to the definition given in the textbook.

_____ 1. actor-observer effect

a. an individual may feel inhibited from taking some action because of the presence of others

_____ 2. altruism

b. our behavior is caused by the situation; other person's is caused by his or her disposition

_____ 3. bystander effect

c. a new approach to understanding social forces and interaction by studying cognitive processes

_____ 4. central route for persuasion

d. exphasizes emotional appeal, focuses on personal traits, and generates positive feelings

_____ 5. cognitive dissonance

e. increased tendency for irrational or antisocial behavior when less chance of being identified

_____ 6. conformity

f. our judgments based on the jobs people perform or the social positions they hold

_____ 7. deindividuation

g. contain behaviors that we associate with familiar activities, events, or procedures

_____ 8. event schemas or scripts

h. finding the causes or someone's behavior in his or her internal characteristics or dispositions

_____ 9. external attributions

i. tension that motivates us to reduce cognitive inconsistencies by making beliefs consistent

_____ 10. foot-in-the-door technique

j. presents information with strong arguments, analyses, facts, and logic

_____ 11. fundamental attribution error

k. probability of compliance to a second request is up if person complies with a small, first request

_____ 12. group cohesion

l. our judgments about the traits that we and others possess

_____ 13. groupthink

m. attributing our successes to our dispositions and attributing our failures to the situations

_____ 14. internal attributions

n. explaining person by focusing on disposition or personality traits and overlooking the situation

_____ 15. obedience

o. helping, often at a cost or risk, for other reason than expectation of a material or social reward

_____ 16. peripheral route for persuasion

p. behavior performed because of group pressure, even though it might not involve direct requests

_____ 17. person schemas

q. finding the causes of someone's behavior in the external circumstances or situations

_____ 18. role schemas

r. behavior performed in response to an order given by someone in a position of authority

_____ 19. self-serving bias

s. togetherness, determined by how much group members perceive shared common attributes

_____ 20. social cognition

t. occurs when discussions emphasize cohesion, agreement over critical thinking, best decisions

Multiple-Choice

_____ 1. Rod Plotnik introduces us to Harvard Law School student Lawrence Graham and neurosurgeon Fran Conley to make the point that
   a. pioneers in any previously closed area are always subjected to ill treatment
   b. African-American men can be just as sexist as white men
   c. how people behave is more significant than what they believe
   d. how we perceive and evaluate others has powerful consequences

_____ 2. When we ask someone, "What do you do?" we are trying to get more information about the person by drawing on our
   a. person schemas
   b. role schemas
   c. event schemas
   d. scripts

_____ 3. If I look for the causes of your behavior in your disposition and personality traits, and overlook how the situation influenced your behavior, I am guilty of the
   a. fundamental attribution error
   b. covariation model factor
   c. actor-observer effect
   d. self-serving bias

_____ 4. "I creamed the chem exam because I studied my a-- off! The psych exam I flunked? Well, you know he always asks tricky questions." Sounds like the _____ in action, doesn't it?
   a. fundamental attribution error
   b. actor-observer effect
   c. self-serving bias
   d. whiner effect

_____ 5. Which one of the following is *not* a component of an attitude?
   a. cognitive
   b. genetic
   c. affective
   d. behavioral

_____ 6. In Leon Festinger's boring task experiment, the subjects who were paid only $1 to tell other students it was interesting (a lie) dealt with their cognitive dissonance by
   a. convincing themselves that it was somewhat interesting after all
   b. hoping the students they lied to realized it was just part of the experiment
   c. insisting that they should also be paid $20 for telling the lie
   d. begging Festinger and his assistants not to reveal their names

_____ 7. Daryl Bem (self-perception theory) interprets the above experiment somewhat differently. Bem believes we
   a. consult our attitudes, then adjust our behavior accordingly
   b. observe our behavior, then infer what our attitudes must be, given that behavior
   c. observe our emotional state and adjust our attitudes according to our feelings
   d. govern our behavior according to the kind of person we think we are

_____ 8. Candidate Roberta Reformer, who has an excellent plan for better government, will take the _____ route to persuasion; her opponent Boss Bluster, who plans to label her a bra-burning radical, will take the _____ route
  a. direct ... indirect
  b. honest ... dishonest
  c. central ... peripheral
  d. logical ... emotional

_____ 9. When Solomon Asch had his confederates deliberately choose an obviously incorrect matching line, the lone naive subject _____ went along with the group
  a. always
  b. never
  c. often
  d. rarely

_____ 10. Tell you what... before you quit just do one more of these questions, O.K.? [I'm using the _____ technique on you in my efforts to get you to do all the questions.]
  a. foot-in-the-door
  b. compliance
  c. conformity
  d. soft-soaping

_____ 11. In Stanley Milgram's electric shock experiment, most subjects continued to give shocks
  a. only up to the point they considered dangerous
  b. even beyond the point they believed was dangerous
  c. only if they had been paid a considerable amount to participate in the experiment
  d. only as long as the shocks seemed to be helping the "learner" do better

_____ 12. Milgram's famous experiment could not be conducted today because
  a. a new code of ethics screens experiments for potential harm to the subjects
  b. the experiment has been so widely written about that everyone is in on the secret
  c. few would be fooled by the fake lab, since psychologists are known for deception
  d. people today are too rational and scientific to obey orders they don't agree with

_____ 13. Which one of the following decisions was a classic example of groupthink?
  a. atomic bombing of Japan in World War II
  b. assassination of President Kennedy
  c. Bay of Pigs invasion of Cuba
  d. withdrawal of Shannon Faulkner from the Citadel military college

_____ 14. Contemporary social psychologists would be highly unlikely to agree that aggression
  a. occurs when our goals are blocked and we become frustrated and angry
  b. is learned through observation and imitation
  c. can be controlled by draining off or releasing emotional tension
  d. is directed by mental scripts stored in memory and used as guides for behavior

_____ 15. Why is rape so common? Researchers point to the fact that
  a. there are other motivations for rape, like aggression, power, and control, that may be more important than sex
  b. women are much bolder today, yet still like to be actively pursued, a situation that leaves men confused about what women really want
  c. Hollywood movies keep our sexual urges in a state of almost constant arousal
  d. unfortunately, rape is as natural as male hormones and female flirtatiousness — but it probably gets reported more often today

Answers for Module 25

True-False	Flashcards	Multiple-Choice
1. F	1. b	1. d
2. F	2. o	2. b
3. T	3. a	3. a
4. F	4. j	4. c
5. F	5. i	5. b
6. T	6. p	6. a
7. F	7. e	7. b
8. T	8. g	8. c
9. F	9. q	9. c
10. T	10. k	10. a
	11. n	11. b
	12. s	12. a
	13. t	13. c
	14. h	14. c
	15. r	15. a
	16. d	
	17. l	
	18. f	
	19. m	
	20. c	

Appendix

Prefix, Suffix, & Root Dictionary

For the Language Enhancement Guide

Jack Kirschenbaum

The following tables contain alphabetically arranged prefixes, suffixes and roots and their definitions and examples. These tables contain word parts that cover a large majority but not all of the terms used in the textbook. You will find that memorizing these roots, prefixes and suffixes and using them to determine the meaning of words will help you increase your reading vocabulary, speed up your reading rate, and improve your understanding of the textbook.

However, you must remember that many words in the English language are made up of separate word parts that have been borrowed from many other languages, such as Latin, Greek, Spanish, German, etc. This can create a problem for word analysis when the same prefix or suffix is borrowed from different languages and has different meanings. Word analysis therefore requires you to examine the context of the sentence for clues for the meaning intended. You must be cautious in your word analysis because as helpful as it is most of the time there will be times when you can and will make errors. With practice, and by checking a dictionary when you are in doubt, your word analysis skill will improve.

Prefix Table

Prefix	Definition	Examples
a	in/on	asleep, aboard
a/an	not/without/lacking/from	anorexia, analgesia, anesthesia, apathy, amoral
ab/abs	away from	abnormal, abstract, abstinence
anti	against	antibiotic, anti-abortion
auto	self	automobile, automatic
bene	good/well	benefit, beneficial
bi	two	biracial, biweekly, bilateral
clu/clud/clus	close/shut	conclude, exclude, exclude, include
co	together/with	co-therapist, co-author, coexist, codetermine
con	with/together	consecutive, configure
contra/contro/counter	against/opposite	contradict, contradiction, controversy
de/dis/ab	down/off/away from/out of/reversal	decelerate, depress, depart
dis/ab/de	away from/apart/not/without	discomfort, disadvantageous, disbelief
dys	bad	dysfunctional
e/ex	out/from/former	exclaim, ex-president, emit, erect, evict
equ/equi	equal	equate, inequality, inadequate, equitable

extra/extro	outside	extrovert, extraordinary
hemi-	half	hemisphere
hetero	different/opposite	heterosexual, heterochromic
homo	same/same kind	homosexual, homogeneous
hyper	over/too much	hyperactivity, hypersensitive
im	without	impotent, imperfect
in/ill/ir	in/into/within	illuminated, illustrated, incision
in/im	not/without	inactive, immature, inadequate, insensitivity
inter	among/between	interaction, international, intercede
intro	into/inside	introspect, introvert, introduce, introduction
ity	being	activity, sincerity, reality, hostility
mal	evil/bad/badly/poor/poorly	malfunction, malformed, maladjusted
metri	measure	metric system, symmetrical
mis (1)	bad/wrong	mistake, misconception, misunderstand, misbehave, miscalculation, mislabel
mis (2)	to hate	misogamy, misanthrope
mono	one/single	monotone, monogamy
multi	many/much	multicultural, multipurpose, multiracial
neur/neura/neuro	nerve/nervous system	neurology, neurotic, neurosurgery
non	not	nonsense, noncognitive, nonexistence
ob	against/to/toward	object, objectionable, objector
per	through/throughout	perception
poly	many	polychrome, polytheism
post	after	postsynaptic, postgraduate
pre	before	prehistoric, premature, precognition
pro/proto	forward/ahead/before/first/original	propose, proactive, proposal, prototype
re	back/again	recall, reheat, replace, resell
retro	back/backward/behind	retroactive, retrospect, retrograde
sequ/secu	follow	consecutive
sub	under/below/nearly	subgroup, subcommittee, substandard
sub-	under/below/inferior	subordinate
syn/sym	with/together	synthesize, symmetrical, sympathy, synchronize, synonym, synonymous
trans	to send/carry across/change	transmit, transform
tri	three	triangle, triweekly, trichromatic
un/under	not/opposite	undo, unnatural, uneven, unloved, unfair
uni	one/single	uniform, unify, unity

Suffix Table

Suffix	Definition	Examples
able/ible	able to/able to make	sensible, visible, readable, curable
al	like/being/belonging/ characterized by/ process/conditions	musical, comical, seasonal, racial, arrival, approval, international, temperamental
alg/algia	pain/ache	algesia, neuralgia
ance/ancy/ence/ency	being/ing	pregnancy, compliance, maintenance, importance, resistance
ant/net	person who is/device for	hesitant, assistant, lubricant
ate	having/resembling/holding office/specializing in	moderate, concentrate, graduate, doctorate
ced/cede/ceed	go/move/surrender (cede = yield, surrender)	precede, intercede, succeed, exceed, concede
en	made of/to make	woolen, silken, soften, harden, ripen
ence	quality/state/condition/ act/means/results	sequence
ent/ant	being/having/doing/ performing/showing/ device for	inconsistent, intermittent
er	one who	plumber
fer	bring/carry	transfer, confer, refer, defer, prefer, infer, reference, conference, suffer
ful	full of	truthful, harmful, thoughtful
gam	marriage	monogamy, polygamy
graph	writing/recording	biography, autograph, demography
gress	go/move/come	progress, regress, transgress, regression
ia	quality/condition/act/ state/result of/result of/ process of	amnesia, anorexia, analgesia, anesthesia
ian	a person who is/does/or is a specialist	librarian, electrician, dietitian, musician
ian/an	native of	American, Mexican, Indian, African
ic	characteristic/having to do with/having the power to/ belonging to	behavioristic, domestic, optimistic, psychiatric
ify	to make/to become	modify, electrify, codify
ion/tion	act/process/means/ results of	celebration, conversation, explanation, deceleration
ion/tion	the process/the act of	motion, transportation, repression
ish	acting like/native of	childish, Spanish
ism	belief/practice/doctrine/ theory/system	behaviorism, alcoholism, racism
ist	a person who practices or studies/a believer	therapist, psychologist, typist, artist, psychiatrist
ity	act of being	activity, sincerity, hostility, legality
ive	tending to (be)/having to (be)	effective, retrospective, proactive, secretive

ize	to make/to use/to become	memorize, mechanize, reorganize
ject	throw	reject, eject, project, projection
logy	study/science	psychology, zoology, anthropology
ly (1)	in the manner of/to the degree/in the direction of	generally, gladly, badly, carefully, conceptually, normally
ly (2)	having the characteristics of/happening at a specific time period	seasonally, totally, daily, yearly
ment	act/means/result of/ process of	improvement, government, management
mit	send	transmit, emit, commit, admit
ness	having the characteristics of/being	goodness, messiness
or/tor/er	person who/something that	doctor, conductor, member, motor, engineer
ous/ious	full of/having to do with	religious, mountainous, famous, envious
pel/pul	drive/push	compel, compulsive
phil	love	philosophy, philanthropy
phobe	excessive fear	homophobic
plete/pleta	fill/full	complete, deplete, completion
pos/pose/posi	put/place	compose, propose, impose, expose, suppose, transpose, depose
tech	skill	technique
tri	three	triangle, triweekly, trichromatic
ure	being	exposure, mixture, rupture, procedure, conjecture
vers	turn	reverse
vert	turn	introvert, convert, invert, revert, subvert, convertible

Root Table

Root	Meaning	Examples
alg	pain/suffering	analgesia, neuralgia
analyze	to break something into its parts, stages or categories	analysis, psychoanalysis
andro/andr	man/human	anthropology, polyandry
audio	sound/hearing	audio-visual
cede	yield/give/assign/transfer	proceed
centr	center/a stationary point	egocentric
ceptive	aware/see	perceptive, perception
chrom/chroma/chromato	color	chromatology, trichromatic, monochrome
chrono	time/in order	chronic, chronology, chronometer
cir/circum	walk around/surround/circular/around	circumnavigate
clu/clud/clus	close/shut	conclude, exclude, include
clude	to shut/end/constrain	preclude
code	arbitrary symbols used to represent words or ideas	encode, decode, codify
cognn/cogni/cogno	to think/to be aware/to know	cognition, cognitive, recognize, cognizant
complex	made of many parts	complexity
comply	to yield/consent/agree	compliance
controvers	turn against/dispute/debate	controversial
discrim	divide/separate/show differences	discrimination
dispose (1)	tendency/bias	disposition
dispose (2)	distribute/arrange	disposal
duc/duct/duce	lead/take/bend	deduct. conduct, transducer, induce, reduce, deduction, ductility
dynamic	movement/interaction/conflict	psychodynamic
ego	I/self	egocentric, egomaniac, egotism, egoist
esthe	sensation/feeling	anesthesia
ethn/ethno	nation/tribe/same culture	ethnic, ethnocentric
fin	end/limit	infinite, finite, finish, final, finalist, define
flex/flect	bend/curve	flexible, reflex, reflect, reflection
flux/flu	flow	fluent, fluency, fluid, influence, influx
form	shape/appearance	transform, format
gen/gene/genea	race/kind/produce	genetic, genetics, genealogy, genocide
gyne/gyn/gyneco	women	gynecology
habit	to hold/to have	inhibit, habituate
hes/her	stick	cohesive, adhesive, coherent, adherence
hesive	to stick to/to cling	cohesive, adhesive
mand	order	command, demand, mandate, commander

mani/mania/maniac	crazy/insanity	manic depressive
mature	completely grown or developed/ripe	immature, maturation
med	medicine/medical doctor	medicate
mediate	middle	intermediate
mene	to recall/to remember	amnesia
ment	mind	mental, mentality, demented
metr/meter	measure/measuring equipment	speedometer
mit	to send	transmit
mo	move	motion, movement, mobile, motive
mobile	move/change position/ to affect emotions	mobility, automobile, autonomous
natal	birth	prenatal
ordinate	arrange	coordinate, subordinate
orex	desire/appetite	anorexic
path	disease/feeling/suffering	pathology, psychopath, pathologists
phob	fear/terror/panic	phobia
plant	to place/put	transplant
project	to throw forward	projection
sci	knowledge/know/aware	science, conscious, conscience
scribe	to write	transcribe
sepsis	decay/infection	antiseptic
soma	body	psychosomatic
soph/sophy	wisdom/knowledge	philosophy
spect	to look/to see	introspection
sphere	a ball like shape	spherical
stabil	firm/established/fixed/ durable/steady	stable, stability, stabilize, establishment
termin	to end/to limit	terminate
therap/therapy	treatment/cure	psychotherapy, drug therapy, therapist
tort	to twist/turn	distortion, contortion
trieve	to find	retrieve
trinsic	the nature of/belonging to	intrinsic, extrinsic
trude	to thrust/to push forward	intrude
vary	change	variation, variability
vis/visi/visual	see	visible, invisible, visualization, visualize
voc/vok	call/voice	invoke, revoke, evoke, provoke, revocable, vocalize, vocalist, vocation, convocation

TO THE OWNER OF THIS BOOK

May I ask a favor? It would be very helpful to know how well the *Study Guide for Plotnik's Introduction to Psychology*, 4th ed., worked for you. I would like to have your reactions to the different features of the guide and your suggestions for making improvements. Please fill out this form, fold and seal it, and drop it in the mail. Thanks!

Matthew Enos

School _____

Instructor's name _____

Used the Study Guide because: Required_____ Optional_____ Comment_____

What did you like most about the Study Guide?_____

_____

What did you like least about the Study Guide?_____

_____

Was the Study Guide interesting and informative? _____

_____

Did the Study Guide help you with the course? _____

_____

Did you use the Language Enhancement sections (by Jack Kirschenbaum)? _____

Were they helpful? _____

Please check ☑ the parts of the Study Guide you used and share your reactions to them:

☐ Module introduction_____

☐ Effective Student Tip_____

☐ Key Terms list _____

☐ Outline_____

☐ For Psych Majors Only sections _____

☐ Special Quizzes _____

☐ True-False Questions _____

☐ Flashcards Matching Questions _____

☐ Multiple-Choice Questions _____

Additional comments about the Study Guide _____

_____

_____

_____

_____

OPTIONAL

Your name _____ Date _____

May Brooks/Cole, the publisher, quote you in promotion for the Study Guide or in future publishing ventures?

Yes_____ No_____

Your own psychology tutor for just $16.25!

Studying is easier and more fun with the **Electronic Study Guide** for Plotnik's *Introduction to Psychology, Fourth Edition*, available now from Brooks/Cole for DOS, Windows®, and Macintosh® systems. Pop the disk into your computer and let the Electronic Study Guide help you prepare for exams, master concepts, and more.

As you work through the self-tests that are built into the program, you'll get immediate feedback on both correct and incorrect answers. If you give a wrong answer, you'll get an immediate explanation, along with page references to the main text for further study.

TO ORDER:

Use our toll-free number, (800) 354-9706, or use this order form. We accept VISA, MasterCard, and American Express. Be sure to include: type of credit card and account number, expiration date, and your signature. We pay shipping charges on credit card orders unless you request special handling. Prices subject to change without notice. Checks or money orders should be made payable to Brooks/Cole Publishing Company. We pay shipping unless you request special handling. Do not send cash through the mail.

ORDER FORM

SPECIAL OFFER! Students ordering with this coupon receive a 10% discount on any purchase!

Quantity	Unit Price	10% Discount	Total
_____*Macintosh version* *Electronic Study Guide* for Plotnik's **Introduction to Psychology, Fourth Edition** (ISBN: 0-534-34030-X)	$16.25	$14.50	_____
_____*DOS version* *Electronic Study Guide* for Plotnik's **Introduction to Psychology, Fourth Edition** (ISBN: 0-534-34031-8)	$16.25	$14.50	_____
_____*Windows version* *Electronic Study Guide* for Plotnik's **Introduction to Psychology, Fourth Edition** (ISBN: 0-534-34032-6)	$16.25	$14.50	_____

*(Residents of AL, AZ, CA, CO, CT, FL, GA, IL, IN, KS, KY, LA, MA, MD, MI, MN, MO, NC, NJ, NY, OH, PA, RI, SC, TN, TX, UT, VA, WA, WI must add appropriate sales tax.)

Subtotal _____

Payment Options:

*Sales Tax _____

_____ Check or Money Order enclosed.

Total _____

_____ Charge my: _____ VISA _____ MasterCard _____ American Express

Card Number _____ Expiration Date _____

Signature_____

Please ship to: (Billing and shipping address must be the same.)

Name_____

School _____

Street Address _____

City _____ State_____ Zip+4_____

Phone number (_____) _____

Detach and return to:

Brooks/Cole Publishing Company
PlotSG4
511 Forest Lodge Road
Pacific Grove, CA 93950-5098

You can fax your order to us at 408-375-6414 or e-mail your order to: info@brookscole.com or detach, fold, secure, and mail with payment.

SECURE WITH TAPE